DETROIT TIKI

A History of Polynesian Palaces & Tropical Cocktails

RENEE TADEY

Foreword by Dave Chow

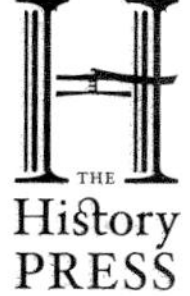

Published by The History Press
Charleston, SC
www.historypress.com

Front cover, clockwise from top left: The Chin Tiki Polynesian Revue. *Courtesy of Kawehilani*; Mauna Loa entrance. *Courtesy of Scott Schell*; The Mauna Loa. *Courtesy of Sven Kirsten*; Chin Tiki signature mug. *Private collection, photo by Nick Hagen.*
Back cover, top: Chin Tiki. *Courtesy of Sven Kirsten*; *bottom*: Vintage large Tropics postcard, circa 1942. *Author's collection.*

First published 2022

Manufactured in the United States

ISBN 9781467145329

Library of Congress Control Number: 2021950504

This book is dedicated to memories—yours and mine.
To the past, the present and the future.
Cheers!

CONTENTS

Foreword, by Dave Chow 7
Preface 9
Acknowledgements 11

PART I. THE EARLY DAYS 13
1. The Beginning 15
2. The Tropics at the Hotel Wolverine 18
3. Elsewhere in Detroit 26
4. Tropical Fever 28

PART II. THE PEAK 31
5. Hawaiian Gardens 33
6. The Chin Tiki 52
7. The Mauna Loa 87
8. Trader Vic's 113

PART III. THE AFTERLIFE 119

Index 125
About the Author 127

FOREWORD

The city of Detroit has always had a reputation of being the world capital of transportation. The factories produced cars, tanks, airplanes and all manner of vehicles—so naturally, there had to be a tiki culture here. Not only did Detroit help transport people all over the world with its vehicles, but its few tiki bars carried its working class to exotic locales. For a few hours, one could forget about their blue-collar job and sit in some thatch-covered space enjoying exotic cuisines.

The tiki bars were an escape—not only from the Midwest mindset but also from the long, cold winters. Tiki's brightly colored drinks and elaborate floor shows contrasted the gray, flat existence. In their glorious heyday, these venues were the last time in America when it was reputable (some would even say enviable) for a married couple to leave their kids with a sitter, imbibe potent concoctions and see scantily clad women gyrate to throbbing drumbeats. It was escapism at its best!

Just like some of the gas-guzzling products, tiki sadly fell out of favor for a while. Detroit has tried to rebrand itself many times, with varying degrees of success. But like a dormant volcano, the city's tiki scene never really left. The iconic palaces are no longer, but the young working class in the area still desire a venue to escape. With any luck, they'll stick around and offer a vehicle to the warmer climes and happier times within their walls.

—Dave Chow

PREFACE

As I write this, the theme song from *Hawaii Five-O* plays in my head—the image of the colossal wave curling over itself and scenes with dancers, surfers and glowing-hot lava burned into my brain. When I was growing up in the 1970s, Hawaii was big. In 1972, sitting in front of my television set in Michigan, *The Brady Bunch* took a family vacation to Honolulu and the Hawaiian Islands, and I marveled at the way hula dancers could move their hips. I wished for a lei made from exotic flowers. Peter and Bobby found a tiki idol at a construction site that brought them bad luck; they were kidnapped and tied to giant tikis. Looking back, it is funny how tiki was a part of everyday life, even in the north.

My grandma went to Hawaii on vacation and brought me back a necklace made of puka shells and souvenir-sized tubes of different-colored sand; the black was my favorite. Don Ho sang on television, you could purchase a Hawaiian shirt at K-Mart, liquor came in tiki-style glazed bottles. My parents ordered fruity rum drinks at restaurants; tiki torches burned brightly at outdoor gatherings. Hawaiian and Polynesian culture seeped into everyday life across the United States.

As an adult, Mid-Century Modern design caught my eye, I felt a fondness for a time I had not experienced personally. I cannot say that Michigan is the first place that comes to mind when most people conjure up images of tulip chairs, glass-walled homes, blonde wood or Herman Miller furnishings. It should. After all, some of the biggest names in Mid-Century design lived and worked in the metro Detroit area: Eliel and Eero Saarinen, Marshall Fredericks, Minoru Yamasaki, Harry Bertoia, Ray and Charles Eames, Florence Knoll, Carl Milles—you get the idea. There is a Marshall

Fredericks sculpture just a mile from my home; his pieces were readily found in shopping malls and city squares, with children climbing all over them.

I quickly discovered tiki bars, mugs, menus and décor were a large part of Mid-Century design. While I was lucky enough to be surrounded by works of some of the world's best Mid-Century designers, there was not a tiki bar to be found. What we did have was Chinese restaurants. For those of you scoffing right now, you must understand the Chinese restaurant experience in the 1960s and '70s was quite different from today's carry-out joints. Going to a Chinese restaurant was a big deal when I was growing up; our family favorite was called China Palace. Restaurants were atmospheric, experiential; lovely lamps with Chinese scenes and red tassels hung over every white-starched table-clothed table. Framed Chinese artwork hung on walls. There were a multitude of servers delivering egg drop soup, egg rolls and finally your entrée. I can clearly picture those heavy stainless-steel serving dishes. War Su Gai (that's almond boneless chicken to you and me) came in a low oval dish, white rice in a pedestaled round one. Dessert arrived in the form of almond and fortune cookies. When you took your bill up to the cash register, you were tempted to purchase several items, from fancy chopsticks and tea sets to wax paper bags filled with fortune cookies.

For decades, my husband, Kris, would tell me the story of his visit to the Mauna Loa in Detroit as seen through the eyes of a six-year-old. He told tales of waterfalls and a little stream that coursed through the restaurant; tiny bridges took you from one side to the other. He swears there were fish swimming in the water. He remembers torches and palm trees in front of the building on West Grand Boulevard. His fascination drew me in. My sister-in-law had dinner after her high school prom at the Mauna Loa, and her description is much the same as her brother's. Kris and I would drive down the boulevard pointing to where the Mauna Loa once stood. Every antique shop or flea market brought an opportunity to find an old relic—a matchbook, mug, anything. Always keeping an eye open for any mention of local tiki palaces—Mauna Loa, Chin Tiki, The Tropics and Hawaiian Gardens—I was sucked in. Websites, blogs, eBay and Facebook pages fed my hunger for information, but I needed more.

Writing this book sent me on a journey back to a time when a night on the town was special. A time when spending thousands or millions to create a secluded world to come to, forget your troubles and just have fun was not unthinkable. It was a time of fantasy, escapism, a tropical getaway nestled in a big city. Sometimes the creators are as much the story as the places. Along the way, I have come to know fascinating people and visited amazing places—some real and some in my imagination. I hope you have as much fun reading this book as I did writing it. Aloha!

ACKNOWLEDGEMENTS

When I began this project, I didn't belong to a tiki group, wasn't a member of a forum and didn't know any specific tikiphiles. Having never worked on a project of this size, I was a little bit intimidated; much thanks to Joe Grimm, who assured me I could do it. My journey began at the library. Thank you to Cassandra Miron, Holly Township Library; Jason Bias, Genesee County Library; Meghan McGowan, Detroit Public Library; and Elizabeth Clemens, Walter P. Reuther Library. I perused the websites of Tiki Central, Critiki, South Seas Cinema, Newspapers.com and Pinterest to help round out my knowledge. I found my way to amazing locals who opened their homes, shared their knowledge and revealed their collections; they were happy to help in any way. Thank you to Marlin Chin, Stephen Lim, Marshall Chin, Dave Chow, Marcyanna Parzych, Tim Shuller, Janis Glotkowski, Kim Fujiwara, Zach Roberts, Louis Devaney, Michael Zadoorian and Eric Haynes. Huge thanks to Barbara Soloko and Jenine Grover, who brought Fred Barton and Hawaiian Gardens to life for me. Thanks to Mark Hill, Doug Williams, Linda Lee and Father Thomas Marble for their memories and stories. Mahalo la 'oe to Joe and Arlene Codilla for your contributions; you went above and beyond. A big thank-you across the country to California: Scott Schell, who did not hesitate for a second to share his immense collection; Sven A. Kirsten; LeRoy Schmaltz; and Bob Van Oosting. To my dear friends and photographers Amy Sacka and Nick Hagen, you are awesome. Thank you for bringing these pages to life. Heartfelt thanks to my family and best friend Kelly Taylor. Love and gratitude to my husband, Kris. In memory of Jim Bowman.

Part I

THE EARLY DAYS

Chapter 1

THE BEGINNING

Legends of the South Pacific began filling the minds and imaginations of Americans in the late 1800s. Writers such as Herman Melville, Robert Louis Stevenson, Jack London and William Somerset Maugham told exciting tales of their South Seas adventures in novels such as *Treasure Island*, *In the South Seas*, *Typee*, *Amoo* and *Mardi*. The writers described their wild journeys through the South Pacific and everyday island life with the Natives. The colorful stories captured the attention of readers across the country; they could not get enough. A new literary genre was born. The early 1900s brought titles such as *South Seas Tales*, *The Moon and Sixpence* and *Mystic Isles of the South Seas*. The popularity of the books was indisputable. In 1922, Burlingham Travel Pictures released *The Lure of the South Seas*, a documentary giving ordinary folks a real insider look at that part of the world. By the late 1920s, Hollywood had taken notice of the trend and decided to jump aboard. With manuscripts in hand, they got to work. In 1928, they released a silent film adaption of Frederick O'Brien's *White Shadows in the South Seas*, filmed in Tahiti. The year 1935 brought Clark Gable and Charles Laughton to the big screen in *Mutiny on the Bounty*. The fad continued with Dorothy Lamour in 1937's *The Hurricane*, *Lure of the Islands* in 1942 and Michael O'Shea and Susan Hayward in *Jack London* in 1943. And these are just the tip of the iceberg. Hollywood had the ability to re-create the beauty of the South Seas right there in sunny California. Artists and set designers turned palm fronds, weathered wood, tapa cloth, tufa rock, hemp rope, primitive weapons, masks, nets and Japanese glass fishing floats into exotic locales.

While visions of island paradise filled movie houses, Hawaiian music was delivered on radio waves to living rooms across the United States. In 1924, Frank Ferera rerecorded the song "Aloha 'Oe," and it landed on the popular music charts of the day. The song was so well loved it was recorded by a new artist every decade from 1911 to 1965. Bing Crosby's version came out in 1936, Andy Williams did it in 1959 to celebrate Hawaii's statehood and Elvis Presley included it on his album *Blue Hawaii* in 1961. Webley Edwards hosted *Hawaii Calls*, a popular radio show, from 1935 to 1975, recorded beneath the banyan tree at the Moana Hotel. Hawaiian music began seeping into everyday American culture. The 1920s and '30s brought droves of wealthy tourists to the big island and are known as the golden years of Hawaiian tourism.

Tiki culture began to gain foothold in 1933 when Ernest Raymond Beaumont Gantt (who later changed his name to Donn Beach) opened a Polynesian-themed restaurant in Hollywood, California, called Don the Beachcomber; today, he is credited as being the founding father of tiki culture. Using relics he collected from his travels throughout the South Pacific, he decorated the space with flaming torches, rattan furniture, straw matting and bright-patterned fabrics. It did not take long for a competitor to join the scene. After hearing about its success, Victor J. Bergeron hung out at Don the Beachcomber's for about a week studying the restaurant and its customers. He decided he could "build a better mousetrap." He redecorated his first restaurant, Hinky Dinks in Oakland, California, to resemble a South Pacific trading post, tore down the Hinky Dinks sign and reopened as Trader Vic's. Prohibition ended in 1933, and rum was cheap and readily available; exotic rum drinks are Trader Vic's trademark. Vic himself originated the Mai Tai. According to the Trader Vic's website:

> *In 1944 after success with several exotic drinks, a bit of serendipity happened that would not only place Trader Vic at the forefront of cocktail mixology, but would also earn him a place in history. That day in Oakland, The Trader pulled down a bottle of 17-year-old Jamaican Rum, added a squeeze of lime, a dash of rock candy syrup, a splash of orange curacao, some French Orgeat and poured the concoction over cracked ice. He handed it to a visiting friend from Tahiti who immediately exclaimed, "it's Mai Tai Roa Ae!" (Tahitian for Out of this world—the best) and the first Mai Tai was born—Paradise in a glass.*

Ideas were plucked straight from the movies and turned into Polynesian-themed restaurants and bars. The Coconut Grove, Christian's Hut and the Hurricane all came from the big screen. The image of a woman in a sarong or grass skirt was snatched from movie posters and applied to tiki bar menus, matchbooks, mugs and promotional items. They even borrowed special effects such as rain on the roof and storms. The movement that started in California and the West Coast headed across the country to New York and Florida and then infiltrated metropolitan cities such as Chicago, Detroit, Pittsburgh and Columbus. Let's face it; things were pretty grim at the time. The Great Depression paralyzed the United States from 1929 to 1939, and then World War II broke out in 1939. Who wouldn't want to escape into a carefree world of tropical leisure where your troubles were left at the door?

Chapter 2

THE TROPICS AT THE HOTEL WOLVERINE

Detroit joined the crowd in 1941 with The Tropics at the Hotel Wolverine. The *Detroit Free Press* published an article on June 15, 1941, announcing the upcoming opening of an "atmosphere nightclub" called The Tropics. It is described as a "triple level affair created in the mood of the South Seas, with bamboo, palm trees and other tropical touches." The article goes on to say, "The novel touch of bamboo and palm-leaf huts instead of the all-too-familiar booths, in the Village Room are a distinct innovation which should catch the public fancy." While the United States would not declare war until December 7, 1941, signs of trouble filled newspaper headlines. The front page of the June 20, 1941 *Detroit Free Press* had the following headlines: "Strict Rations of Rubber Announced by OPM; Tire Production to Be Slashed," "House Groups for Doubling Income Tax," "Suicide Blitz Engulfs the Irish," "Axis Orders Consulates of US Closed." But on page fourteen, the big story is "City Night Lifers Discover It's Fun in 'The Tropics.'" The article describes the club in great detail:

> *It was a case of Mohamet and the mountain Thursday night in Detroit where those after-dark pleasure seekers of the Motor City who couldn't go to the tropics for relaxation, found the "Tropics" brought to them with all the trimmings. In short Detroit's newest and gayest night spot, "The Tropics" opened at the Wolverine Hotel Thursday, to a large crowd who found its décor in sub-equatorial mood, strictly to their taste. Giant palm trees and bamboo huts; throbbing drums and gay colors; waitresses in sarongs and Hawaiian leis and a general color scheme of light green and gold lent*

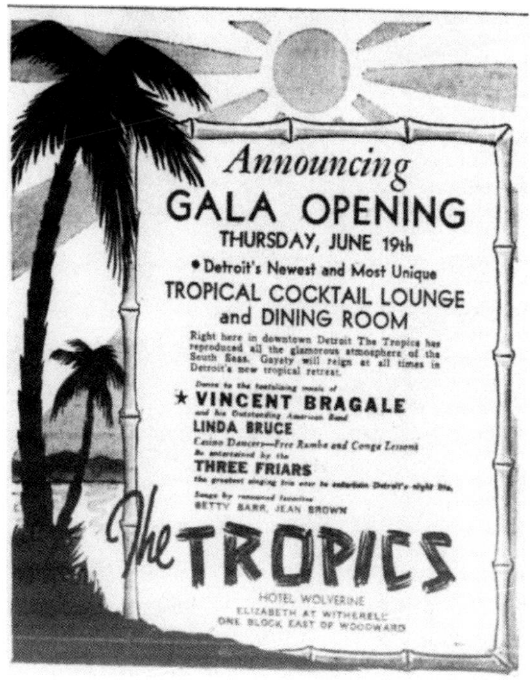

The Tropics gala opening newspaper announcement. *Author's collection.*

atmosphere to this club which bids fair to be the gathering place with those with the South Seas on their minds. An imposing entrance, complete with a green neon palm-tree marks the outside of the club, and inside, on the street level, there is a long double bar built in the style of a shelter, complete with tin roof from which rain drips steadily and noiselessly before lighted murals of distant landscapes. Behind this bar the bartenders in brightly colored shirts, add their tropical touch to the scene. At the far end of the bar a small gallery with bamboo railing looks down upon the "Tropical Village," in which bamboo huts replace the customary booths, and a small stage is located for the band to play. There is another bar on the lower level, leading to "The Village." Upstairs, there is a triple-level dining room, with dancefloor and bandstand, and the bands, by means of an hydraulic lift can be shifted from the "Village" to the dining room in double-quick time. The effect of spaciousness is cleverly created by the use of mirrors on one wall. Special lighting effects plus the yellow and light green furniture coverings add freshness and coolness to this triple-tiered fun spot. The throbbing drums are part of the contribution of Vincent Bragale, whose Latin rhythm orchestra, aided by charming Betty Barr, and Jeanne Brown, vocalists keep things going at a lively pace from floor to floor. Then there

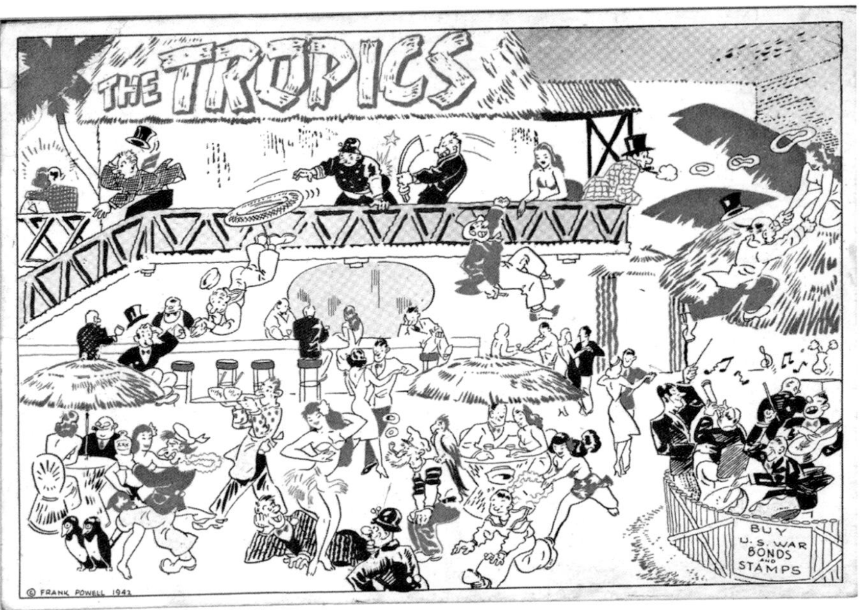

Vintage large Tropics postcard, circa 1942. Looks like fun to me! *Author's collection.*

> *are "The Three Friars," a musical trio with rhythm in their fingers and vocal cords, who alternate with Bragale throughout the evening. For dancing there is Linda Bruce who with her five assistants gives rhumba and conga exhibitions and will teach those who feel the rhumba urge, to learn the steps. Thus there's never a dull moment at this club, which has novelty, color, pace and atmosphere to attract pleasure seekers and to transport them, if only temporarily, to the land of the soft winds, the blue lagoons and the bright skies. It's topical to be tropical today in Detroit.*

Don't you wish you could go there right now? Me too. Imagine a hidden paradise tucked in between skyscrapers, the bell of the streetcars, the swish of automobiles halted at the entrance. Here was your chance to experience the things found only in the movies. The Hotel Wolverine was built in 1921 at a cost of $3 million. The Beaux-Arts and Italian Renaissance–style building rose seventeen stories in red brick. At the time, it was Detroit's newest and finest hotel, catering to the rich and famous of the day. Former Detroit Tigers Hank Greenberg and Al Kaline lived at the hotel for a time. Famous musicians who stayed at the hotel include Duke Ellington, Glenn Miller, Stan Kenton and Horace Heift. In 1941, a sign was added at the top of the building: Tropics Room.

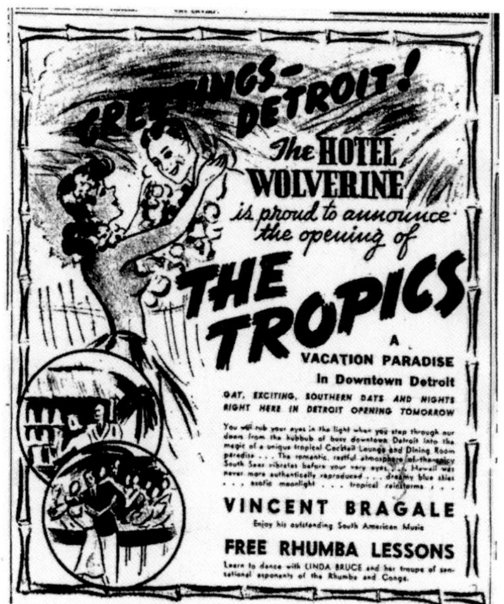

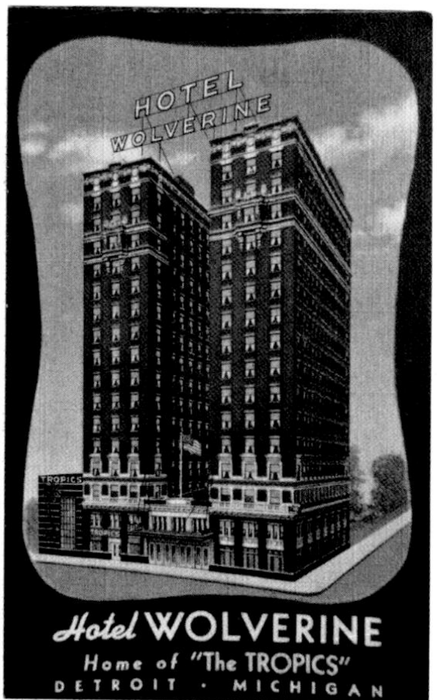

Left: Hotel Wolverine newspaper ad announcing the opening of The Tropics, a vacation paradise. *Author's collection.*

Right: Wolverine Hotel postcard. Home of the famous Tropics. *Author's collection.*

Vintage postcards display renderings of thatch-covered bars, palm trees, huts constructed from bamboo poles, straw matting and a night sky. The text brags of air-conditioned comfort—a big deal in 1941. The most unique feature is "America's only traveling band stand." Can you picture it? A full orchestra plays tunes on the first floor and then is magically lifted to the second to play another set and finally the third floor. Sure beats packing up your instruments and carrying them up the stairs only to set up all over again. That had to be amazing to see. The postcard description of the Native Village says: "In this authentic replica of a South Sea island Native Village, there is skillfully captured all the beauty and charm of far-off tropical lands." It continues, "Connected with the Tropics Village is the very charming and unusual Tropics Cocktail Lounge, which is also designed in the South Seas motif. The Tropics, Michigan's most unusual night spot and cocktail lounge." The cocktail lounge postcard brags, "Here indubitably is one of the most unusual cocktail lounges to be found anywhere. The Authentic South Sea island motif in which it is designed is convincing even to the patter of rain on the roofs of the unique Rainfall Bars." The cocktail menu is extravagant for the day: six pages of fancy cocktails, spirits, cordials, imported and domestic champagnes and wines and thirty-four kinds of imported Scotch whiskies. Looking down the list of cocktails, the Zombie is at the top, the price a mere dollar. There's a Puka Puka Punch, also $1.00; the most expensive drink is the Wow, a Tropics special, for $1.50—no description, unfortunately. Lots of traditional cocktails for the time—Old Fashioned, Alexander, Martini, Orange Blossom and Bacardi—could be had for under $0.50. For perspective, a local bottle of beer was two bits ($0.25), and a Coke cost $0.15. A November 30, 1941 advertisement describes The Tropic's Love Charm Punch: "flavored with the mystic fruits of the tropics—tang—zest—excitement—a unique drink that brings Tahiti to you—drink it and hear the jungle drums throb out savagely beautiful rhythms." That had to be some punch.

The Tropics' opening announcement in local newspapers called it a "vacation paradise in Downtown Detroit." Renderings of dancing couples wearing leis, palm trees and pretty girls in grass skirts filled newspaper advertisements. They lured customers with free rhumba lessons and an invitation to wine, dine and dance on a multicolored lighted floor where "the romantic atmosphere of the spicy South Seas vibrates before your eyes. Hawaii was never more authentically reproduced...dreamy blue skies... exotic moonlight...tropical rainstorms." Entertainment was another key

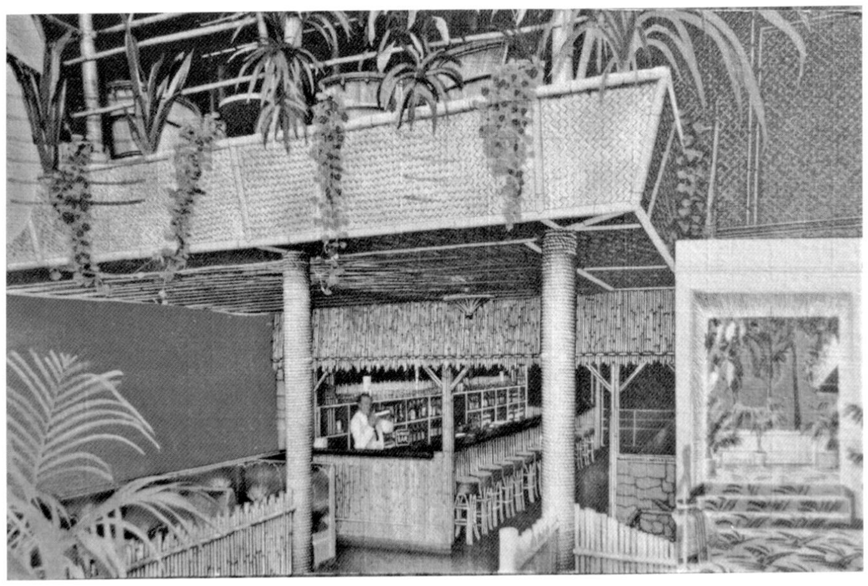

The Tropics Cocktail Lounge postcard. *Author's collection.*

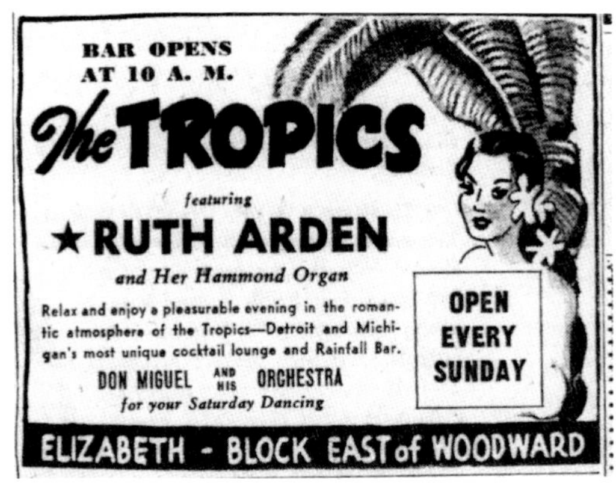

Tropics advertisement. Notice the bar opens at 10:00 a.m. *Author's collection.*

to getting people in the door. The "Dance of Knives," where two young men "shoot sparks from their clashing knives"; Vincent Bragale and his South American music; Ruth Arden and her Hammond organ; Don Miguel and his orchestra; and Royce Merrwll and his Velvetones are just some of the entertainers. Many advertisements beckoned folks to "go where the celebrities go." The war ended in 1945, sending GIs back home with stories and pleasant memories of downtime spent in the Pacific Theater; they flocked to theme restaurants and bars connecting with the atmosphere. Articles and ads continued to appear in Detroit-area newspapers throughout the 1940s and '50s.

In *Ohio Tiki*, Jeff Chenault tells the story of George Rudin, a man who moved from Middletown, Ohio, to Detroit during World War II to work in his cousin's tire shop. While living in Detroit, George rented a room at the YMCA, which happened to be across the street from the Hotel Wolverine. George visited The Tropics and was clearly taken with it. When he returned home to Dayton, Ohio, in 1947, he obtained a liquor license and turned his grocery store into a restaurant and Hawaiian-themed cocktail lounge. It was quite popular; it was just the beginning of what would eventually become an elaborate Polynesian supper club. What did he name it? The Tropics, of course.

The Tropics remained in business at the Hotel Wolverine throughout ownership changes and unstable times. In 1963, The Tropics was no more. In its place was The Stables, a theater located above the hotel bar that was formerly part of the Tropic Room. A December 1963 *Detroit Free Press* article states, "The place is still rather exotic, with lots of bamboo doo-dads tacked on here and there, but it is an excellent small theater with room for 150 people grouped around little tables on main floor and balcony." In 1967,

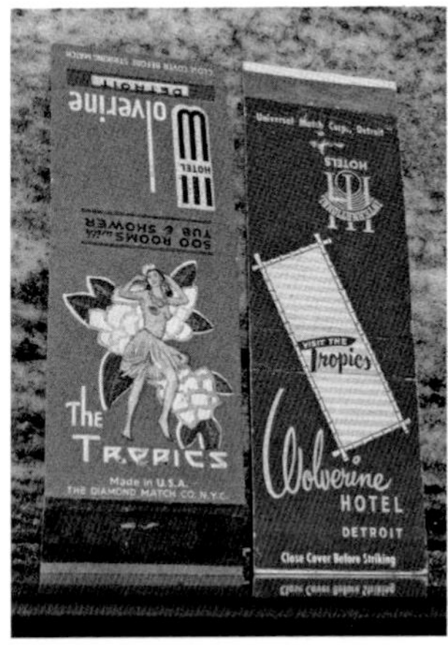

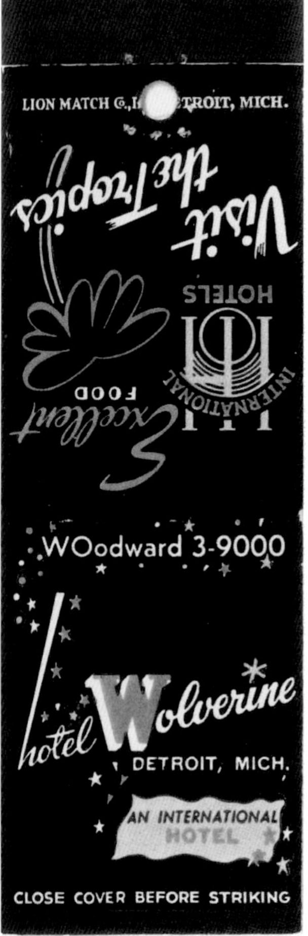

there's mention of the Tropics Theater in the *Free Press*: "The Tropics in the Wolverine Hotel at 55 E. Elizabeth, was launched by John Kinney and Rodger Heiple. Richard P. Brown and Raymond Morin will be *The Dumb Waiter* and Mary Tracy and Greg Larkin in *The Tiger*." According to HistoricDetroit.org, "By 1968, the Wolverine was already near the fringes of poverty areas. The bands had been silenced. The Tigers had moved out. The Wolverine called it quits." The once-opulent hotel would be turned into a federally subsidized senior housing facility. Upon hearing of the closure, people trickled back to the hotel to take one last look, maybe have one last cocktail drinking in the memories. The *Port Huron Times Herald* ran a story on the closing with the headline "Onetime Detroit Show Biz Mecca to Be Old Folks Home." In it, former patrons shared their memories. A man from Oregon recalled, "When I was at Romulus Airfield during World War II, if I had been a Jap or Nazi spy, I'd have hung out at the Wolverine. That's where all of the Air Force came." Bartender Henry Flowers said, "I used to sit upstairs looking down at the dance floor, and I couldn't see how anybody wanted to dance, because the floor was so crowded."

Top: Souvenir matchbooks. *Author's collection.*

Bottom: Hotel Wolverine matchbook. "An international hotel" invites you to visit The Tropics. *Courtesy of Scott Schell.*

> *Flowers remembered that on his honeymoon—before he ever dreamed he would spend nearly a decade at being the hotel's last bar manager—he paid $5 just for a ticket for him and his wife to sit on the balcony and watch dancers and the bands. "This used to be the hotel of the professional people—the doctors, the lawyers, the show people. Duke Ellington. Glenn Miller, all of the bands stayed here" Flowers said. "And Horace Heidt and Stan Kenton," cut in John Murray, a onetime manager of minor league baseball teams who has lived in the hotel for 20 years. "And all the baseball and hockey players used to stay here." The Tropics Club retains its bamboo fixtures. Replicas of South Seas trees sway in the corners, but their onetime occupants—paper mache animals—have long since gone. And so have the people. At one side of the Tropics is a huge cavern—now just dank and dirty. But once, when lit up, the top was domed and as blue as an early nighttime sky. An orchestra performed on a hydraulic lift, floating from one floor to the other. Behind the bar, water used to flow overhead, bubbling into a well-lit tropical scene, producing a rainfall effect.*

After the senior citizens left, the building became rundown and eventually was abandoned. Then-owner Mike Illitch teamed up with the City of Detroit to build a new stadium for his Detroit Tigers on the property occupied by and surrounding the Hotel Wolverine. The hotel was the first building to go on March 22, 1997; the implosion was filmed for the Learning Channel. After more than sixty years, there was now a vacancy in the skyline where the hotel once stood. Comerica Park opened in 2000.

Chapter 3

ELSEWHERE IN DETROIT

Turning once again to newspaper archives, the October 26, 1945 *Detroit Free Press* announces, "Bali Opens as Newest Night Club." The article reads, "Bali, luxuriously appointed, is the latest bidder for public favor, featuring a Sarong Room. With John F. Maher as proprietor, it opened Thursday night. Music is provided by the Johnny DiCicco Trio and Paul Mallory." Club Bali was located at 808 West McNichold at Third, about six miles from downtown Detroit. The *Detroit Free Press* featured an After Dark column listing entertainment and special features at the local hot spots. Large advertisements beckoned guests to "dine amidst tropical splendor" in the Sarong Room or Zebra Room or dance to Johnny DiCicco and his Smartones in the Balinese Dance Room. Musicians and comedians such as George Scotti, Charley Chaney, Smilin' Jim DeLand, Nan Blakstone, Leonard Stanley, Duane Lockard and pianist Al Whyte played Club Bali. The club showed up regularly in the listings. Then, on Tuesday, July 11, 1950, the headline on page fifteen of the *Detroit Free Press* read, "Club Bali Is Swept by $200,000 Blaze." A two-alarm fire gutted the luxurious nightclub; four firemen were overcome by smoke as the fire raged out of control for two hours. The fire started in the electrical behind the wood paneling at the bar. Five adjacent stores were damaged by smoke.

Another club that pops up in 1947–49 is the Tropical Show Bar at the Bowl-O-Drome. According to *Before Motown: A History of Jazz in Detroit, 1920–1960*, the Bowl-O-Drome was a bowling alley with a bar on Dexter

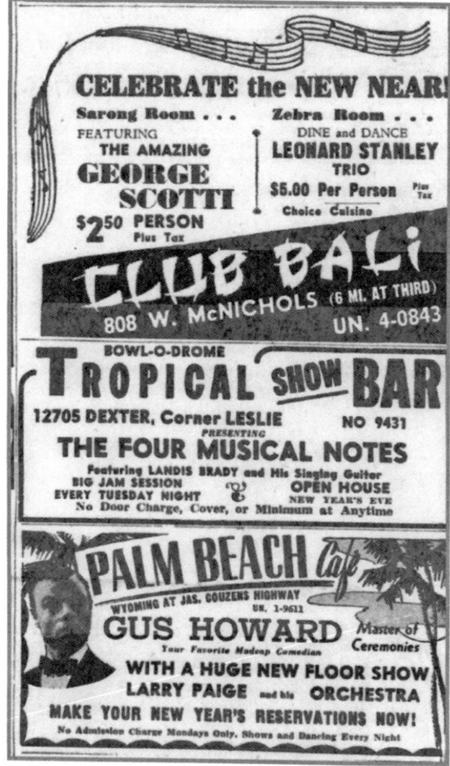

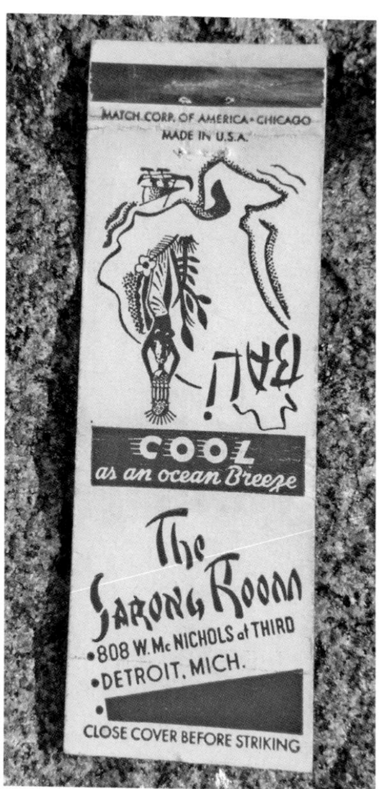

Left: *Detroit Free Press* ad featuring three tropical-themed venues. *Author's collection.*

Right: The Sarong Room at Club Bali matchbook. *Author's collection.*

Avenue at Leslie. There was a separate entrance to the bar on Dexter. Run by former Purple Gangster Lou Jacobs, the bar featured some of Detroit's top jazzmen. A string of advertisements in 1948 lists Club Bali, Tropical Show Bar and Palm Beach Café. A new trend had begun.

Chapter 4

TROPICAL FEVER

The mood had lightened across the United States, the boys were back from the war, the economy was flourishing and confidence was in the air. Americans continued their love affair with the South Seas. James Michener wrote a Pulitzer Prize–winning collection of short stories based on his own observations while stationed in the Pacific as a lieutenant commander in the U.S. Navy. The book was titled *Tales of the South Pacific*. Published in 1947, the book was then loosely adapted into the 1949 Broadway musical *South Pacific*. The Rodgers and Hammerstein musical film adaption was released in 1958. In 1947, Thor Heyerdahl, a Norwegian anthropologist, captured the attention of the world when he set out on an expedition across the South Seas from Peru to French Polynesia by raft. He named the raft *Kon Tiki* after the Inca god. The 101-day journey was immortalized first in a book by the same name and then as a 1950 Academy Award–winning documentary film. James Jones's debut novel, *From Here to Eternity*, was published in 1951. Set in Hawaii in 1941, the story is about members of a U.S. Army infantry company in the months leading up to the attack on Pearl Harbor.

In the 1950s, tikis began creeping into the mainstream; they could be seen on signs and in décor for motels, restaurants, bowling alleys, miniature golf courses and, of course, bars and restaurants. All of that thatch, bamboo, Moai, palm trees and tiki mugs came to be known as Polynesian Pop. In 1956, Bob and Jack Thornton opened the Mai Kai in South Florida. They say it cost $300,000 to build and grossed $1 million in its first year. In 1959,

Hawaii became the fiftieth state, and Americans welcomed it with open arms. People quickly embraced the laid-back lifestyle—luaus, limbo, sweet fruity drinks. Exotic music by Martin Denny and Les Baxter saturated the airwaves, and movie screens played host to island-themed films like *Drums of Tahiti*, *Song of the Sarong*, *His Majesty O'Keefe*, *Swiss Family Robinson* and *Blue Hawaii*. Television followed suit with *Follow the Sun*, *Hawaiian Eye*, *Adventures in Paradise*, *Gilligan's Island*, *McHale's Navy* and *Hawaii Five-O*.

Part II

THE PEAK

The 1960s were the peak of tiki in Detroit. It was during that time that escapism thrived. From pearl divers to hula girls, George Nakashima to Al Kaline, Holly to Hollywood, the Detroit scene was spectacular and left a lasting impression on all who visited.

Chapter 5

HAWAIIAN GARDENS

My journey to Hawaiian Gardens began with a simple matchbook on eBay. I casually knew about the tropical paradise in Holly, Michigan, before my encounter with the listing. The cover looked like a watercolor painting of a faraway vacation land. There was something about that cardboard rectangle that really appealed to me—the rendering of the sailboat on the lake, umbrellas on a beach, the Polynesian longhouse and the writing inside: "Hawaiian Gardens. Touch of the Tropics at Door of Detroit." I won the auction. My curiosity was piqued.

Hawaiian Gardens Resort sprouted up in a little town called Holly in 1961. At that time, the city's population was just over three thousand; the nearest big city was Flint, about eighteen miles away. The reason for the location is a wonderful story of chance.

Let me begin with Hawaiian Gardens' creator, Fred Barton, a born dreamer who came into the world in Saginaw, Michigan, in 1907. After graduating from high school, Barton joined the coast guard, moved to Sault Ste. Marie in Michigan's Upper Peninsula, married Elsie Cracknell and welcomed daughters Barbara and Diane. After leaving the coast guard, he had a difficult time finding work, so he packed up his family and moved to sunny California. Fred, always thinking, planning and dreaming, was known as an idea man. It was there in California that he began putting those ideas to work. In 1947, he created a formula to stop a radiator leak from within; it has become America's best-known brand of leak-stopping products, Bar's Leaks. The "Bar's" comes from the first three letters of his last name. By

1950, Bar's Leaks had entered the traditional automotive aftermarket: jobbers, warehouses, repair garages.

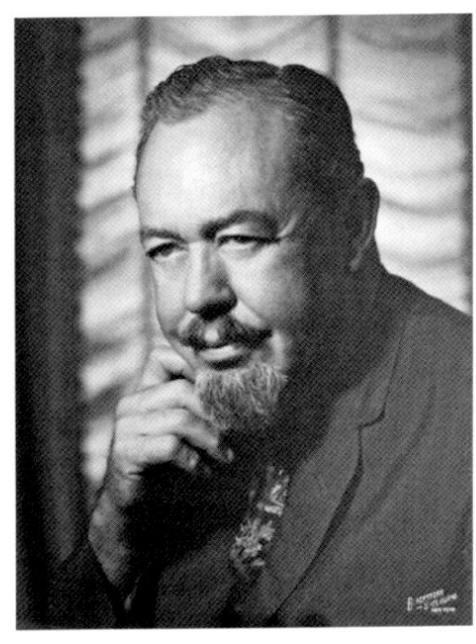

Entrepreneur Fred Barton. *Courtesy of Barb Soloko.*

But Fred had bigger aspirations. To accomplish them, he needed to be closer to the Big Three automakers. He boarded a train headed to Michigan in search of a location for his factory. On the train, he struck up a conversation with a fellow passenger named Raymond Addis. Fred explained to Addis that he was looking for a place to build a factory back home, Addis asked Fred if he had any place in mind and Fred responded by saying his mother had lived in Holly and he'd always liked it there. Addis replied saying he happened to own property in Holly and was interested in selling it. Fred purchased several plots of land from Addis, built a factory on one of them and moved Bar's Leaks headquarters to Holly in 1951.

Fred went to work immediately meeting with major U.S. automakers like GM, located just a hop and a skip away in Flint. His pitch was successful; beginning in 1952, Bar's Leaks products were used in regular and heavy-duty assembly lines as OEM treatments by the automakers. The year 1958 made Bar's Leaks a household name. The summer Olympics were being held in Melbourne, Australia, that year. The swimming events almost came to a halt when a leak was discovered in one of the pool's mechanisms, but Bar's Leaks came to the rescue and fixed the problem. That same year, the nuclear submarine USS *Nautilus* was attempting to make a historic mission to be the first submarine to travel under the North Pole. During the mission, a small saltwater leak was discovered in one of the vessel's nuclear reactor steam condensers. Previously, pinpointing the leak would have been impossible. But sailors were able to get their hands on seventy quarts of Bar's Leaks. They poured it into the submarine's condenser system, and the leak stopped. Mission accomplished.

Fred's first marriage had broken up in California. With the success of the business, he needed to be where the action was. Building a modest home near the factory, he moved back to Holly and married Ethel "Jane" Mercer. Fred loved adventure, travel and exploring; the success of Bar's Leaks gave him the financial means to do so. He and Jane traveled all around the South

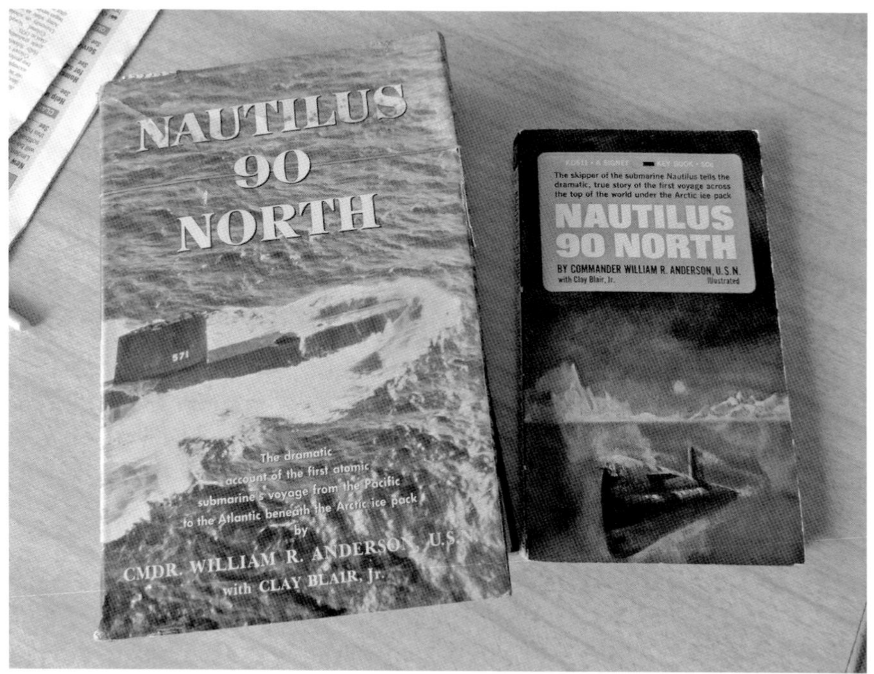

Books written about the USS *Nautilus* historic mission. *Courtesy of Barb Soloko.*

Pacific, Hawaii, Polynesia and New Zealand. He found the islands of Hawaii bewitching, so much so that he was compelled to build a place where others could enjoy a bit of the magic of Hawaii and the South Pacific too.

As stated earlier, Fred was full of ideas. Once he got something in his head, there was no stopping him. He purchased the land where he would build Hawaiian Gardens, and Jim Livingston of James H. Livingston Associates Architects out of Ann Arbor, Michigan, was hired. Jack Klempp of Holly was brought in as general contractor, and the dream was set into motion. The project began in 1960 with a modest twenty-four-room motel; with no overnight accommodations in the area, it provided visiting skiers from nearby Mount Holly and traveling businessmen a convenient and comfortable place to stay. Construction continued with the twelve-thousand-square-foot building that would become Huki Lau Restaurant and a large motel lobby that would connect the two buildings. The once-swampy area was perfect for lake building, so Fred built several lakes in the area. Using his unique lake-building skills, he had a huge dredge brought in on the railway from Florida. In a newspaper article, close friend and fellow Holly businessman Don Winglemire said Barton called the dredge Sand Bar #1:

"He was so proud of that thing, he christened it with a bottle of champagne and everything." And thus, scenic Lake Oahu was born.

Linda Lee lived down the road on Grange Hall, and her school bus passed the building every day. Her mom worked for Fred for years. She can remember the breezeway of her family home being filled up with dishes Fred purchased in Hong Kong while waiting for the restaurant to be finished. Everyone I talked to expressed the sense of excitement that filled the village; they felt it would put Holly on the map. Holly also had the good fortune to be served by the Grand Trunk Railway (the depot still stands today). Visitors could come from all over. Even though Hawaiian Gardens was on the outskirts of town, it did bring in business, as visitors liked to check out the village.

The resort complex consisted of fourteen acres of land, the motel, a honeymoon cottage, two lakes, a par-three golf course, a greenhouse and a restaurant. Guests could fish, canoe and swim in the summer months and ice skate in winter on the lake. If water's not your thing, you could go horseback riding on the trails, do a little hunting (not sure how that worked) or perhaps spend the day on the golf course; there were plenty of outdoor activities to keep guests busy. At first glance, the resort looked like a series of structures built in different styles—A-frame, thatch roof, geodesic dome. A huge outrigger filled with rowers pierced the skyline, and a giant carved wooden Easter Island figure (Moai) was perched atop a stone wall. The parking lot was vast. Flowers were planted all around the restaurant, and a dragon figure lurked among the plants. Huki Lau restaurant was unlike anything ever seen before, not only in Holly but likely the whole state of Michigan at that time. Three pages of the dinner menu contain personal messages to guests, a sort of love letter to Hawaii and Polynesia. The inside cover reads, "In our many trips through the area we were mainly intrigued with the Maori in New Zealand and naturally the Hawaiian. Hawaii has always represented a profusion of beautiful plants and colors, and the feeling of warmth that is extended the traveler is beyond description."

It was big; one advertisement reads "capacity from 10 persons to 1200." The Bartons went all out decorating the place, making it as authentic as possible. Palm trees were brought in from Florida, lava rock from Hawaii and island timbers, thatch and stone from the islands. They built waterfalls, tropical gardens, woven grass and bamboo walls. The lobby was an equatorial paradise; a waterfall cascaded down a lava rock wall, and lush plants and vines transported visitors to the South Pacific. Maharini chairs, colorful lanterns, bamboo-legged tables and chairs, fresh flowers and lakeside views filled the dining rooms. Food was Polynesian or American. The wine cellar

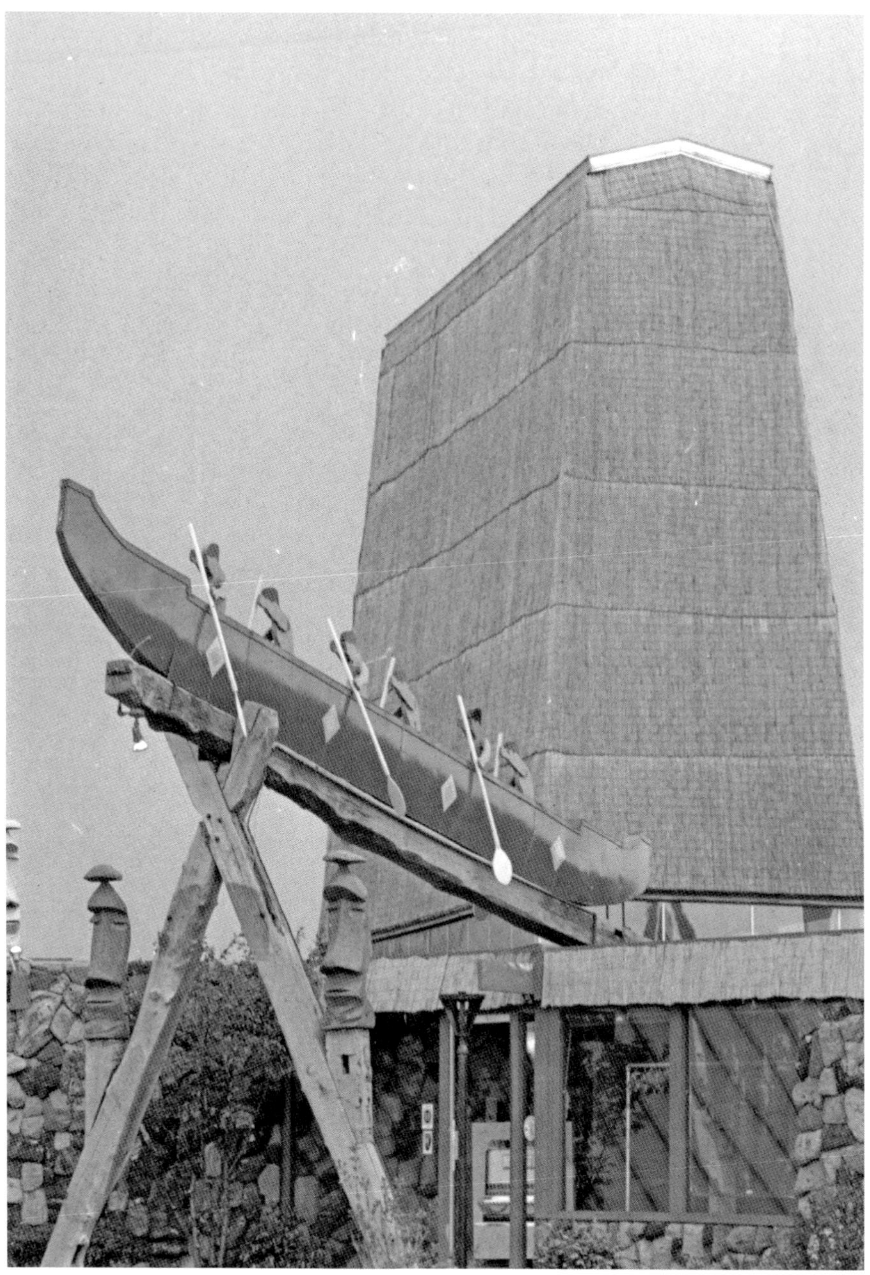

Hawaiian Gardens entrance. *Courtesy of Walter P. Reuther Library, Archives of Labor and Urban Affairs, Wayne State University.*

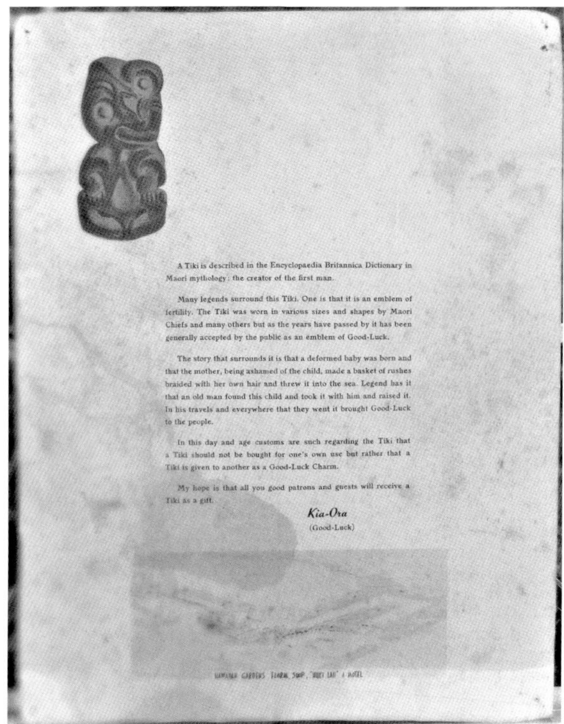

A Tiki is described in the Encyclopaedia Britannica Dictionary in Maori mythology: the creator of the first man.

Many legends surround this Tiki. One is that it is an emblem of fertility. The Tiki was worn in various sizes and shapes by Maori Chiefs and many others but as the years have passed by it has been generally accepted by the public as an emblem of Good-Luck.

The story that surrounds it is that a deformed baby was born and that the mother, being ashamed of the child, made a basket of rushes braided with her own hair and threw it into the sea. Legend has it that an old man found this child and took it with him and raised it. In his travels and everywhere that they went it brought Good-Luck to the people.

In this day and age customs are such regarding the Tiki that a Tiki should not be bought for one's own use but rather that a Tiki is given to another as a Good-Luck Charm.

My hope is that all you good patrons and guests will receive a Tiki as a gift.

Kia-Ora
(Good-Luck)

Back cover of Huki Lau menu. *Author's collection.*

was temperature controlled by fifty-one- to fifty-three-degree water that flowed constantly through a cabinet; the wine selection was extensive and impressive.

The restaurant was divided into three sections by glass sidewalls all connected by tropical courts. Plants acted as dividers; you could not see from one room to the next. The dividing walls/doors could be opened, creating one huge space. The Banyan Court, designed in the style of a Manu (Polynesian chief's house), was the largest of the three. A brochure reads, "Shaggy barked poles over 50 feet high support the sky-lighted, thatch-roofed Manu in Banyan Court." Divided into three rooms—the Tahitian, the Samoan and the Hawaiian—each could be screened off with grass blinds for privacy. The space enchanted guests with a waterfall, a miniature stream crossed with a bridge and carpeting the "color of grass-in-the-sun." Sunlight seeped in through the specially made skylight into the garden filled with trees, wisteria and bougainvillea. Melodies of island music played softly in the background; light flickered from hanging lanterns. The entire room gave the feeling you were on an outdoor patio. The back wall was glass and overlooked beautiful Lake Oahu.

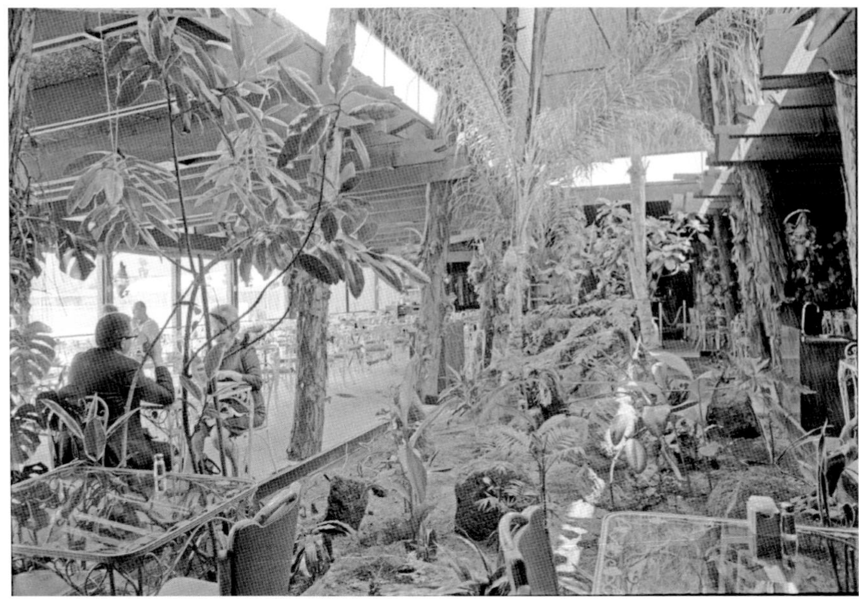

Banyan Court's fifty-foot skylighted, thatch-roofed Manu. *Courtesy of Walter P. Reuther Library, Archives of Labor and Urban Affairs, Wayne State University.*

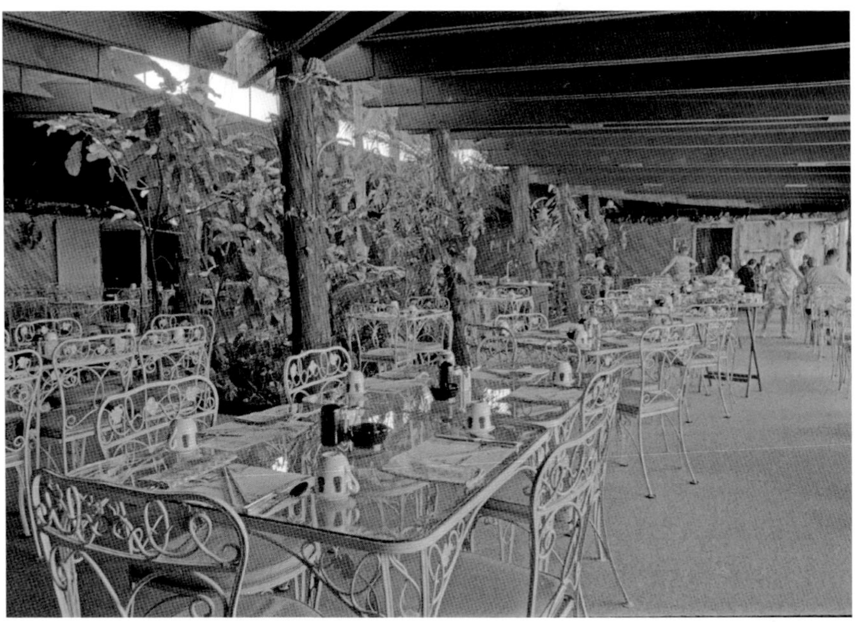

Dining tables in Banyan Court. *Courtesy of Walter P. Reuther Library, Archives of Labor and Urban Affairs, Wayne State University.*

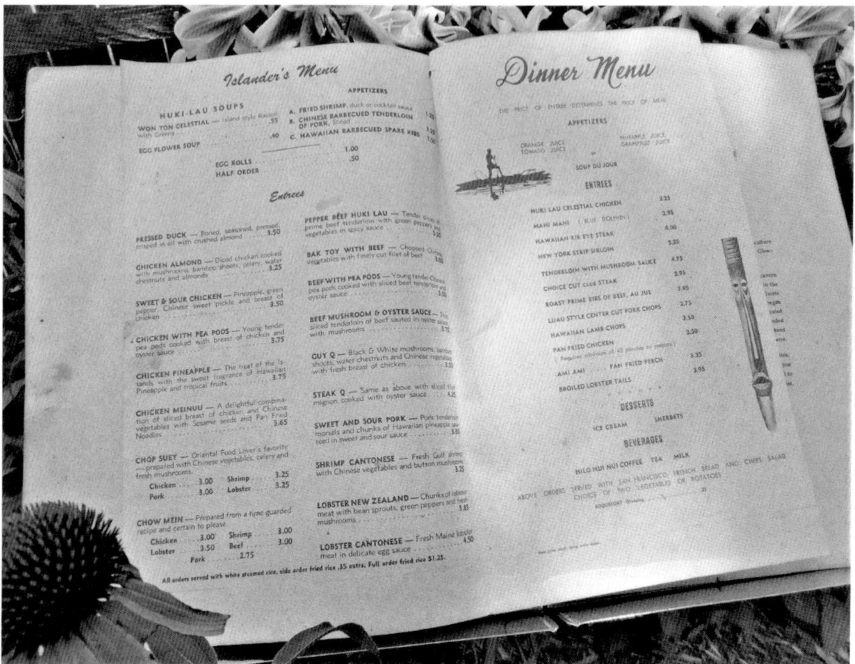

Huki Lau menu selections. *Author's collection.*

The Polynesian Longhouse was situated among bamboo walls, monkey pod wood, timbers and colorful lanterns. The back of a vintage postcard reads, "Here each item of food is an individual creation cooked especially for you. The dishes are varied and utilize the best efforts of our experienced native chefs using their original recipes." A vintage Huki Lau menu boasts some of the more exotic-sounding dishes, like Chicken Meinuu, Pepper Beef Huki Lau, Bak Toy with Beef and Lobster New Zealand.

The Kahili Room was completely different from the others in design and function. This was the room under the geodesic dome. Tables lined the circumference of the space, a large lantern hung in the center of the room and potted tropical plants lined a shelf circling the bottom of the dome. This is where the Fabulous Sunday Buffet was served and where the Exciting and Enchanting Royal Hawaiian Luau took place. Hawaiian Gardens played host to the big bands of Frank James, Clark Williams, Andy Zelenak and Don Pablo. Linda Howe performed her Hawaiian-Tahitian dance exhibition regularly. Stan Kenton, Lee Castle, the Jimmy Dorsey Orchestra and Frank Sinatra Jr. played here, as well as Guy Lombardo and his Royal Canadians, who performed here in June 1969.

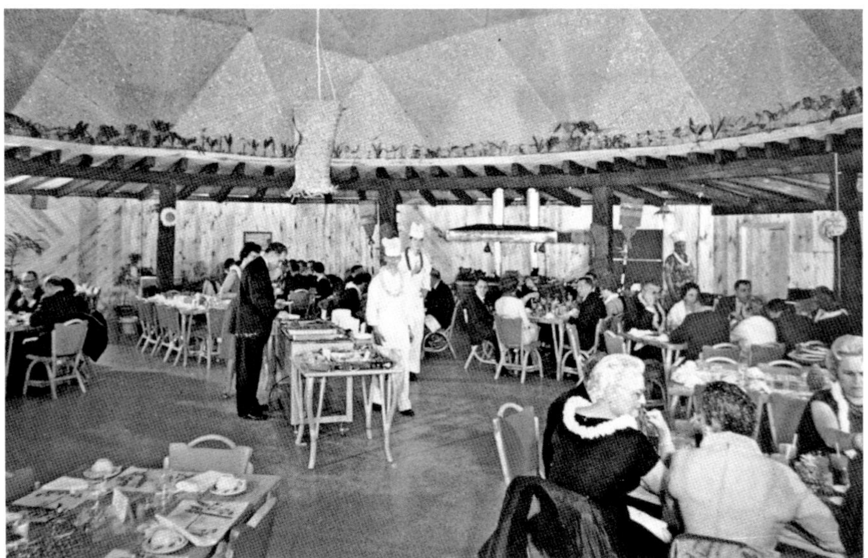

The geodesic dome of the Kahili Room. *Author's collection.*

The Waitoma Grotto Lounge is what many remember the most. The armchair bar and cocktail lounge served the finest Hawaiian drinks in real coconuts, fancy glasses or generic tiki mugs. Drinks arrived with tiny umbrellas, miniature fans or, if ordering something extra-fancy, smoke. Overlooking scenic Lake Oahu, the back wall of the lounge featured variegated lava rock, a ceiling of glimmering glowworms and a live volcano. Well, sort of...The Bartons describe their visit to the Glowworm Grotto in New Zealand in the Huki Lau menu as a phenomenon that is almost indescribable. They say as their boat pulled into the Glowworm Grotto, "we detected a splendor overhead, duplicated only on the clearest type of starlit night, as thousands of tiny glowworms suspended overhead twinkled and glowed." It made such an impression on them that they decided to re-create it right here in Holly. In a newspaper article, Don Winglemire recalled, "Fred paid a Girl Scout troop a penny per bead to make the glowworms for the ceiling." He estimates the girls strung three or four thousand beads that would flicker overhead. As for the volcano, patrons swayed to Hawaiian music on a lighted glass dance floor near the bar. Throughout the evening, the Mauna Loa volcano (named after the real thing on the island of Hawaii) would erupt. It would go like this. A recording of a volcano eruption would play; at first it was quiet, with a slight rumble, and then it would grow stronger and louder until it turned

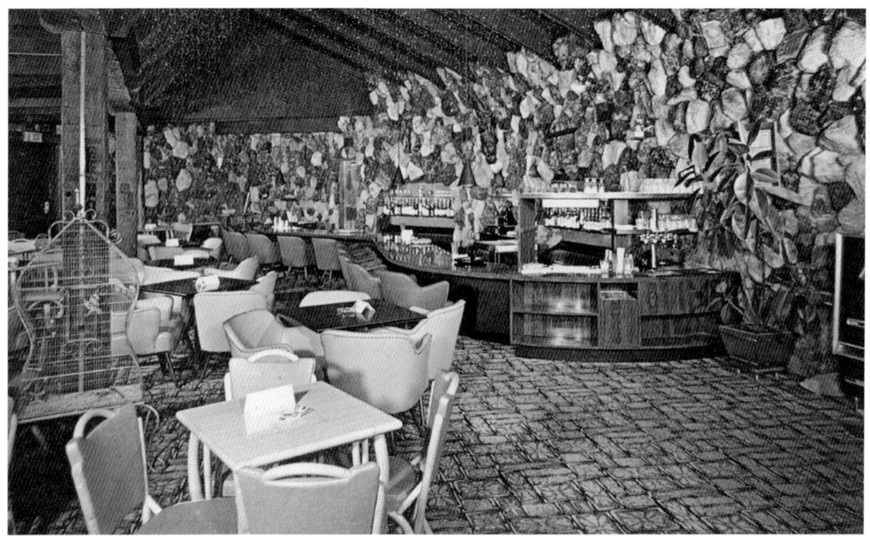

The Waitoma Grotto Lounge. *Author's collection.*

into a roar. Lights would dim in the bar, the dance floor would glow red—a mass of "lava" beneath their feet—the floor would begin to shake and then slowly it would subside. How cool must that have been in 1961 (or now)? All done electronically, it was a one-of-a-kind experience that thrilled visitors.

Hawaiian Gardens was all about escapism, fine dining and entertainment. This was the place you went to celebrate a special occasion, eat an extravagant meal, have a Mai Tai or a Singapore Sling and dance the night away. Fred and Jane paid attention to details, and staff members were trained to give outstanding service; dirty dishes were removed immediately, tables were cleaned off and reset quickly. Uniforms were Hawaiian shirts for men and floral sarongs for women. There were hat check girls, usually local teenagers paid five dollars a night. Doug Williams, who started working at the restaurant in 1962 as a busboy, worked his way up to head waiter. As he was young and athletic, his adult co-workers convinced him he'd make a perfect torch runner. When sunset came, Doug would head outside, taking flame to a torch. Starting at the pool, one by one he would light the torches and then make his way to those surrounding Lake Oahu, running around the perimeter until all were aglow. Customers got a kick out of seeing him in action; it often resulted in bigger tips. As head waiter, he had the good fortune to wait on Gordie Howe and Nancy Sinatra. Other famous visitors to Hawaiian Gardens include Frank Sinatra and Muhammad Ali.

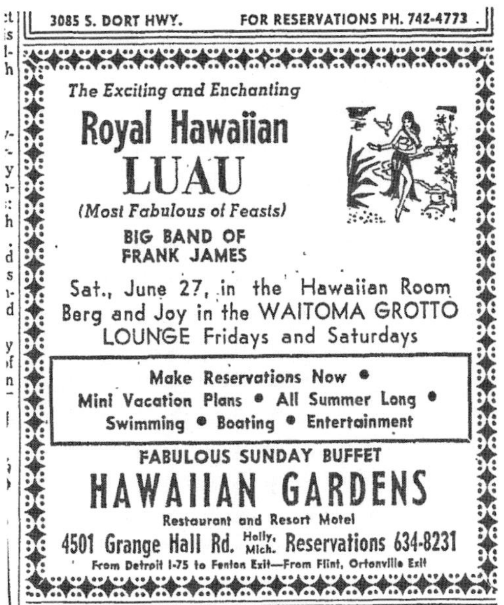

An advertisement for the Royal Hawaiian Luau at Hawaiian Gardens. *Author's collection.*

In addition to the restaurant and lounge, one could also visit the Wonderworld of Imports Gift Shop. Here you could purchase Hawaiian Gardens souvenirs such as postcards and chopsticks. Fred made regular trips overseas to stock the gift shop. You could buy lovely Asian clothing like a cheongsam dress, kimono, brocade pant sets or pajamas; clothes from Singapore with Mandarin collars were popular. How about a pair of shoes to go with that new dress? Don't forget the handbag. Porcelain chopstick holders came in the form of bunnies, turtles and fish. They sold serving dishes, imitation jade statues, tiki keychains, Buddhas on a wooden base, fancy dolls from Asia, hand-painted fans and parasol-style umbrellas made of wood and wax paper. Hand-knit sweaters came from Hong Kong. It really was a wonder world of imports. Tropical plants grown in the greenhouse and placed in lava planters constructed by Hawaiian Gardens employees were also available.

Fred did his best to build and outfit the resort using as many local businesses as possible. From contractors, plumbers and electricians to the supplies, food, butcher, furnishings and employees, he involved the entire community. Don Winglemire, who owned Winglemire Furniture in the Village of Holly, said, "All of the furniture in the restaurant and bar, all of the motel furniture, the beds, light fixtures, televisions—everything right down to the Kleenex tissue holders were furnished by us." Employees came from Holly, Fenton, Grand Blanc and Clarkston. Local

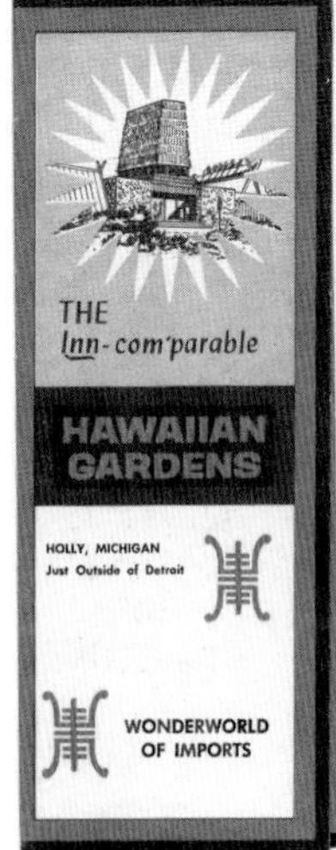

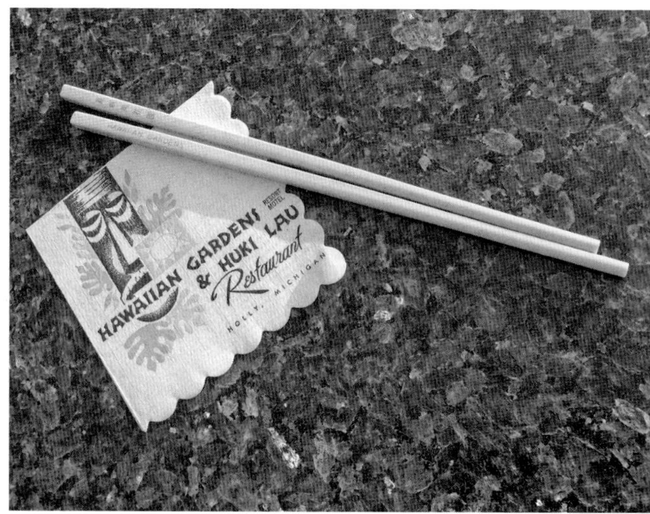

Left: The front of the Hawaiian Gardens menu noting the Wonderworld of Imports. *Courtesy of the Holly Township Library.*

Right: A cocktail napkin and chopsticks. *Author's collection.*

teens served as dishwashers, busboys, hat check girls and lei-makers and mowed the lawns.

Opening night was a huge deal for the Bartons and residents of Holly. To get ready for the big opening, Fred had boxes of exotic flowers flown in from Hawaii. Local teens were called upon to string the leis. Linda Lee recalled sitting in the cooler stringing flowers. They were taught specifically which order the flowers were to be strung in and which colors went next to each other. Linda can still remember her hands being so cold she couldn't feel her fingers; she was having so much fun it didn't matter. As each lei was finished, it hung in the cooler waiting to be placed around the neck of a guest. Opening night was invitation only. James Michener, author of the novel *Hawaii*, was invited but did not attend.

According to the July 20, 1961 *Herald Advertiser*:

> *Hawaii came to Holly Tuesday evening when Mayor Eddie Tam and Mrs. Tam of Wailuku Maui, Hawaii were guests of Mr. and Mrs. Fred Barton of Hawaiian Gardens for a dinner in their honor in the Huki Lau restaurant. About 30 newspaper, television and radio representatives were also guests for dinner. Guests were welcomed with leis of miniature orchids and other South Sea island flowers, and cocktails were served in one of the*

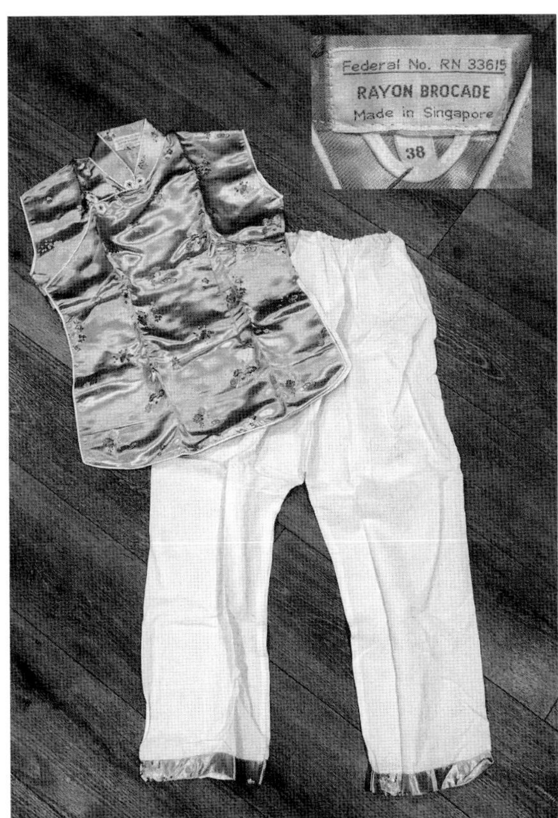

Right: A brocade pant set sold in the Wonderworld of Imports. *Courtesy of Jenine Grover.*

Below: Mandarin collars adorned much of the clothing sold in the Wonderworld of Imports. *Courtesy of Jenine Grover.*

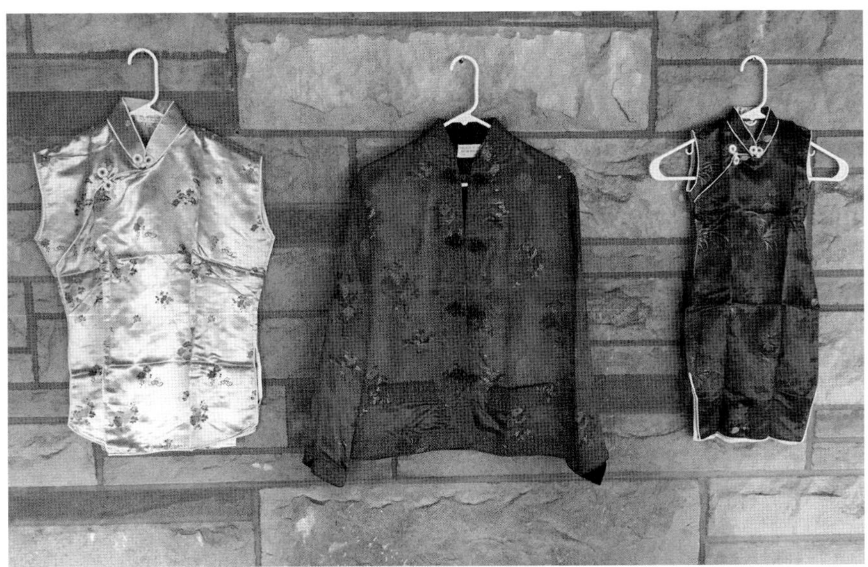

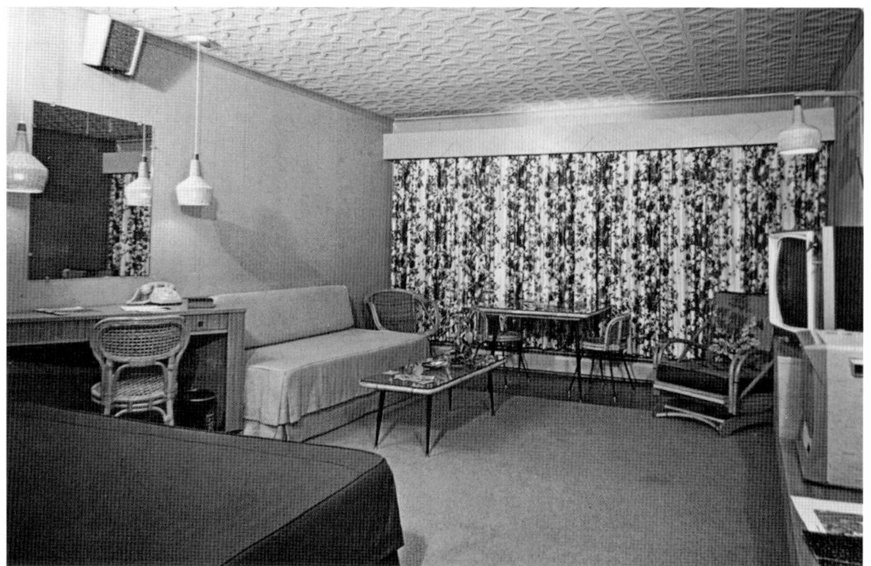

A motel room at Hawaiian Gardens Resort. *Courtesy of Barb Soloko.*

> *private dining rooms where the refreshment table was centered with a four-foot ice carving of a hula girl surrounded by pineapples, fresh flowers and tropical greens.*

The following week, Holly merchants held their second annual Hawaiian sidewalk sale. The first year was a tribute to our newest state. In its second year, the Bartons worked with the local merchants to make the event even more authentically Hawaiian by including "gayly decorated streets and several entertainment features," as a newspaper account put it. In an old family movie, there are outdoor scenes of a woman (presumably Linda Howe) in a grass skirt performing an island dance up on a stage.

Imagine what it must have been like back then. Picture a snowy, frigid Michigan winter day; you drive around the parking lot looking for the closest space to the door as the wind howls. You step inside to a completely different environment—warm, extravagant and exotic. The three-foot snow piles in the parking lot have evaporated from your mind. The soothing sound of Hawaiian music and natural light wash over you as you are shown to your table. An enormous buffet is laid out—shrimp, lobster, Hawaiian pineapple, tropical fruits; you take a little of everything. Outside the window, people in heavy coats, scarves and mittens ice skate on the frozen-over Lake Oahu. Inside, the luau begins; grass skirts shake on the hips of dancers. You are

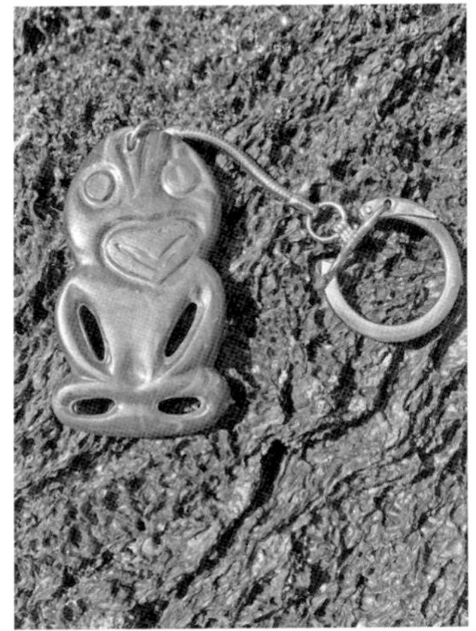

Left: Hawaiian Gardens keychain. *Courtesy of Jenine Grover.*

Below: Waitoma Grotto Bar. *Courtesy of Walter P. Reuther Library, Archives of Labor and Urban Affairs, Wayne State University.*

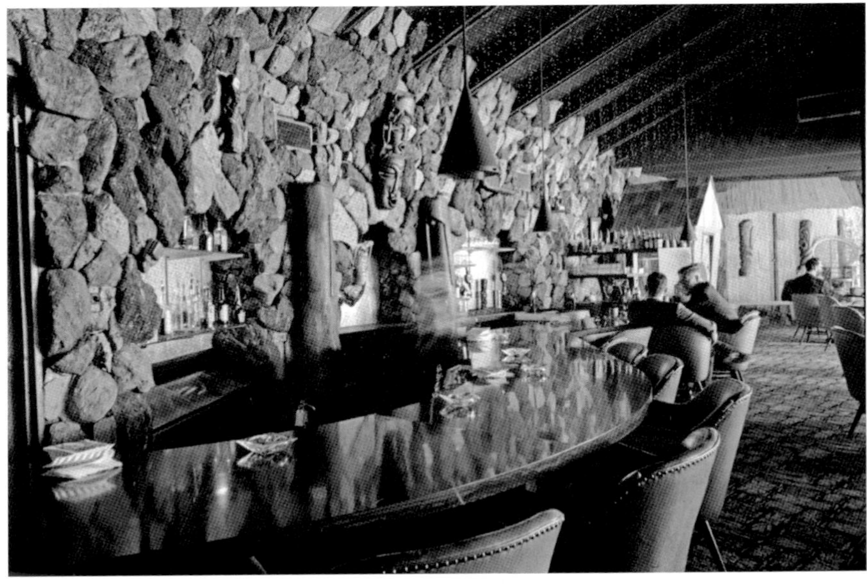

surrounded by island beauty. By the time the show is over, you have finished your meal, and a cocktail sounds perfect. You grab the tiki keychain that has been left on your table for good luck and make your way to the lounge. While sipping on your sweet rum drink in the Waitoma Grotto, you marvel at the glowworms above, feeling like you are on vacation in a faraway place. When your glass is empty, you wander among volcanic rock and palm trees to the gift shop. You purchase souvenirs just like a tourist would do, something to take home and show your friends when you tell them about your *trip.* It was not unusual to see a long line of cars creeping down Grange Hall

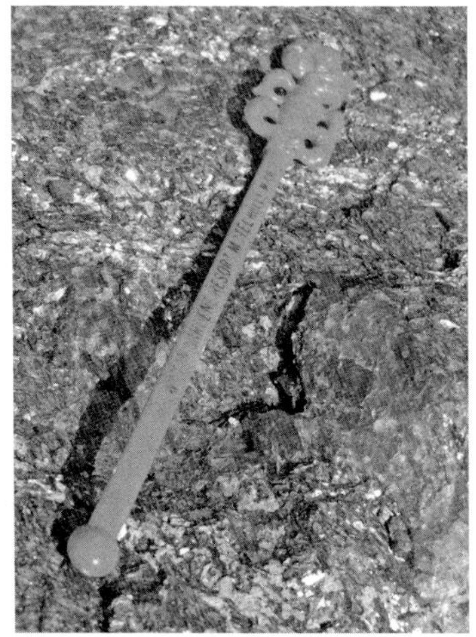

Hawaiian Gardens swizzle stick. *Author's collection.*

Road waiting to get into the parking lot. Mark Hill, who worked as a busboy, recalls that Hawaiian Gardens was very elegant; people dressed up to come. They didn't grab a meal and leave; they lingered, He also says lots of wheelers and dealers came here. Business deals were made under the palm trees to the sound of an erupting volcano and steel drums.

Hawaiian Gardens opened at the ideal time; Hawaii became a state in 1959, and people were fascinated by it—though most could not afford to travel there. Fred Barton transported them there, even if it was only for a few hours. Father Thomas Marble was a dishwasher when he was a teen, and he said the room that held the dishwasher was large, like an army or hospital dish room. As it was the lowest room in the complex, there were uphill ramps leading to the dining room, banquet room, bar and kitchen. The dishwasher was enormous, the size of a F-250 pickup truck. The work was hard, hot and dirty; in the summer, it could reach one hundred degrees in there with the gas-heated machine chugging away. On Sundays when the brunch was winding down, those in the dish room could have all they wanted from what was left on the buffet. Another woman said her mother, Marilyn Davis, was one of the first people hired. Their family dessert recipe, Pineapple Torte, became the house dessert. People had their proms, rehearsal dinners, anniversary parties and significant birthdays at Hawaiian Gardens. At least one couple I know spent their wedding night in the Honeymoon Cottage.

Fred Barton owned Hawaiian Gardens from 1961 to 1965. In that time, his marriage to Jane broke up, and he married the woman he would spend the rest of his life with, OiChun. He met OiChun on one of his buying trips to Hong Kong; her family business supplied the gift shop with beautiful hand-knit items sold there. Granddaughter Jenine remembers receiving many lovely handmade items from OiChun through the years. Fred's dream was centered on bringing Hawaiian Gardens to the people more than the day-to-day operations of the place; it was all about the fun of creating it for him. He had hoped the motel and resort would take off as well as the Huki Lau did, but for the most part, the people who came were local. Mount Holly Ski Resort did not attract enough out-of-town visitors to keep the motel filled.

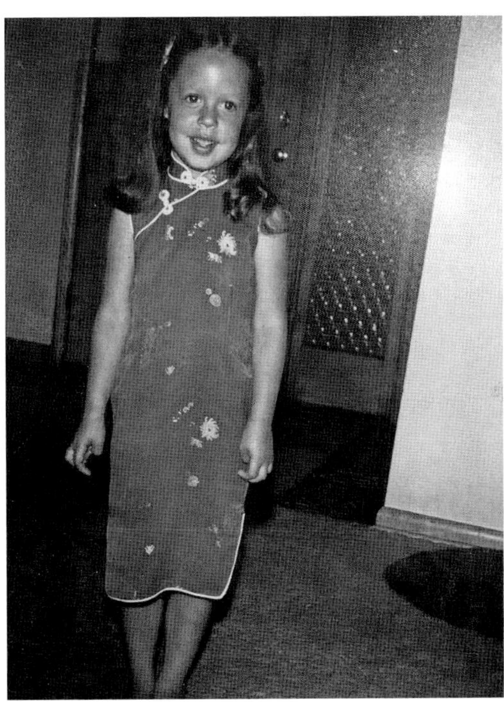

Jenine models a dress given to her by her grandfather Fred Barton. *Courtesy of Jenine Grover.*

In 1965, Fred built Hawaiian Gardens Mobile Home Retirement Village, despite great opposition from the community. A short drive down Grange Hall Road from the resort, it was not a popular development with the locals. Surrounding Lake Mauna Loa (of course), the street names are all Hawaiian. In a strange twist of fate, the mobile home park is still there today, and the restaurant is long gone. Fred had also offered to build a new church building in the Hawaiian style for his parish but was turned down. Fred's generous and whimsical nature was being stifled; the fun was gone. In 1965, Fred sold Hawaiian Gardens Resort to his attorneys, Jim and John Shea. The Shea brothers didn't change anything; they had a good thing going. They were friends of Fred and understood what he had created. Even though he was no longer there, a bit of his personality remained within the walls.

In 1972, Hawaiian Gardens not only changed hands, but the entire theme changed. After three months of construction, the Electric Crater disco opened its doors, catering to those from eighteen to twenty-one years old. The floor of the volcano was converted to a Plexiglas dance floor with different-colored lights electronically synchronized to the music; pool tables and two screens that showed movies minus the sound were also added. When that failed, it reopened as Governor's Gardens Restaurant, and then the restaurant went

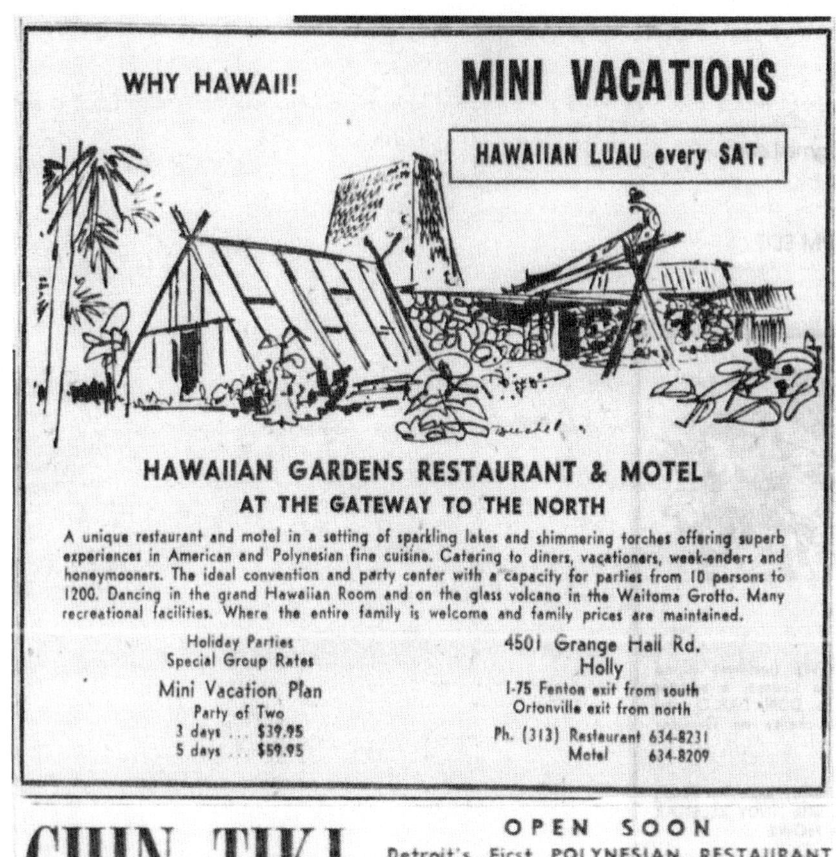

Hawaiian Gardens Resort advertises that a party of two could stay three days for $39.95. *Author's collection.*

back to the old Hawaiian Gardens name. Ownership changed four times in a decade. In 1976, the building was transformed into an Alpine village theme called Vladimir's Inn; in 1979, it was Lake Valley Inn. Nothing ever came close to the success enjoyed by Fred Barton's original Hawaiian Gardens. At some point, Fred got possession of all the old furnishings, decorations and dishes. He rented a storefront in the village and sold everything, and the proceeds went to charity. In 1984, the property was taken over by Holly Gardens, a nonprofit drug and alcohol rehab center, which stayed open until the late 1990s. In 2003, the abandoned buildings became the victims of an

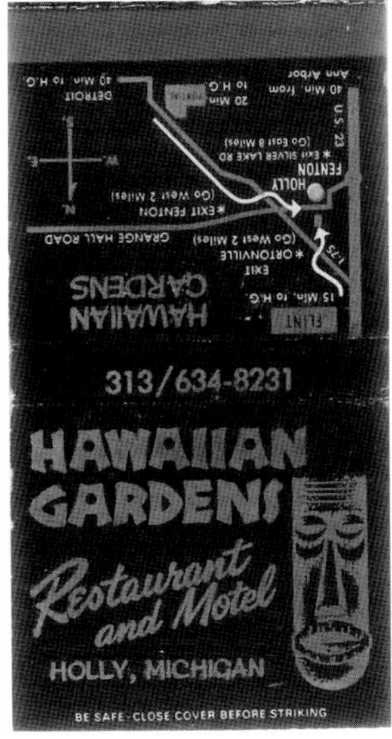

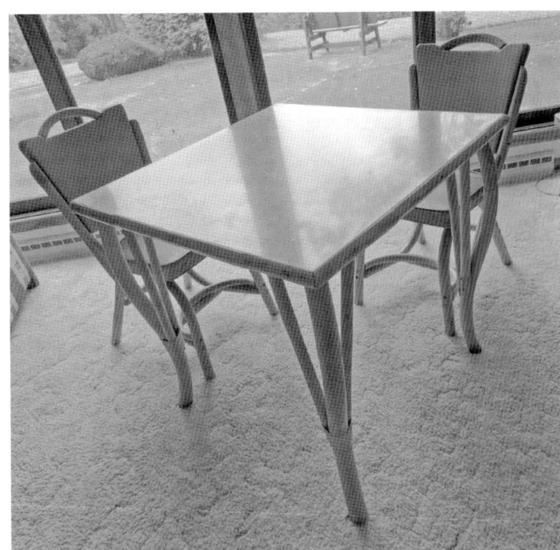

Left: A souvenir matchbook with tiki. *Courtesy of Scott Schell.*

Right: An original Hawaiian Gardens table and chairs. *Courtesy of Barb Soloko.*

arsonist and burned to the ground. Local newspapers were filled with stories of the glory days of Hawaiian Gardens. All that remains today is a section of the parking lot on Grange Hall Road.

At the home Fred Barton built when he was married to Jane, perched overlooking another of the lovely lakes he was so adept at building, a large lava rock rests on the patio. Fred did get to live his dream of living in Hawaii, for he and OiChun lived there for a time. On the big island, he was called Old Gray Beard. Known for his generosity, he gave ukuleles to jailed men so they could learn how to play them in order to have an occupation when released. Fred and OiChun moved to Las Vegas, where the air was better for his health. Fred Barton passed away in Las Vegas in 1975 at the age of sixty-seven. An episode of *Operation Success* hosted by Clinton Reynolds featured Fred. It focused on the success of Bar's Leaks; his multiple business endeavors, including the Shangri La apartments in Reno, Nevada; and Hawaiian Gardens. He has been described as a colorful, bearded industrialist, a world traveler, an entrepreneur extraordinaire. He was quirky, fun-loving, kind and generous. He created, in his words, "a soft, colorful paradise, an atmosphere with an easy state of mind" straight from his imagination; it was unique, just like he was unique. Almost sixty years later, it still brings a smile to people's faces.

Chapter 6

THE CHIN TIKI

The Chin Tiki is Detroit's best-known tiki restaurant. It certainly had the longest tenure; it opened in 1966 and closed in 1980. It was a destination that appealed to all ages, budgets and classes. The lot at 2121 Cass Avenue was once a parking structure owned by the Loyal Order of Moose. Along came Marvin Chin, a multitalented engineer-turned-restaurateur, who transformed the parcel into a Polynesian jungle paradise. Chin Tiki not only hosted celebrities but also became a celebrity itself after appearing in the movie *8 Mile* in 2002. With new life breathing between the mural-adorned, bamboo-clad walls, there was a glimmer of hope for a reopening, but it never came to fruition.

Chin Tiki was not Marvin's first foray into the restaurant business; you could say entrepreneurship runs in the family. In the 1920s, Marvin's father left Canton, China. An article in the February 2008 issue of *Hour Detroit* explains:

> *Jin Chin, who later changed his name to Joe sailed to the United States. He came through Ellis Island in New York, and eventually to Detroit, where he had a Chinese laundry before going into the grocery business. There, the roots of the Chin family food business were planted. For nearly eight decades, the Chin family has been one of the most prominent in Chinese food in the Detroit area. First, as owners of Wah Lee, one of the biggest Chinese-goods stores and importer and exporter-distributor in the original Chinatown area, near the spot where the MGM Grand Detroit now*

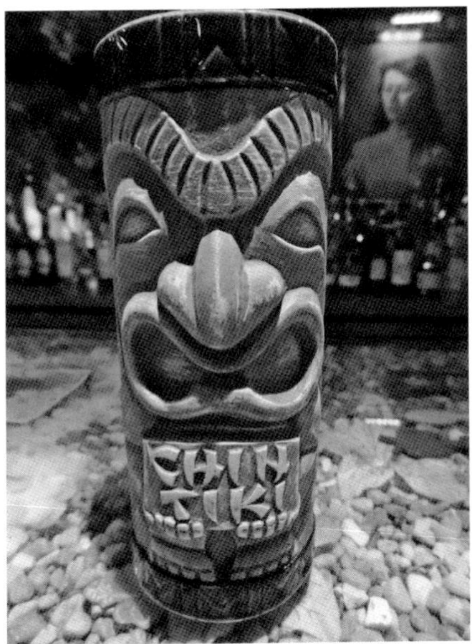

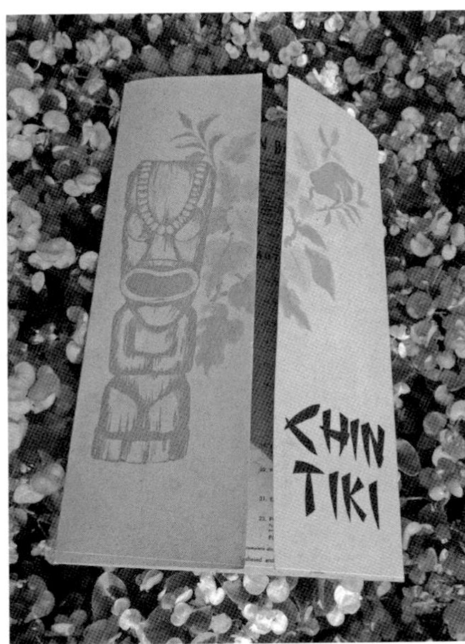

Left: The only mug style to bear the Chin Tiki name. *Courtesy of Tim Shuller.*

Right: Chin Tiki menu. *Author's collection.*

> *sits near Bagley, Third and Porter. The store supplied vegetables, goods and spices to Chinese restaurants throughout the area. Joe Chin's success allowed him to back several restaurant ventures for his extended family, most of whom were Chinese, and other Asian-themed places that operated with the names Chin and Chung as part of their titles.*

Marvin's sister Gloria Suie Chin moved to California in the 1940s with hopes of becoming a movie star. Her first role came in 1947. The movie was *Singapore*, starring Fred MacMurray and Ava Gardner. Gloria—who changed her name to Maylia—married actor Benson Fong. Fong was looking for a steady source of income between acting roles, so Marvin, his father and Fong became partners in a restaurant. A June 15, 1970 *Detroit Free Press* article explained:

> *Chin's first experience in the Chinese food business was a disaster. He and his father and a relative, Benson Fong the movie actor who played the role of Charlie Chan's No 2 son pooled resources to open Fong's in Hollywood on Vine Street. A big bash was staged when Fong's opened. But business never picked it. "It was a recession year and we went broke. Our overhead was*

> *too high," Chin recalls....Chin temporarily erased the restaurant business from his mind and turned his thoughts once again to making cars. But not for long. He and Kitty moved to Livonia "and we discovered there was no place to eat out there."*

According to the family, the couple opened Chin's Chop Suey on Plymouth Road in 1953, followed by Kitty's in Garden City in 1957; both were takeout joints. "In 1965 he bought the Jackson Bar on Gratiot in Detroit and in 1966 he opened the Chin Tiki, a Chinese-Polynesian restaurant and night club in downtown Detroit on Cass." Newspaper articles began mentioning the new restaurant going up on Cass early in 1966. The "Passing Parade" article from the *Detroit Free Press* of February 22, 1966, notes:

> *A quiet youthful-looking mechanical engineer is putting his heart and soul into a building that doesn't look like very much from the outside yet—at 2121 Cass. Marvin Chin, 41-year-old native Detroiter, hopes that by opening day not too many weeks off, the front of the two-story building will be an intriguing expanse of sand sculpture. Inside, a visitor will be introduced to the sights and sounds of a waterfall, murals depicting the South Seas, tables tucked under thatched eaves and Polynesian cookery. Chin spent eight years as a plant engineer at Ford Motor. But his real interest has always been in the restaurant field....Marvin tried his hand at a Polynesian restaurant out there* [California]. *"It was either too soon or I didn't know enough and I failed." Back home, Chin has been active in the management of two family restaurants in Livonia, but his dreams have kept returning to his own Chin Tiki, now seven years in the planning...A brother, William ordered from the islands the huge wooden hand-carved tikis or gods that lend their name to the restaurant....Another native Detroiter, artist Blaine Perrigo, who has done much of his work in Cleveland, returned here to help Chin with the decorating, executed the murals that give the place an outdoors feeling.*

Piecing together newspaper articles, it appears Chin Tiki opened in July 1966. The *Detroit Free Press* of July 31, 1966, mentions "Son of Chan Visits Chin" and that "Benson Fong, noted Chinese-American actor currently appearing in the movie 'Our Man Flint,' is in Detroit to visit his brother-in-law, Marvin Chin, owner of the newly opened Chin Tiki Restaurant, Cass and Grand River."

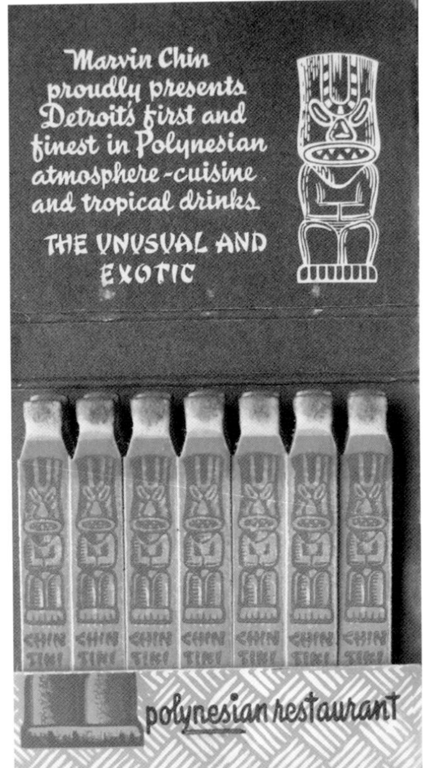

Right: Chin Tiki matchbook. Every match is a tiki. *Courtesy of Sven Kirsten.*

Below: Chin Tiki menu and coaster. *Chin family collection, photo by Amy Sacka.*

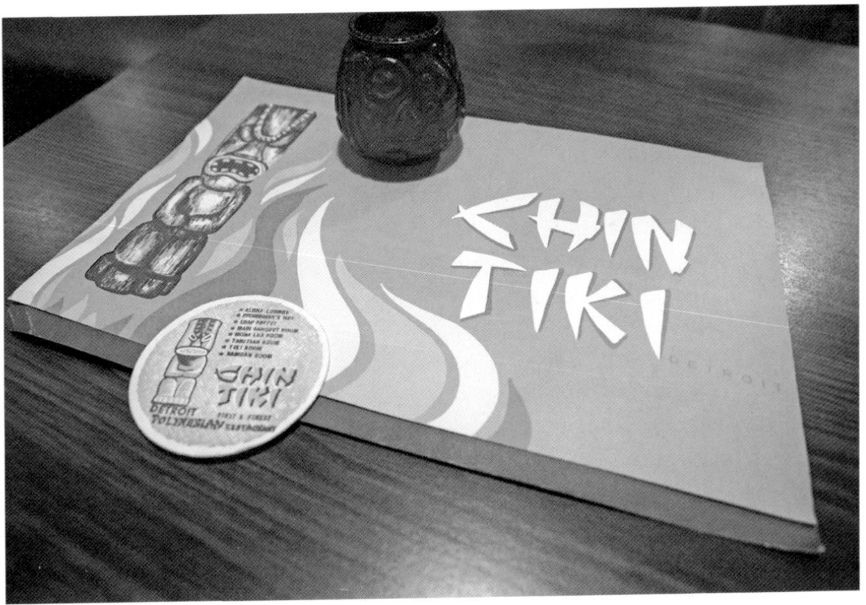

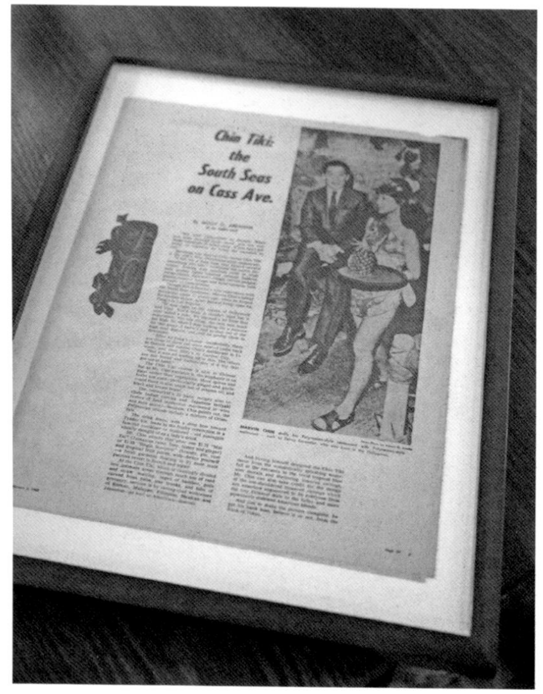

Chin Tiki: the South Seas on Cass Ave.

A framed Molly Abraham newspaper article. *Chin family collection, photo by Amy Sacka.*

Those close to Marvin tell tales of his ingenuity and craftsmanship; his younger brother Marshall speaks fondly of him, saying, "Marvin could do anything." Son Marlin recalls that his dad "loved to build things." He was hands-on, artistic and creative, with an engineer's mindset. Chuck Thurston of the *Detroit Free Press* wrote an article about the Chin Tiki on August 16, 1966; his description allows us to picture it in our imagination.

> *Stepping Out to Polynesia, Right Here on Cass Ave. It wouldn't take much imagination to turn Cass Avenue's traffic rumble into the roar of Pacific surf, so stimulating is Chin Tiki, Marvin Chin's dream of a Polynesian restaurant brought to life at 2121 Cass near downtown.*
>
> *You enter through idol-carved doors beneath flaming torches. The door swings shut and Detroit is 10,000 miles away. You take a moment to adjust your eyes to the jungle light, then crossing a tiny bridge over a rippling stream, you've been taken in tow by a tiny Pacific girl who wraps a lei around your neck and leads you to a table.*
>
> *Some of these Eastern creatures are very small and care must be taken by tall, near-sighted men not to trample any in the dim light. The dim light is a colorful light, though, filtering through a wild assortment of fixtures,*

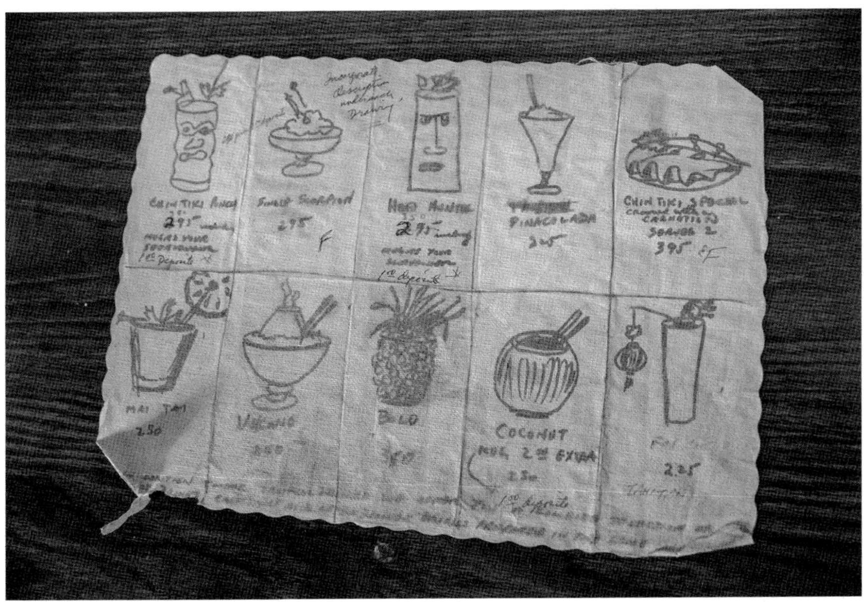

Marvin's rough sketch of the Chin Tiki cocktail menu. *Chin family collection, photo by Amy Sacka.*

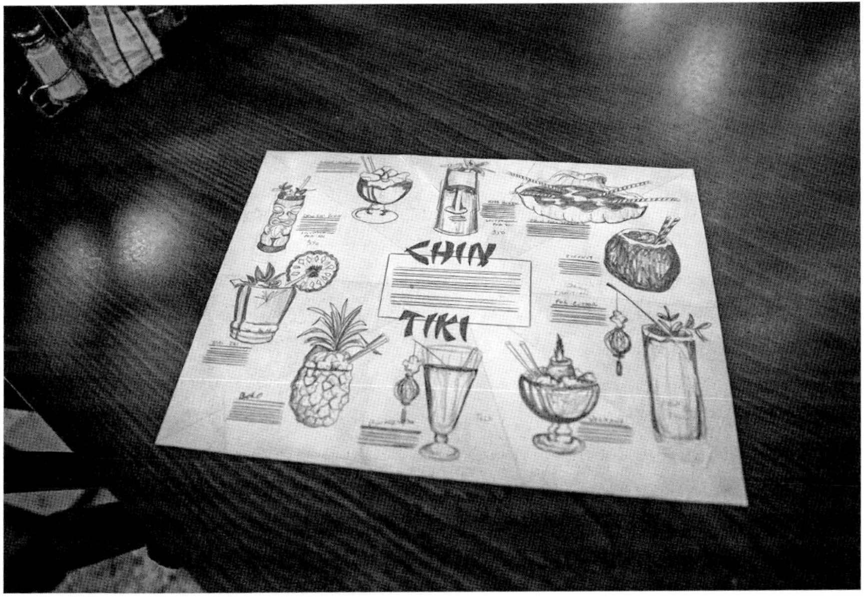

Marvin's refined cocktail menu sketch. *Chin family collection, photo by Amy Sacka.*

many of them handmade wicker baskets, bread baskets and what seem to be size 28½ hats made of reeds.

Marvin Chin and decorator Blaine Perrigo put these things together during 14 months recently. Chin who had done some Polynesian restauranting in Los Angeles some years back started gathering material for this one eight years ago, gradually filling a two-car garage with Oriental-island fixings, including great wicker chairs and exquisite black wooden chairs with splashing colors in their flowered seats.

Blaine Perrigo came up from Cleveland and started painting and carving and creating the atmosphere that transformed a parking garage....

The restaurant is divided into cozy segments separated by bamboo and beaded partitions, the sort that Rita Hayworth might step through. At the bar brightly shirted bartenders concoct huge jugs of smoking, bubbling gardenia-floating drinks. Needless to say, these rum-based potions should be approached with care and respect.

Girl watchers would be well advised to bring along their spectacles. [Remember, this is 1966.] *There are waitresses from Japan, Korea, the Philippines and any number of Pacific Islands. Some are wrapped to the floor in brightly printed shiny cloth and others wear slashed sarongs. Here and there a blond has slipped in but for the most part the girls are right out of the Orient, dark, pretty and often heavily accented.*

There isn't a floor show, but with all those lovely girls, who needs one? And there's magic in the food, too—exotic meats and sauces so dear to the gourmet heart. It's all so, well, different—like being somewhere else for a while.

The August 12, 1966 *Detroit Free Press* entertainment section had this to say:

Always open on Sunday is Marvin Chin's exotic new Polynesian restaurant, the Chin Tiki on Cass, where giant fresh gardenias float on the "scorpions" one of the many unusual tropical drinks and the menu comes straight from the Islands. Specifically remembered, the seasoned meatballs (po po), the curry Shrimp Singapore, the Steak Kow Lapo Lapo (black mushrooms included) and the best of all, Balamaki, thin strips of marinated beef in a secret sauce.

Free Press staff writer Louis Cook reviewed the Chin Tiki on August 14, 1966:

In order to get into Chin Tiki at 2121 Cass you have to reach into an idol's eye, a rather unnerving experience, but once inside, Detroit's new Polynesian restaurant is softly-lit, cool and decorated to make one hear the distant

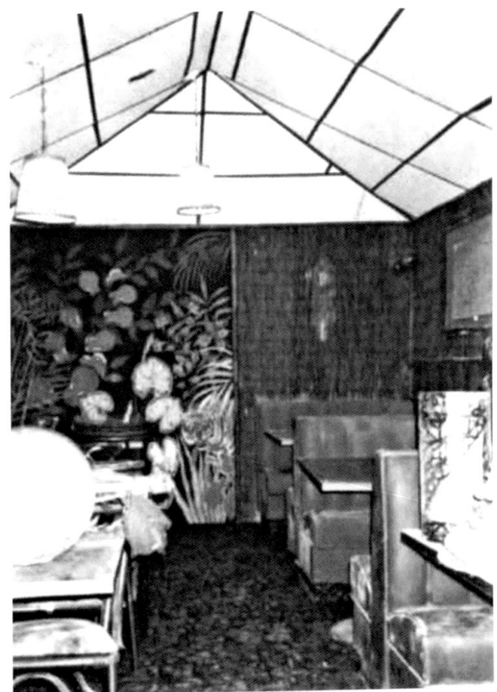

Right: Original Chin Tiki interior.
Courtesy of Scott Schell.

Below: Chin Tiki cocktail menu.
Private collection, photo by Nick Hagen.

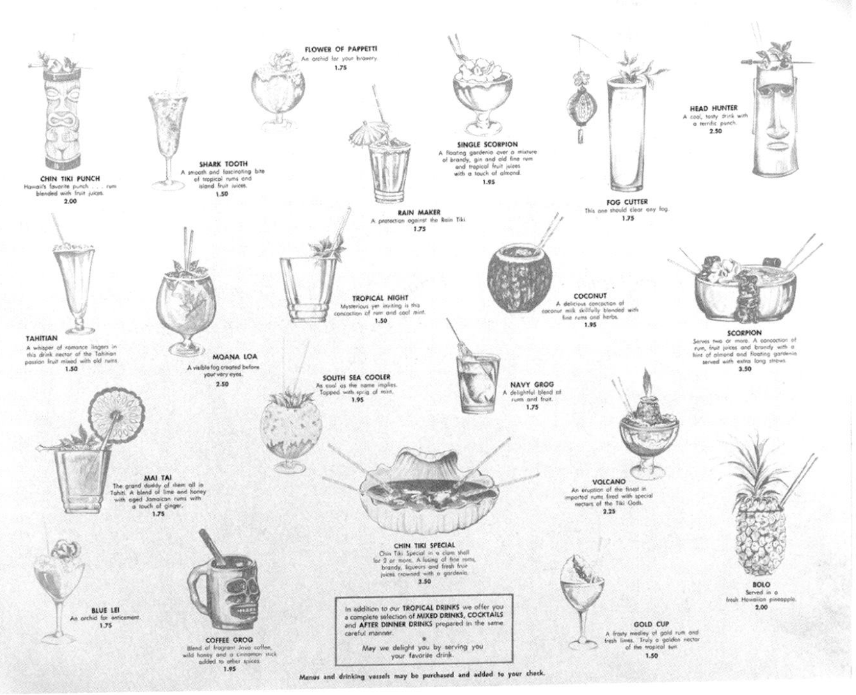

CHIN TIKI PUNCH
Hawaii's favorite punch . . . rum blended with fruit juices.
2.00

SHARK TOOTH
A smooth and fascinating bite of tropical rums and island fruit juices.
1.50

FLOWER OF PAPPETTI
An orchid for your bravery.
1.75

RAIN MAKER
A protection against the Rain Tiki
1.75

SINGLE SCORPION
A floating gardenia over a mixture of brandy, gin and old fine rum and tropical fruit juices with a touch of almond.
1.95

FOG CUTTER
This one should clear any fog.
1.75

HEAD HUNTER
A cool, tasty drink with a terrific punch.
2.50

TAHITIAN
A whisper of romance lingers in this drink nectar of the Tahitian passion fruit mixed with old rums.
1.50

MOANA LOA
A visible fog created before your very eyes.
2.50

TROPICAL NIGHT
Mysterious yet inviting is this concoction of rum and cool mint.
1.50

COCONUT
A delicious concoction of coconut milk skillfully blended with fine rums and herbs.
1.95

SCORPION
Serves two or more. A concoction of rum, fruit juices and brandy with a hint of almond and floating gardenia served with extra long straws.
3.50

SOUTH SEA COOLER
As cool as the name implies. Topped with sprig of mint.
1.95

NAVY GROG
A delightful blend of rum and fruit.
1.75

MAI TAI
The grand daddy of them all in Tahiti. A blend of lime and honey with aged Jamaican rums with a touch of ginger.
1.75

VOLCANO
An eruption of the finest in imported rums fired with special nectars of the Tiki Gods.
2.25

CHIN TIKI SPECIAL
Chin Tiki Special in a clam shell for 2 or more. A fusing of fine rums, brandy, liqueurs and fresh fruit juices crowned with a gardenia.
3.50

BOLO
Served in a fresh Hawaiian pineapple.
2.00

BLUE LEI
An orchid for enticement.
1.75

COFFEE GROG
Blend of fragrant Java coffee, wild honey and a cinnamon stick added to other spices.
1.95

In addition to our **TROPICAL DRINKS** we offer you a complete selection of **MIXED DRINKS, COCKTAILS** and **AFTER DINNER DRINKS** prepared in the same careful manner.

May we delight you by serving you your favorite drink.

GOLD CUP
A frosty medley of gold rum and fresh limes. Truly a golden nectar of the tropical sun.
1.50

Menus and drinking vessels may be purchased and added to your check.

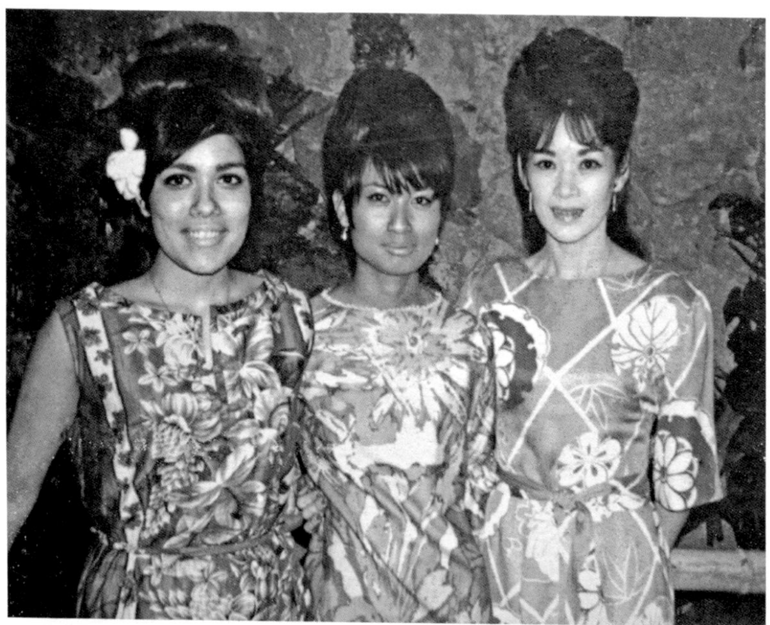

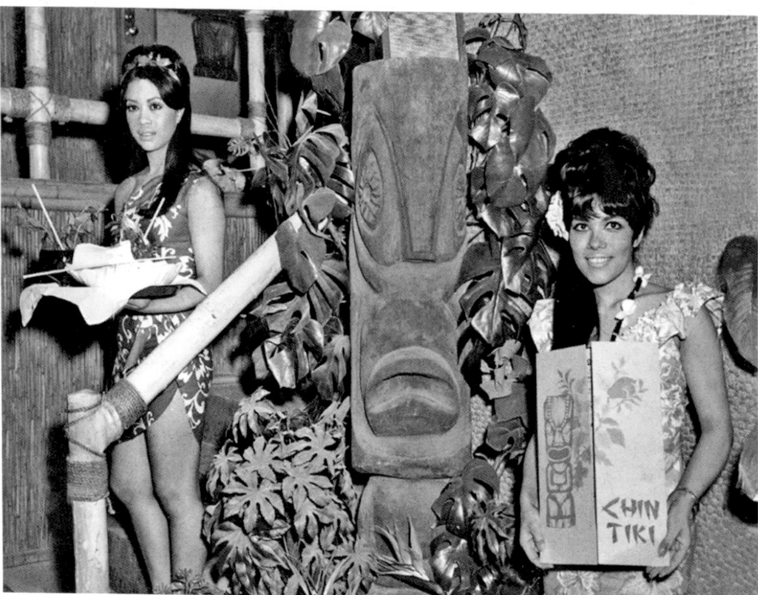

Top: Seating hostesses. Kawehilani worked as a seating hostess and server for Marvin Chin for many years. She was also a dancer in the Chin Tiki Polynesian Revue. She is on the left, and Helen Fujiwara is on the right. *Courtesy of Kim Fujiwara.*

Bottom: Chin Tiki lobby. At left, Belen carries a tray of cocktails; Kawehilani is on the right. *Courtesy of Sven Kirsten, photo retouched by Kim Fujiwara.*

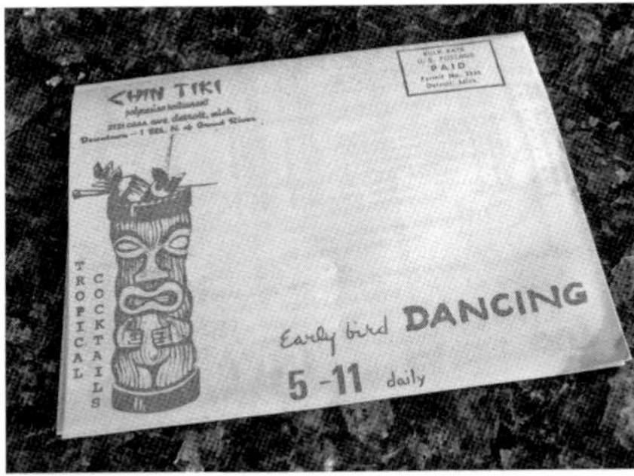

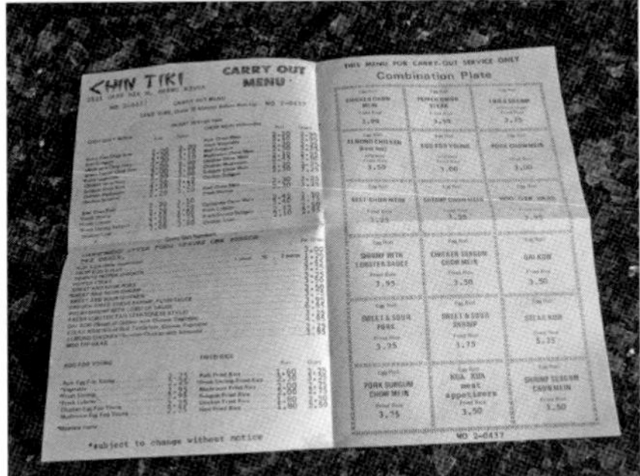

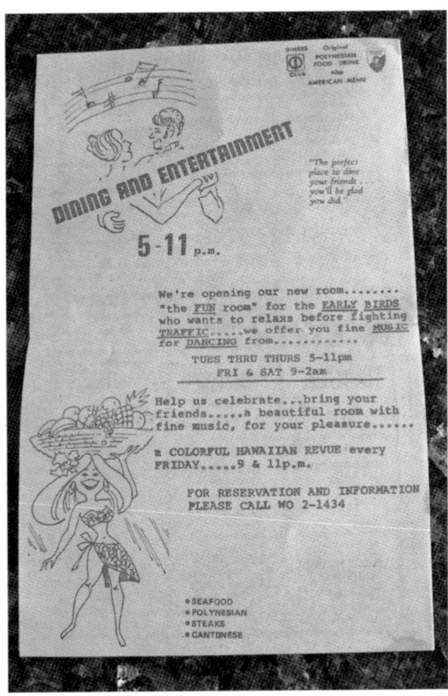

Left, top: Chin Tiki carry-out menu. *Author's collection.*

Left, bottom: The carry-out menu includes combination plates, chop suey, chow mein, fried rice and egg foo young. *Author's collection.*

Right: The menu advertises dining and entertainment: a Colorful Hawaiian Revue every Friday, 9:00 and 11:00 p.m. *Author's collection.*

> *boom of surf on the outer reef of the atoll. It is wise to consult one of the bare-foot waitresses extensively about the menu. But you can't go wrong with Kau Kau (pronounced Koah Koah), which is a collection of things done with fish, pork, chicken and lobster. The Chin Tiki specializes in drinks formulated with exotic and obscure juices but you can get an excellent Martini of you are properly polite.*

Chin Tiki was the place Marvin had waited for, dreamed of. For years, he had an image in his head, and now he had brought it to life. Once you were inside the windowless building, you stood in the lobby, where a stream ran beneath your feet, a counter stood ready to sell you trinkets and novelties and a hat check girl was at the ready to relieve you of your coat and hat. To the left, a lovely hostess was waiting to lead you across a bamboo bridge, past five-foot-tall tikis and a waterfall cascading down tufa rock deeper into

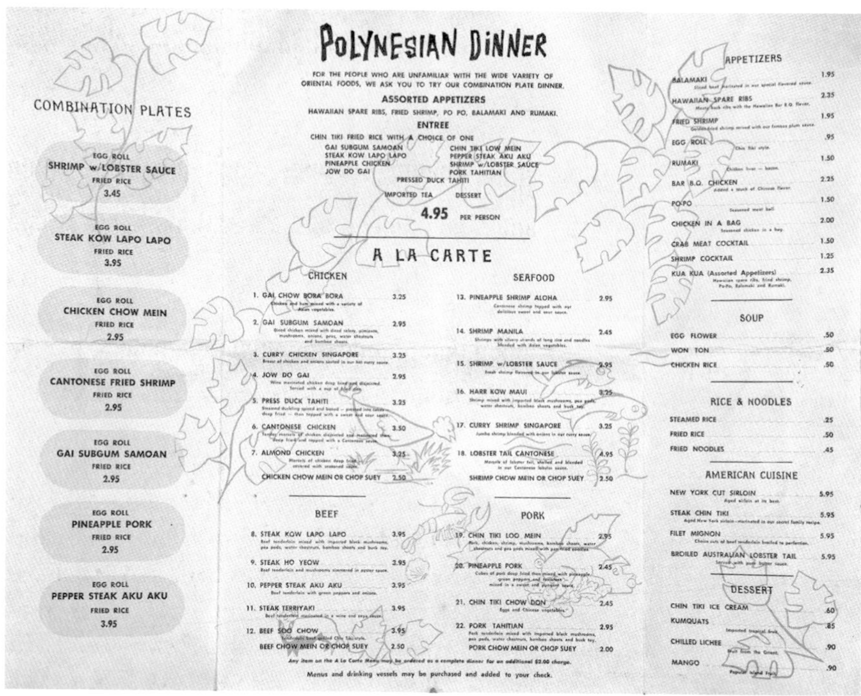

COMBINATION PLATES

EGG ROLL
SHRIMP w/LOBSTER SAUCE
FRIED RICE
3.45

EGG ROLL
STEAK KOW LAPO LAPO
FRIED RICE
3.95

EGG ROLL
CHICKEN CHOW MEIN
FRIED RICE
2.95

EGG ROLL
CANTONESE FRIED SHRIMP
FRIED RICE
2.95

EGG ROLL
GAI SUBGUM SAMOAN
FRIED RICE
2.95

EGG ROLL
PINEAPPLE PORK
FRIED RICE
2.95

EGG ROLL
PEPPER STEAK AKU AKU
FRIED RICE
3.95

POLYNESIAN DINNER

FOR THE PEOPLE WHO ARE UNFAMILIAR WITH THE WIDE VARIETY OF ORIENTAL FOODS, WE ASK YOU TO TRY OUR COMBINATION PLATE DINNER.

ASSORTED APPETIZERS

HAWAIIAN SPARE RIBS, FRIED SHRIMP, PO PO, BALAMAKI AND RUMAKI.

ENTREE

CHIN TIKI FRIED RICE WITH A CHOICE OF ONE

GAI SUBGUM SAMOAN	CHIN TIKI LOW MEIN
STEAK KOW LAPO LAPO	PEPPER STEAK AKU AKU
PINEAPPLE CHICKEN	SHRIMP w/LOBSTER SAUCE
JOW DO GAI	PORK TAHITIAN

PRESSED DUCK TAHITI

IMPORTED TEA DESSERT

4.95 PER PERSON

A LA CARTE

CHICKEN

1. GAI CHOW BORA BORA	3.25
2. GAI SUBGUM SAMOAN	2.95
3. CURRY CHICKEN SINGAPORE	3.25
4. JOW DO GAI	2.95
5. PRESS DUCK TAHITI	3.25
6. CANTONESE CHICKEN	3.50
7. ALMOND CHICKEN	3.25
CHICKEN CHOW MEIN OR CHOP SUEY	2.50

SEAFOOD

13. PINEAPPLE SHRIMP ALOHA	2.95
14. SHRIMP MANILA	2.45
15. SHRIMP w/LOBSTER SAUCE	2.95
16. HARR KOW MAUI	3.25
17. CURRY SHRIMP SINGAPORE	3.25
18. LOBSTER TAIL CANTONESE	4.95
SHRIMP CHOW MEIN OR CHOP SUEY	2.50

BEEF

8. STEAK KOW LAPO LAPO	3.95
9. STEAK HO YEOW	3.95
10. PEPPER STEAK AKU AKU	3.95
11. STEAK TERRIYAKI	3.95
12. BEEF SOO CHOW	3.95
BEEF CHOW MEIN OR CHOP SUEY	2.50

PORK

19. CHIN TIKI LOO MEIN	2.95
20. PINEAPPLE PORK	2.45
21. CHIN TIKI CHOW DON	2.45
22. PORK TAHITIAN	2.95
PORK CHOW MEIN OR CHOP SUEY	2.00

Any item on the A La Carte Menu may be ordered as a complete dinner for an additional $2.00 charge.

Menus and drinking vessels may be purchased and added to your check.

APPETIZERS

BALAMAKI	1.95
HAWAIIAN SPARE RIBS	2.35
FRIED SHRIMP	1.95
EGG ROLL (Chin Tiki style.)	.95
RUMAKI	1.50
BAR B.Q. CHICKEN	2.25
PO-PO (Seasoned meat ball)	1.50
CHICKEN IN A BAG	2.00
CRAB MEAT COCKTAIL	1.50
SHRIMP COCKTAIL	1.25
KUA KUA (Assorted Appetizers)	2.35

SOUP

EGG FLOWER	.50
WON TON	.50
CHICKEN RICE	.50

RICE & NOODLES

STEAMED RICE	.25
FRIED RICE	.50
FRIED NOODLES	.45

AMERICAN CUISINE

NEW YORK CUT SIRLOIN	5.95
STEAK CHIN TIKI	5.95
FILET MIGNON	5.95
BROILED AUSTRALIAN LOBSTER TAIL	5.95

DESSERT

CHIN TIKI ICE CREAM	.60
KUMQUATS	.85
CHILLED LICHEE	.90
MANGO	.90

Chin Tiki dinner menu selections. *Private collection, photo by Nick Hagen.*

the Polynesian fantasyland. Helen Fujiwara, who later married George M. Nakashima, was a hostess; if you could peel your eyes away from Helen's beauty or the tropical scene that lay before you, you might have noticed Marvin's floor treatment of rocks sealed in epoxy. The main floor was divided up into two large and two small dining rooms, separated by beaded curtains and tall tikis; an outrigger hung from the ceiling. The bar area was to the left; the splendid rattan bar could seat approximately thirty people. There were also seven two-top tables in this area. Marvin made his own stunning tabletops from crushed shells and epoxy. Blaine Perrigo painted a lengthy and exquisite aquarium mural behind the bar that glowed under black lights. The Chin Tiki was noted for floating fresh flowers on top of cocktails. In a 2003 interview with the *Metrotimes*, Marvin said, "People would collect [the gardenias] and try to make a lei out of them, but by the time they left, after that many drinks, they wouldn't walk out of the bar, they would fall out." The second floor played host to an even larger waterfall, more tufa rock walls and lots of exotic décor; this space could be rented out for events and private parties.

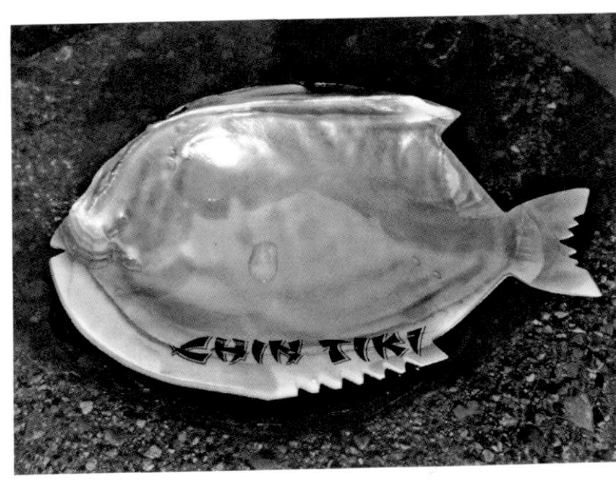

Chin Tiki fish ash tray. *Author's collection.*

Decorative items purchased from Oceanic Arts in Whittier, California, include five-foot-tall carved tikis of Hawaiian war gods, Maori and Tahitian figures made of palm wood, along with blowfish, pufferfish, war clubs and ceremonial paddles. Light fixtures wore shades made of rattan in the shape of baskets, half ball and frame shades. Oriental tiles of red and emerald green were used as partitions; walls appear to be covered in bamboo matting, and rice thatch could be found throughout. Mugs were generic in design and glazed in singular colors; one style bore the Chin Tiki name. Marvin designed everything from the graphics on the front of the building to the menus, matches, ash trays and swizzle sticks. Everything was bespoke by Marvin specifically for Chin Tiki.

Marvin Chin's name would continue to be linked to Benson Fong. Every time Fong made news, there would be something about him in the Detroit newspapers. The June 30, 1967 *Detroit Free Press* informed its readers: "Benson Fong, Marvin Chin's brother-in-law, signed a three-picture deal in Rome. Fong was in Detroit when Chin opened the Chin Tiki Restaurant."

The Chin Tiki was welcomed in Detroit with open arms; there was nothing like it in the area at the time. From the get-go, it was popular with the business crowd, locals, suburbanites, travelers and college kids from Wayne State University. Celebrities in town for performances at the Fox, Masonic Temple, the Fisher and more would stop in for a meal or a cocktail. Even Barbra Streisand may have visited when she was in town. Detroit's professional athletes frequented Chin Tiki; Marvin received a football from one of the Detroit Lions. When the New York Yankees were in town playing the Detroit Tigers, Joe DiMaggio came in every night—he even gave Marvin an autographed baseball. Marlin Chin calls DiMaggio a nice guy, remembering how he would sit and talk with him.

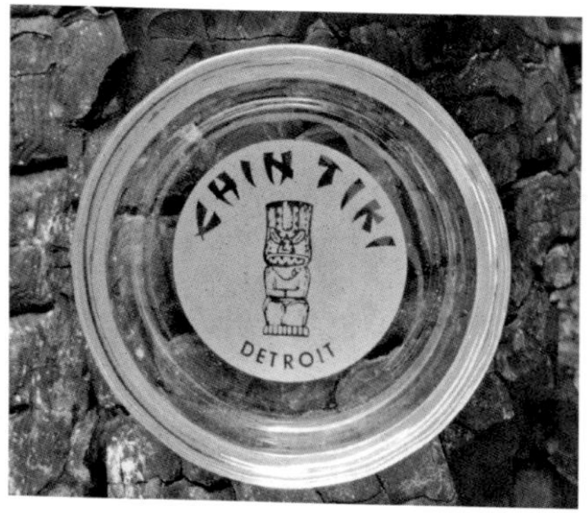

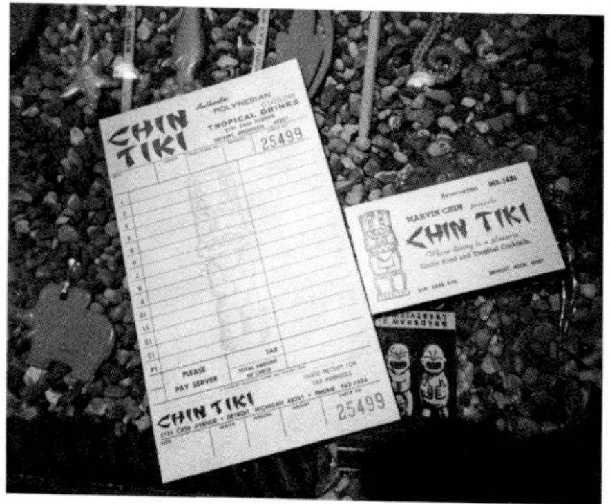

Above, left: Chin Tiki glass ash tray. *Author's collection.*

Above, right: Chin Tiki order ticket and business card. *Courtesy of Tim Shuller.*

Opposite, top: Chin Tiki State Fair Parade float. Debbie Chin is front row, third from left. *Courtesy of Kawehilani.*

Opposite, bottom: The first-place award for the Hawaiian Holiday float is presented to Chin Tiki. That's Blaine Perrigo on the left. *Courtesy of Kawehilani.*

Roughly a year later, in the "long hot summer of 1967," riots broke out in Detroit that lasted five grueling days, July 23–28. Everything changed; people were afraid to go downtown. For the people who worked in the city, there was no choice; they went to work and in time resumed normal activities like going out for lunch and dinner. Slowly, people came back, and Chin Tiki was there waiting for them. Eventually, it was business as usual.

On November 18, 1968, the *Detroit Free Press* printed an article announcing "Chin Tiki Adds Flavorful Show."

> *FIRST NIGHT REPORT: They do this thing with two long sticks. Two crouching Hawaiians hit the sticks on the floor at the count of one and two and on three they smack them together. The dancers move gracefully between the sticks, being careful to have both feet outside on the count of three because if they aren't they get a sturdy wallop and that's an ouch and ouches don't fit in with Hawaiian music at all. At the Chin Tiki, where they have just added entertainment on Thursday and Friday, this particular dance is called Tinikling, or in English Planting Rice. Amateurs are advised to avoid it….Chin Tiki offers a splendid opportunity for students of Pacific culture to study and differentiate between Samoan, Hawaiian, Tahitian and Philippine authentic dances and music. Not a bad place for girl watchers either.*

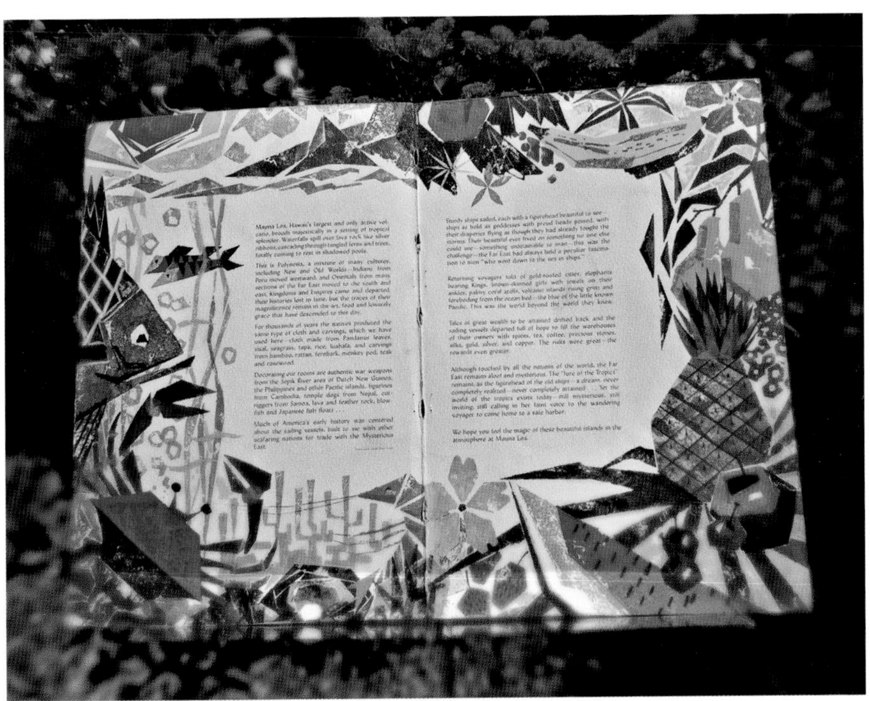

Mauna Loa, Hawaii's largest and only active volcano, broods majestically in a setting of tropical splendor. Waterfalls spill over lava rock like silver ribbons, cascading through tangled ferns and trees, finally coming to rest in shadowed pools.

This is Polynesia, a mixture of many cultures, including New and Old Worlds—Indians from Peru moved westward, and Orientals from many sections of the Far East moved to the south and east. Kingdoms and Empires came and departed, their histories lost in time, but the traces of their magnificence remain in the art, food and leisurely grace that have descended to this day.

For thousands of years the natives produced the same type of cloth and carvings, which we have used here—cloth made from Pandanus leaves, sisal, seagrass, tapa, rice, luahala, and carvings from bamboo, rattan, fernbark, monkey pod, teak and rosewood.

Decorating our rooms are authentic war weapons from the Sepik River area of Dutch New Guinea, the Philippines and other Pacific islands, figurines from Cambodia, temple dogs from Nepal, outriggers from Samoa, lava and feather rock, blowfish and Japanese fish floats . . .

Much of America's early history was centered about the sailing vessels, built to vie with other seafaring nations for trade with the Mysterious East.

Sturdy ships sailed, each with a figurehead beautiful to see—ships as bold as goddesses with proud heads poised, with their draperies flying as though they had already fought the storms. Their beautiful eyes fixed on something no one else could see—something unattainable to man—this was the challenge—the Far East had always held a peculiar fascination to men "who went down to the sea in ships."

Returning voyagers told of gold-roofed cities, elephants bearing Kings, brown-skinned girls with jewels on their ankles, palmy coral atolls, volcanic islands rising grim and foreboding from the ocean bed—the blue of the little known Pacific. This was the world beyond the world they knew.

Tales of great wealth to be attained drifted back and the sailing vessels departed full of hope to fill the warehouses of their owners with spices, tea, coffee, precious stones, silks, gold, silver, and copper. The risks were great—the rewards even greater.

Although touched by all the nations of the world, the Far East remains aloof and mysterious. The "lure of the Tropics" remains, as the figurehead of the old ships—a dream never completely realized—never completely attained . . . Yet the world of the tropics exists today—still mysterious, still inviting, still calling in her faint voice to the wandering voyager to come home to a safe harbor.

We hope you feel the magic of these beautiful islands in the atmosphere at Mauna Loa.

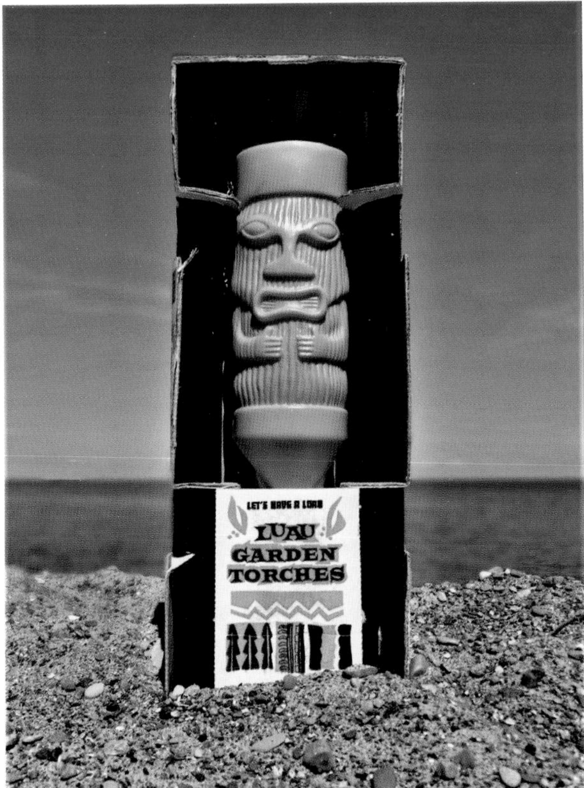

Above: Inside the Mauna Loa dinner menu. *Author's collection.*

Left: A vintage Luau Garden torch. *Author's collection.*

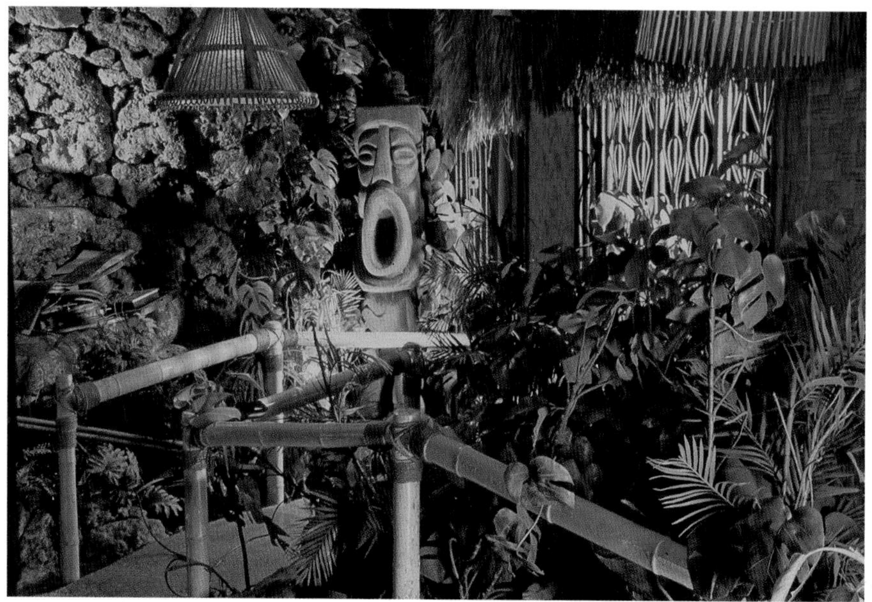

The infamous Chin Tiki bamboo bridge. *Courtesy of Sven Kirsten.*

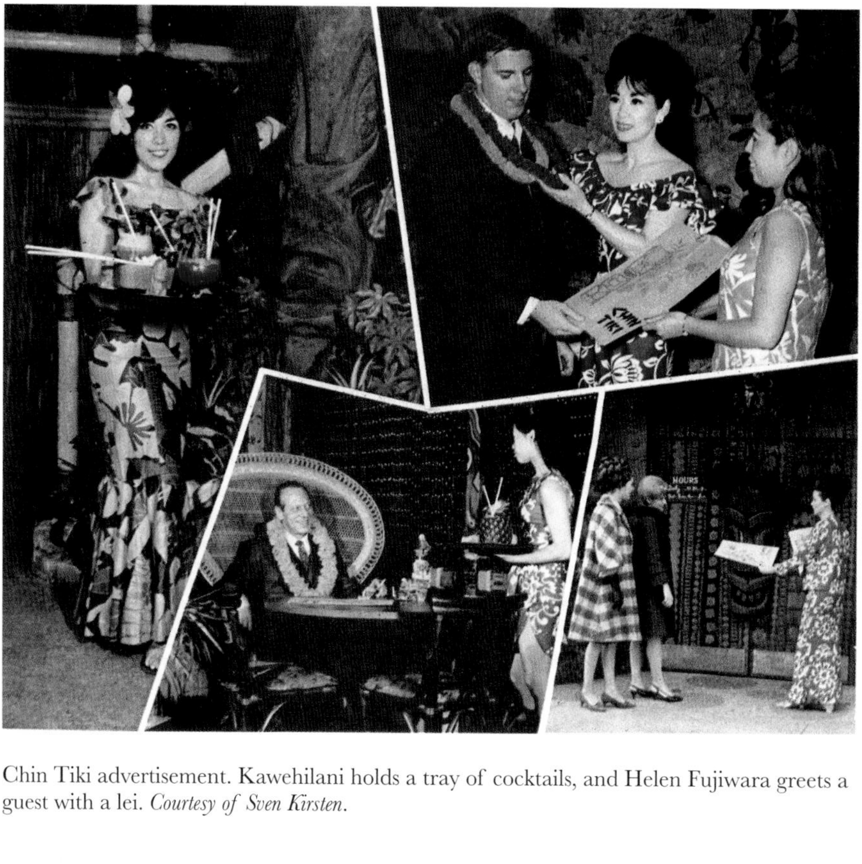

Chin Tiki advertisement. Kawehilani holds a tray of cocktails, and Helen Fujiwara greets a guest with a lei. *Courtesy of Sven Kirsten.*

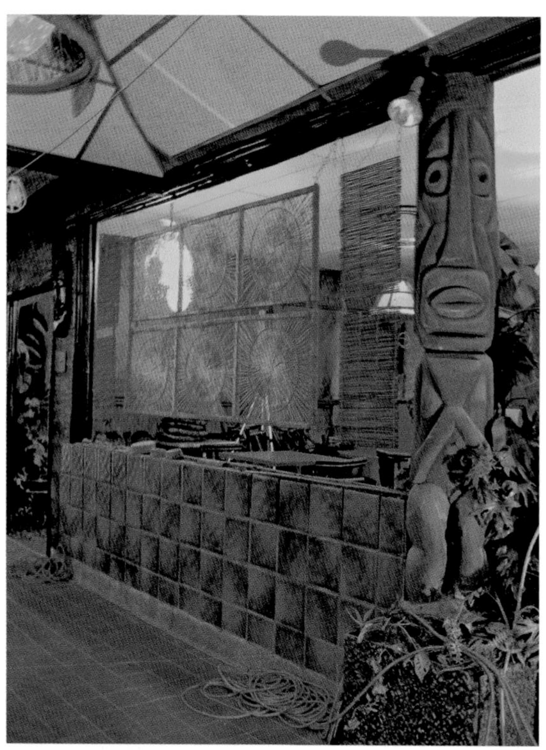

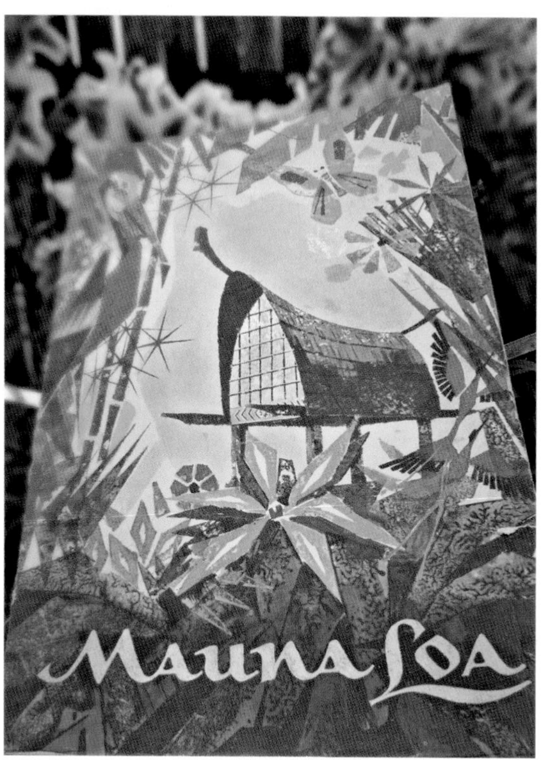

Top: The interior of Chin Tiki as it looked after the filming of *8 Mile. Courtesy of Sven Kirsten.*

Bottom: The much-sought-after Mauna Loa dinner menu. *Author's collection.*

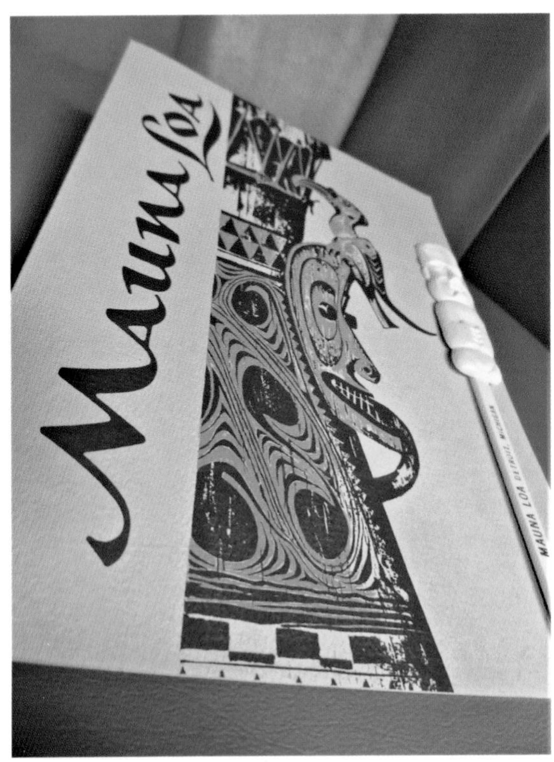

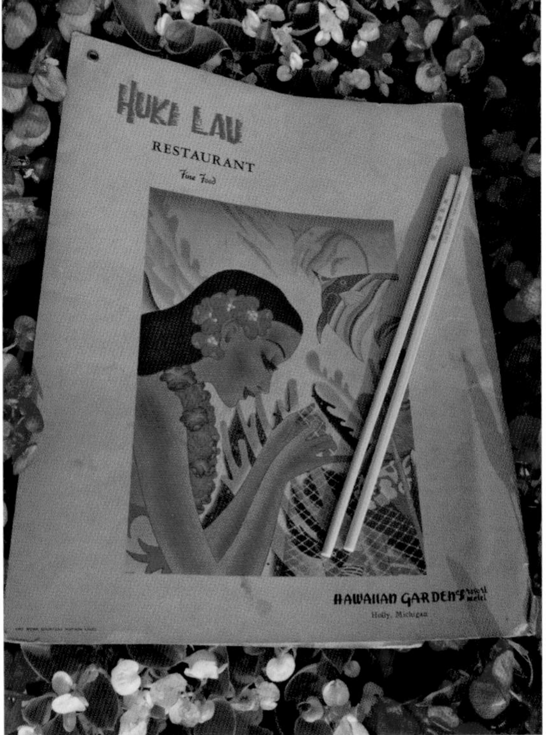

Top: A rare Mauna Loa special occasion menu. *Author's collection.*

Bottom: Huki Lau at Hawaiian Gardens dinner menu with souvenir chopsticks. *Author's collection.*

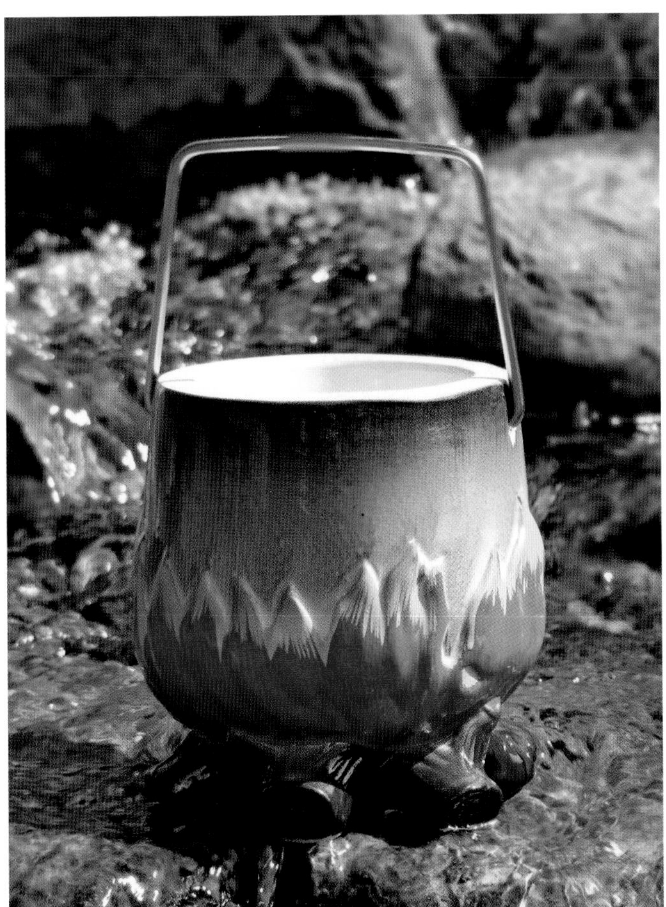

Mauna Loa Cauldron mug. *Author's collection.*

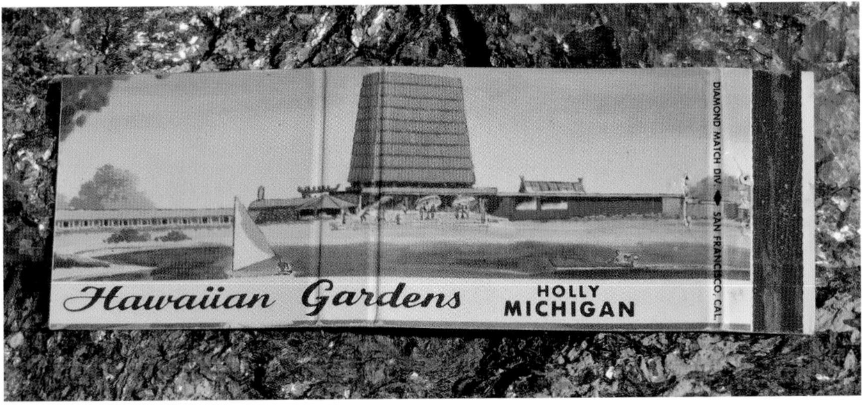

The Hawaiian Gardens Resort matchbook that inspired my fascination with the resort. *Author's collection.*

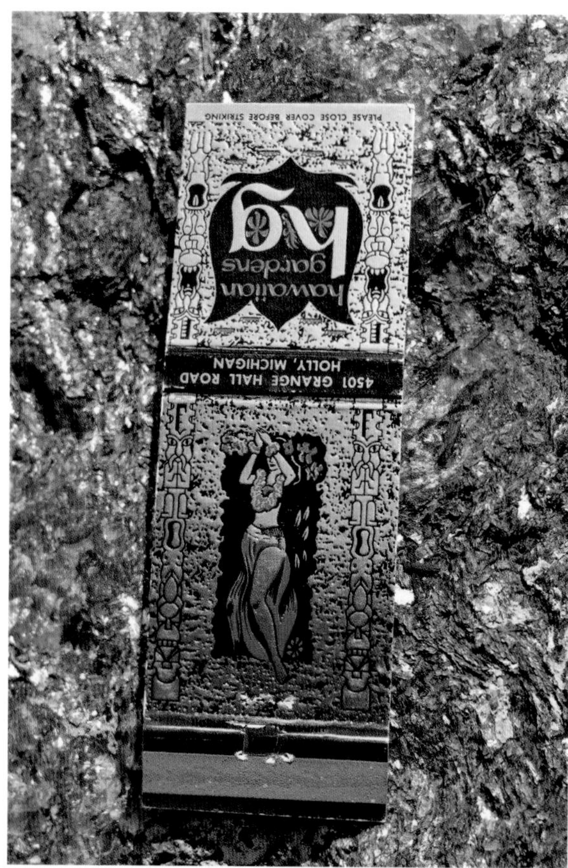

Left: Typical for the time, this Hawaiian Gardens matchbook features an exotic female dancer. *Author's collection.*

Below: This Tropic's postcard features the Native Village, complete with orchestra atop America's only traveling bandstand. *Author's collection.*

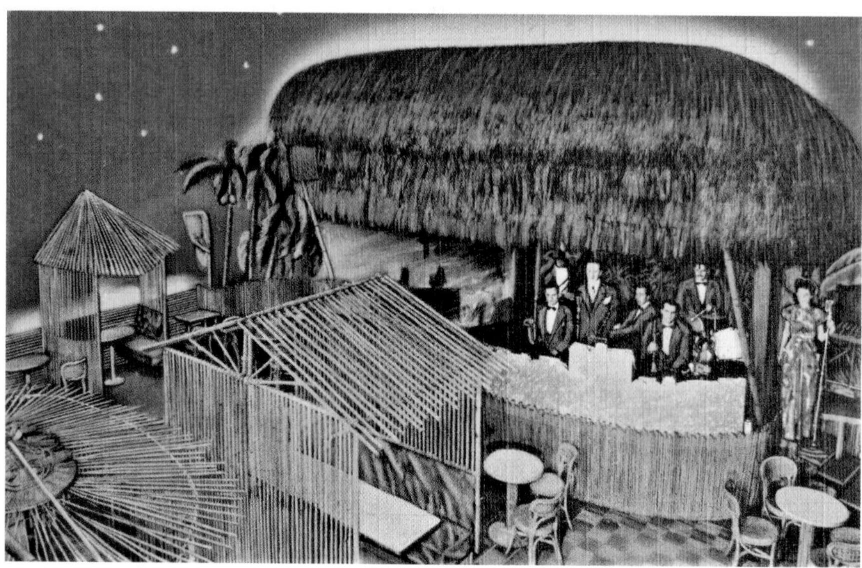

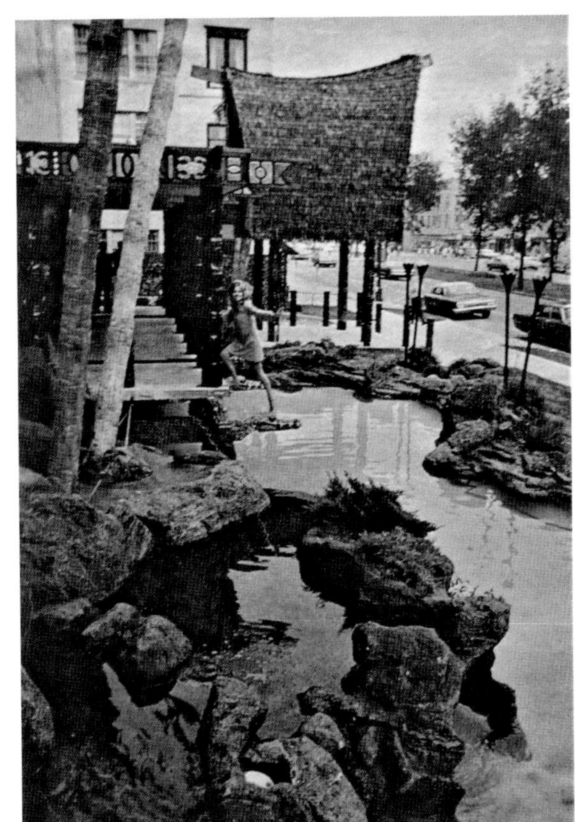

Right: A *Detroit News* photo of the lagoon in front of the Mauna Loa. *Author's collection.*

Below: This Port O' Three menu cover and pics use the same design and characters as Chin Tiki. *Author's collection.*

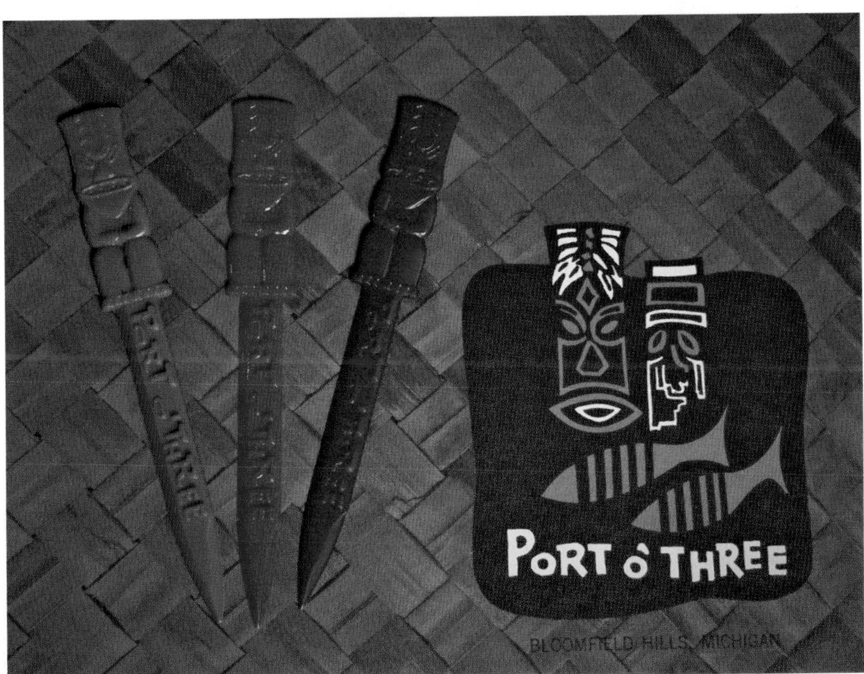

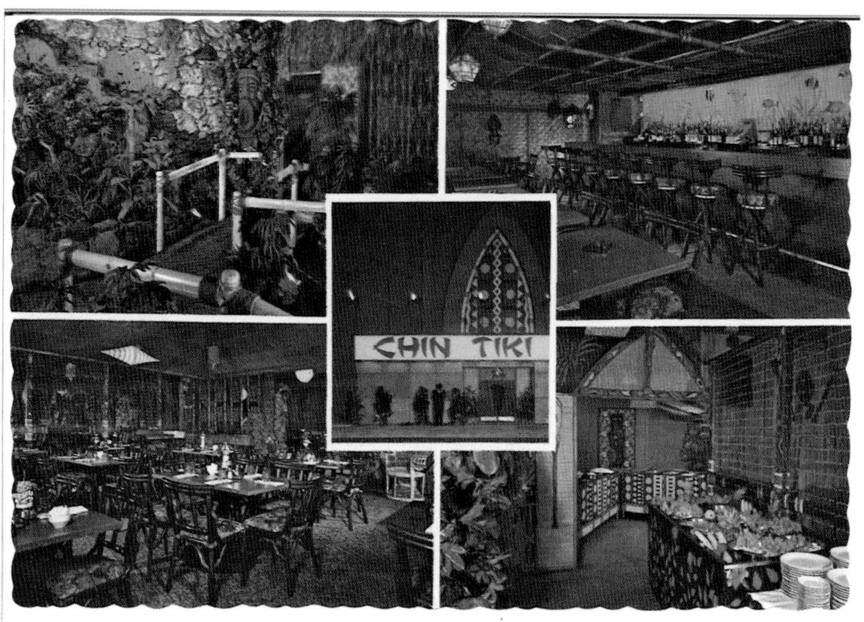

A Chin Tiki postcard highlighting the bamboo bridge, aquarium mural, dining room, buffet and exterior. *Author's collection.*

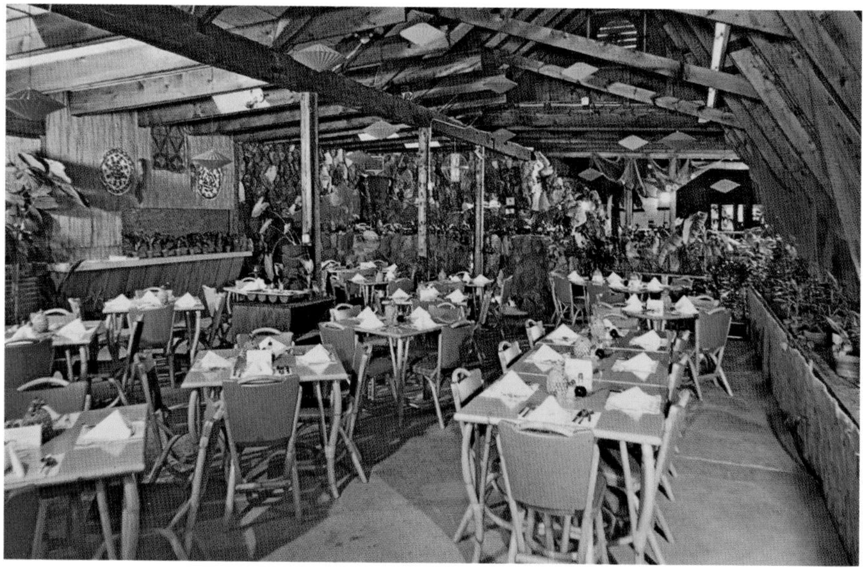

The Polynesian Longhouse at Hawaiian Gardens. *Author's collection.*

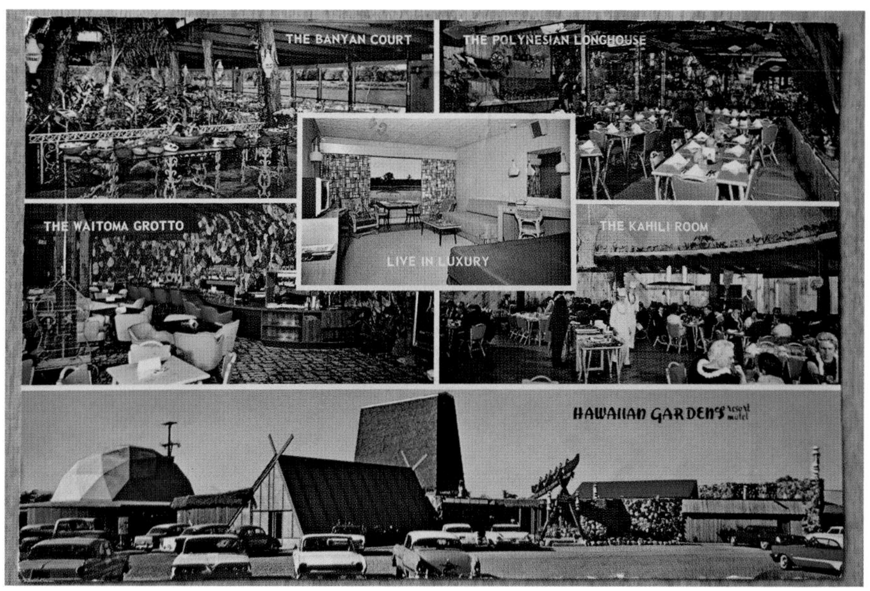

Hawaiian Gardens Resort Motel postcard showing the exterior, dining areas, Waitoma Grotto and motel room. *Courtesy of Barb Soloko.*

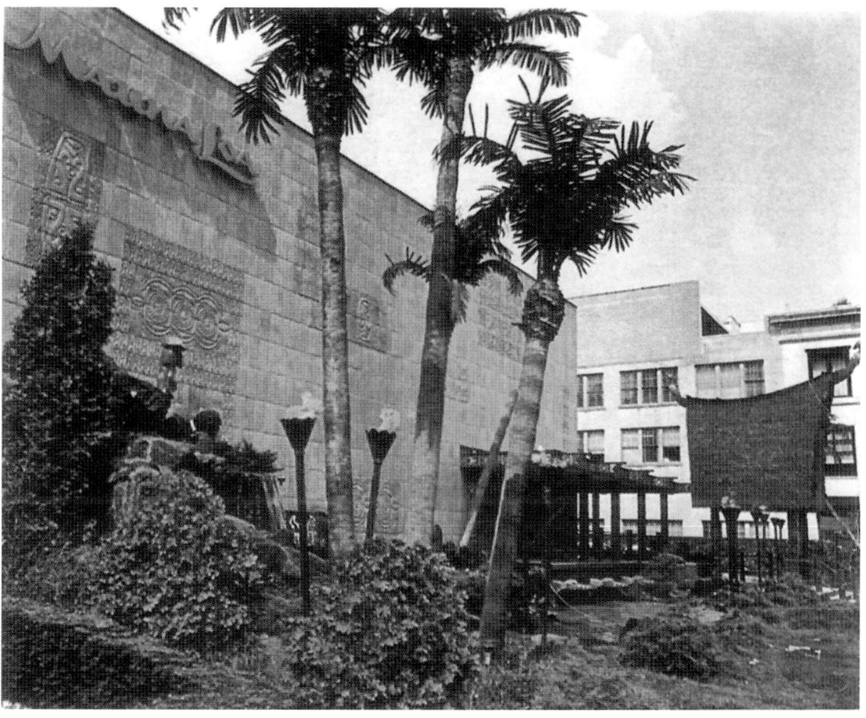

This *Dodge News Magazine* photo of the Mauna Loa shows the fiery torches, waterfall and lagoon. Look closely to see the architectural detail in the stone wall. *Author's collection.*

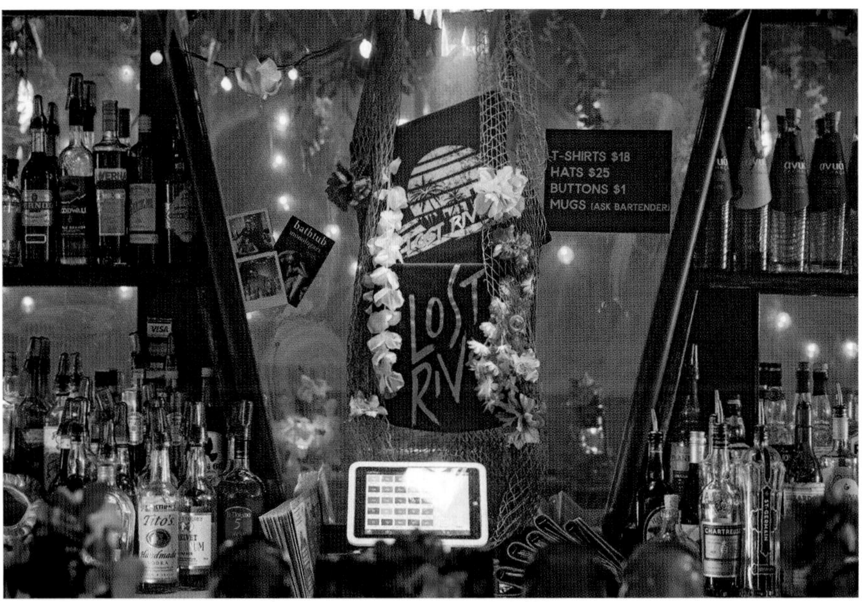

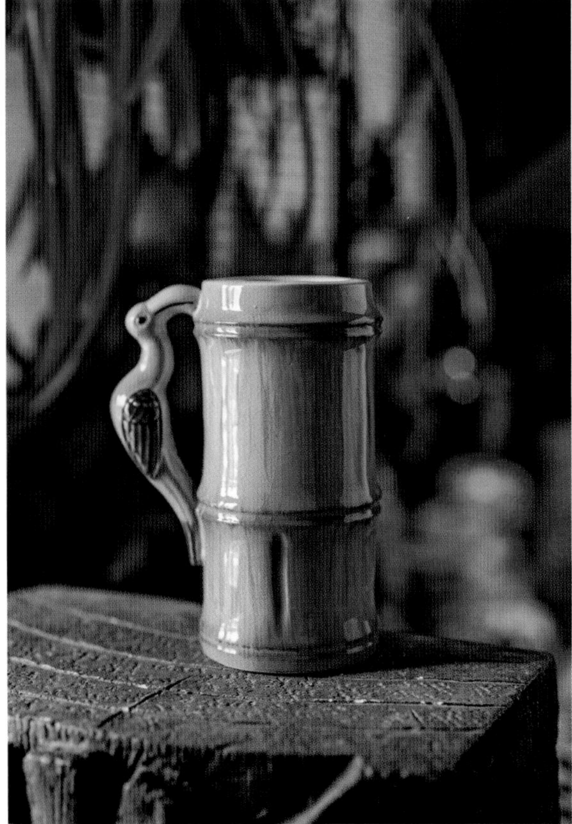

Above: The bar at Lost River in Detroit. *Photo by Nick Hagen.*

Left: Mauna Loa Polynesian Pidgeon mug. *Private collection, photo by Nick Hagen.*

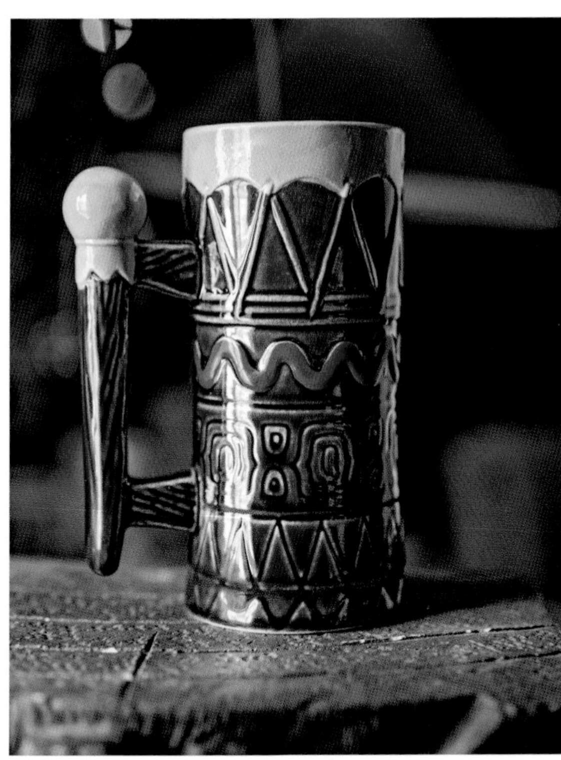

Left: Mauna Loa Drum mug. *Private collection, photo by Nick Hagen.*

Below: The Interior of Chin Tiki as it was in 2003. *Courtesy of Louis Devaney.*

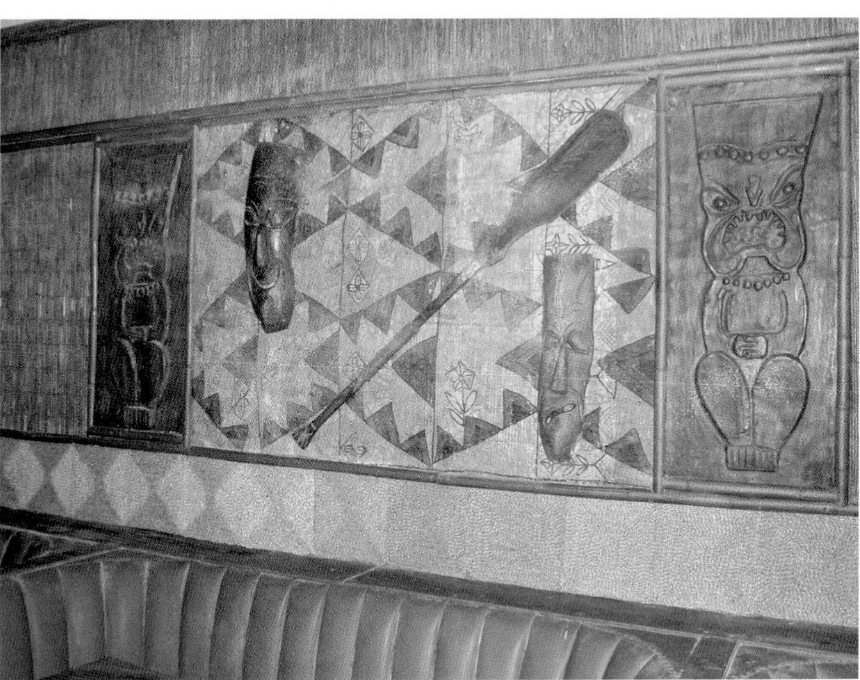

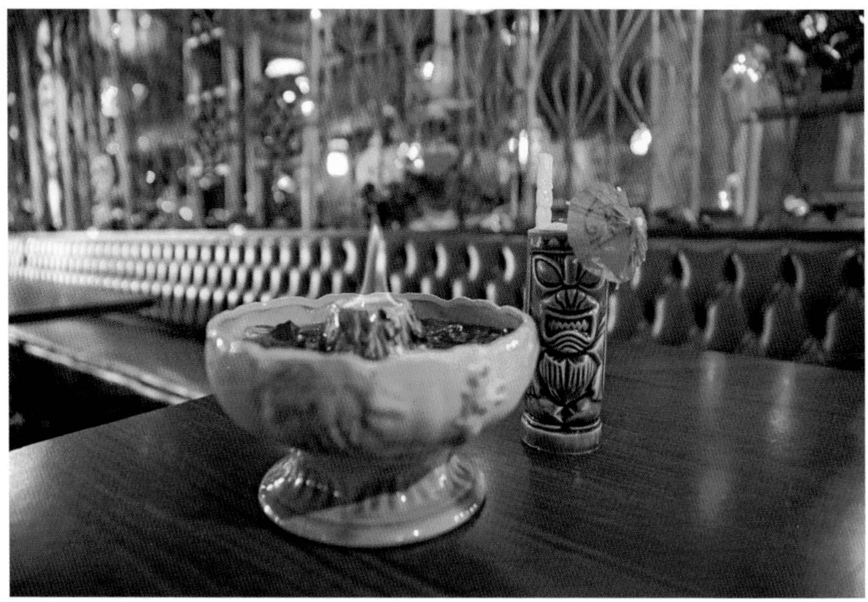

Tiki mugs and volcano bowls brought over from Chin Tiki are now being used at Chin's Chop Suey in Livonia. *Chin family collection, photo by Amy Sacka.*

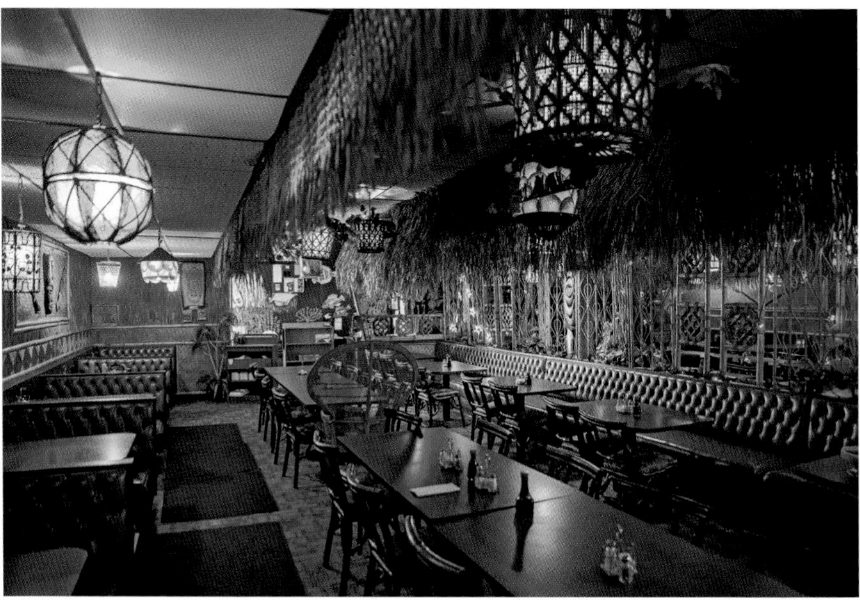

Chin Tiki's little sister, Chin's Chop Suey. *Photo by Amy Sacka.*

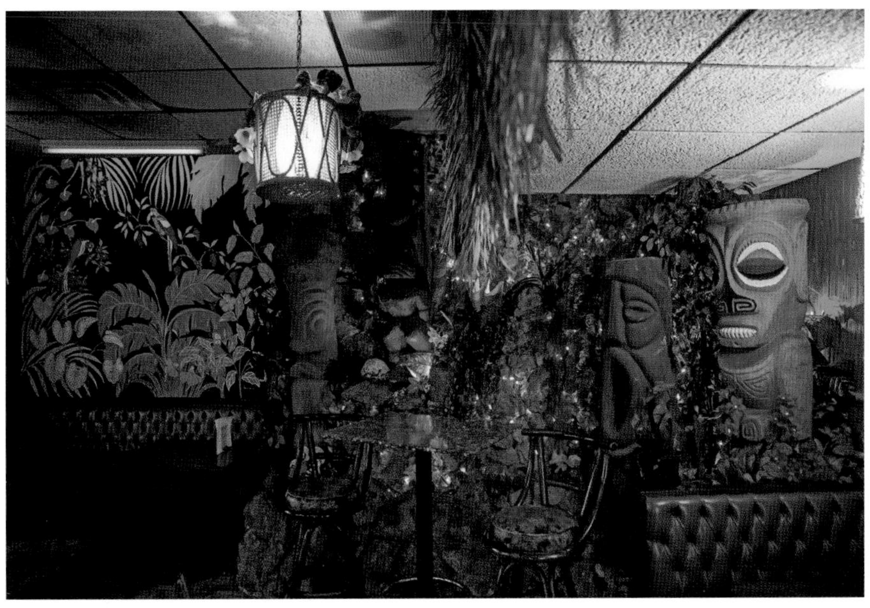

The Blaine Perrigo mural still decorates the wall at Chin's. The waterfall has been turned into a volcano. *Photo by Amy Sacka.*

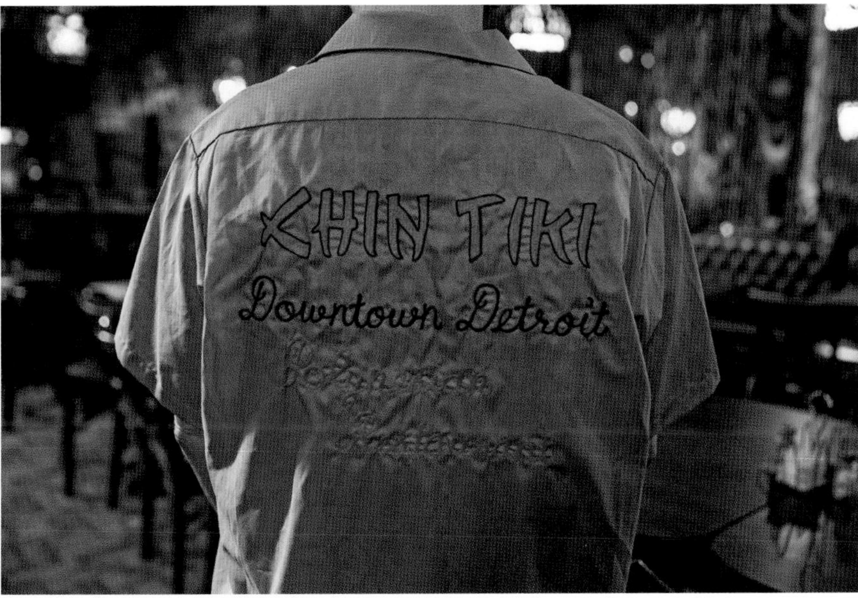

Chin Tiki sponsored a bowling team. Check out this super-cool bowling shirt! *Chin family collection, photo by Amy Sacka.*

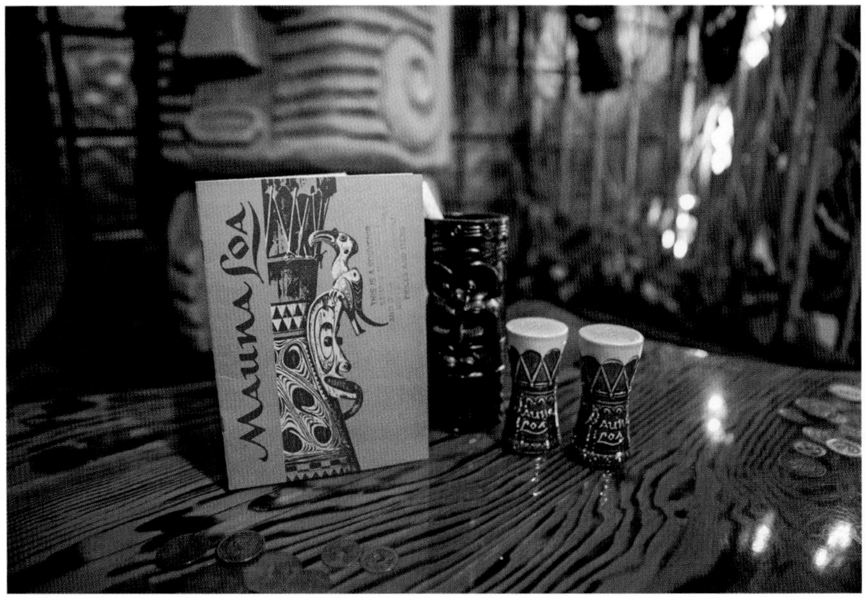

Inside Chin's Chop Suey, the legendary Mauna Loa bar is reunited with an original menu, signature mug and drum salt and pepper shakers. *Photo by Amy Sacka.*

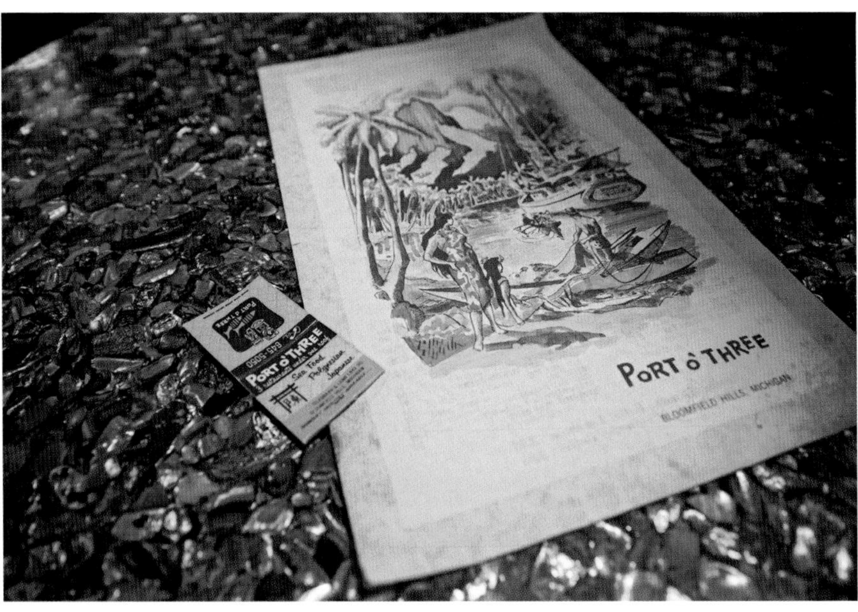

Marvin Chin's creativity is displayed in this hand-crafted tabletop, Port O' Three menu and matchbook. *Chin family collection, photo by Amy Sacka.*

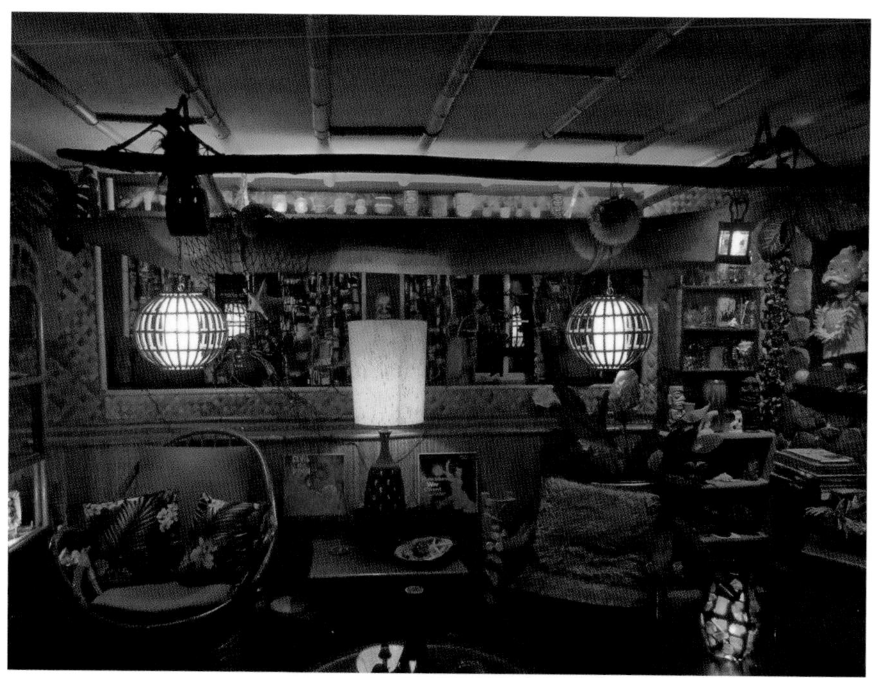

Above: Tim Shuller's basement tiki bar features the original outrigger that once hung in the Chin Tiki. *Courtesy of Tim Shuller.*

Right: A trio of original Mauna Loa table lamps. *Courtesy of Zach Roberts.*

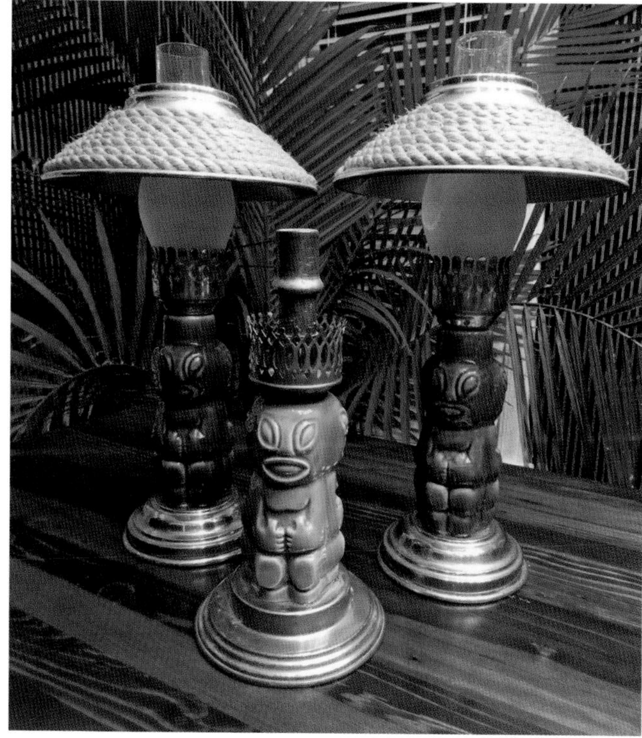

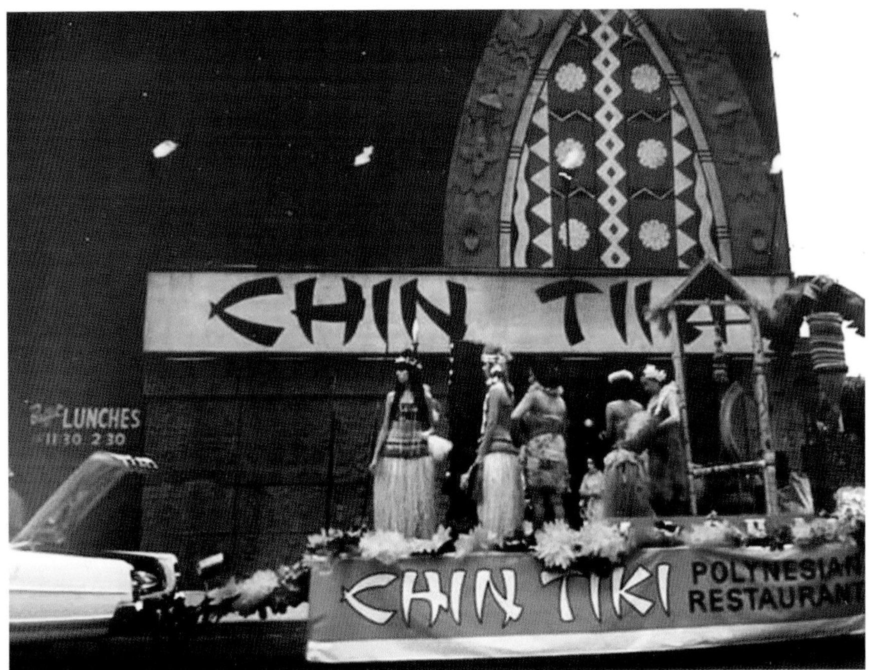

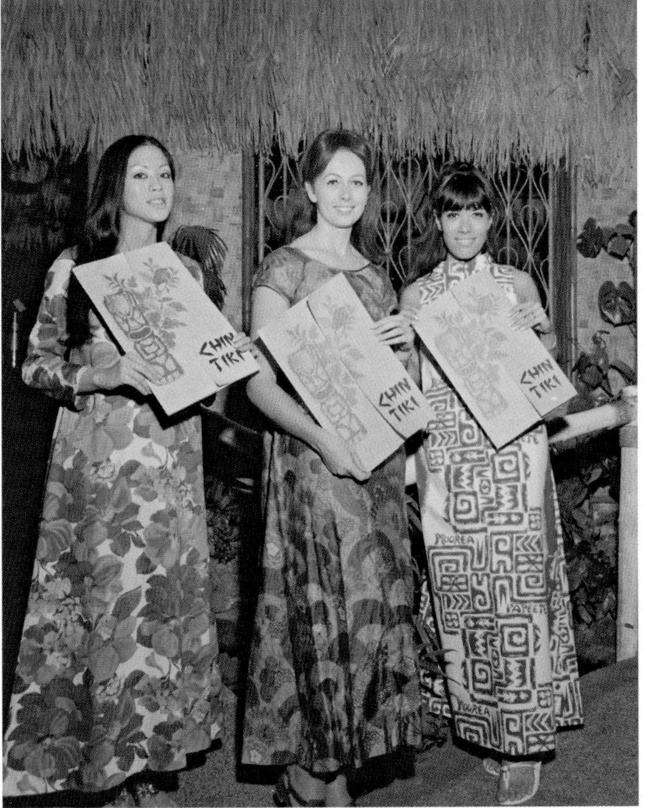

Above: The Chin Tiki float is ready to make its trek down Woodward to the state fair. *Courtesy of Kawehilani.*

Left: Chin Tiki seating hostesses pose for the camera in their muumuus. *Left to right*: Marvin's half sister Margie, Barb and Kawehilani. *Courtesy of Kawehilani.*

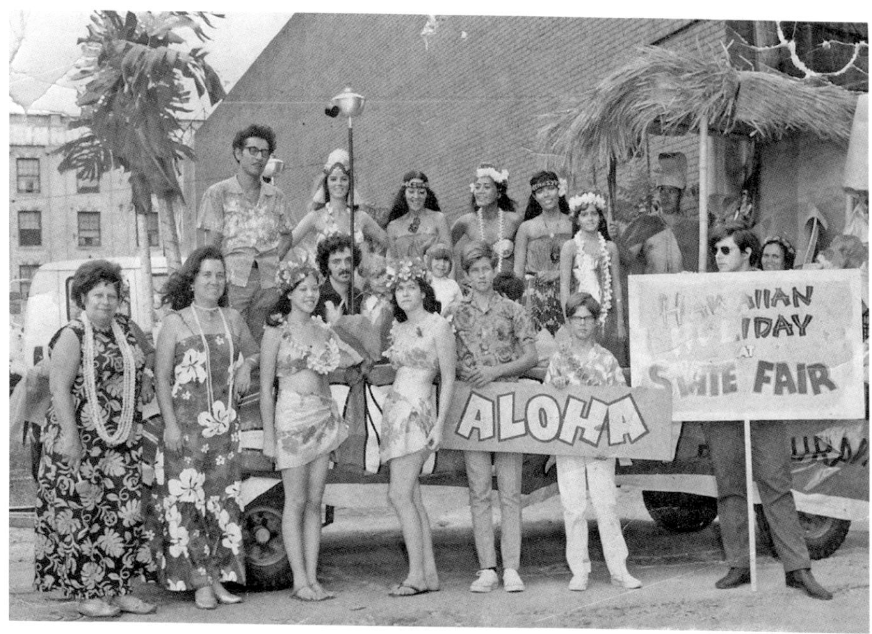
HAWAIIAN
AT
FAIR
ALOHA

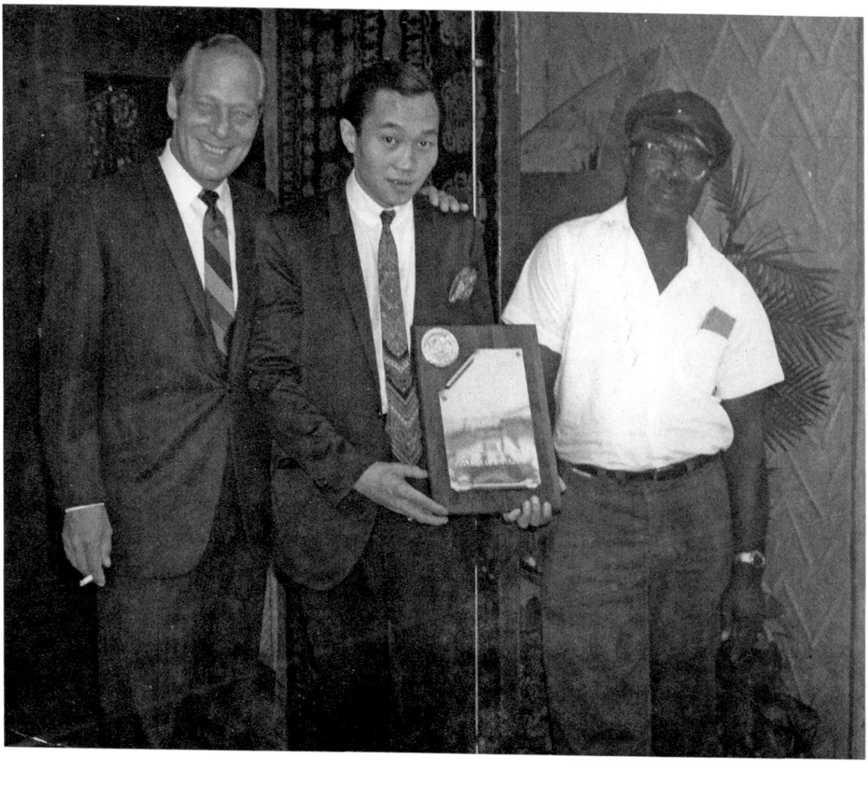

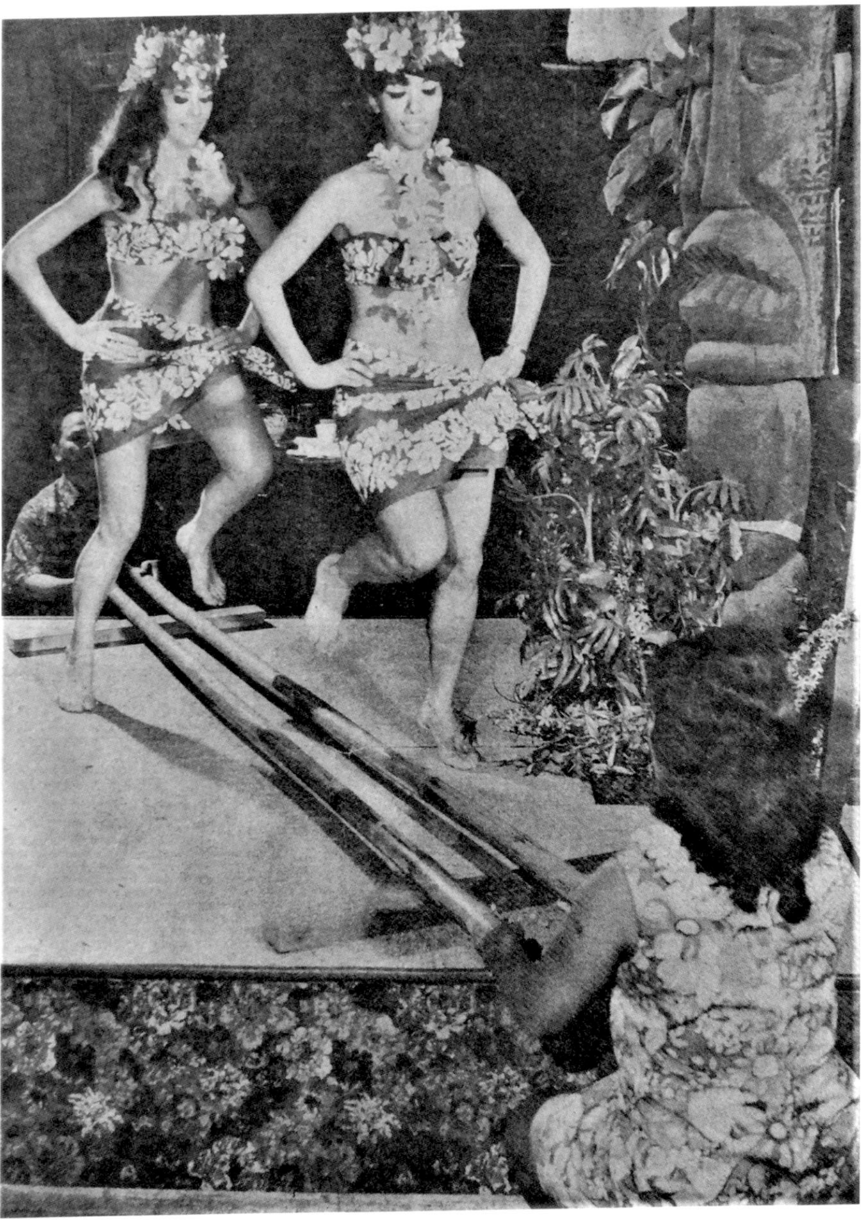

Above: A newspaper photo of a native Philippine dance with long poles. On the left is Leimomilani, on the right is Kawehilani. *Courtesy of Kawehilani.*

Opposite, top: The Chin Tiki Polynesian Review on the main-floor stage. *Courtesy of Kawehilani.*

Opposite, bottom: Dancers Leimomi, Ninipo and Kawehilani. *Courtesy of Kawehilani.*

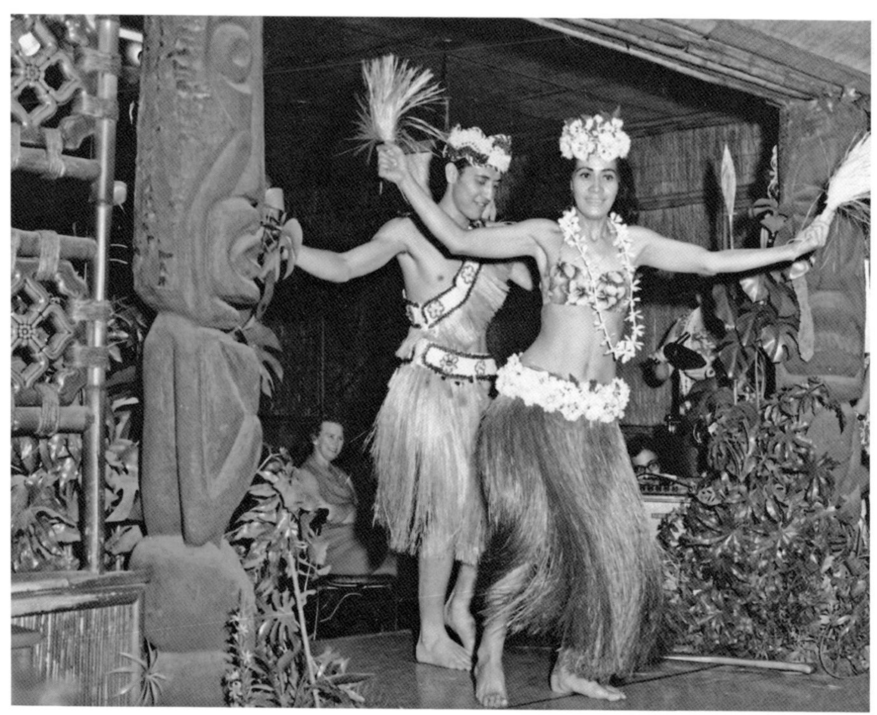

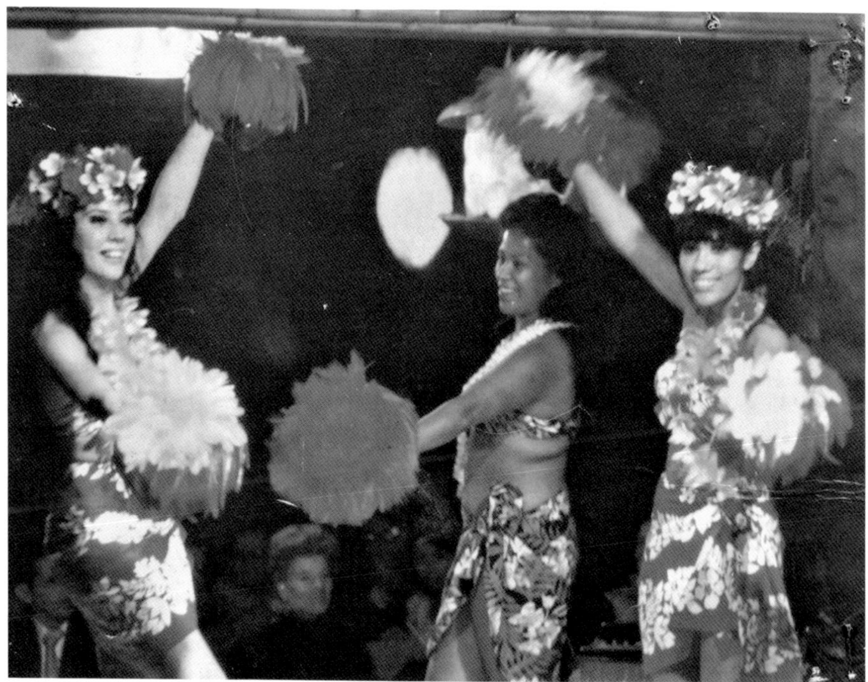

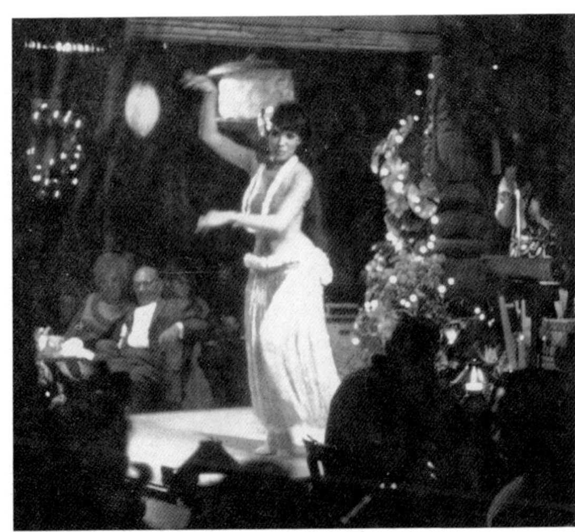

Right: Kawehilani dances for a packed house. *Courtesy of Sven Kirsten.*

Opposite: Chin Tiki pics. *Private collection, photo by Nick Hagen.*

Weekly floor shows took place on Thursday and Friday evenings, with two shows each night. The Chin Tiki Polynesian Revue featured four lovely females and two young Tahitian men performing authentic Polynesian dances to live music. The band featured a steel guitar, two rhythm guitars, drums and a bass. Shows took place on the main floor. On Saturday nights, a live band played contemporary music on the second floor, where patrons could dance the night away.

On February 16, 1969, the *Detroit Free Press* printed the recipe for the Scorpion Chin Tiki:

Scorpion Chin Tiki

2 ounces of spirits (composed of one-third each)
Gin
Light and Dark Rum
Brandy
1 ounce lime juice
1 ounce orange juice
Dash of almond spice powder

Combine liquids in glass container and pour into cocktail shaker, filled with shaved or crushed ice. Mixed vigorously and served in large glass, decorated with appropriate flower, it makes one "outrigger" sized serving.

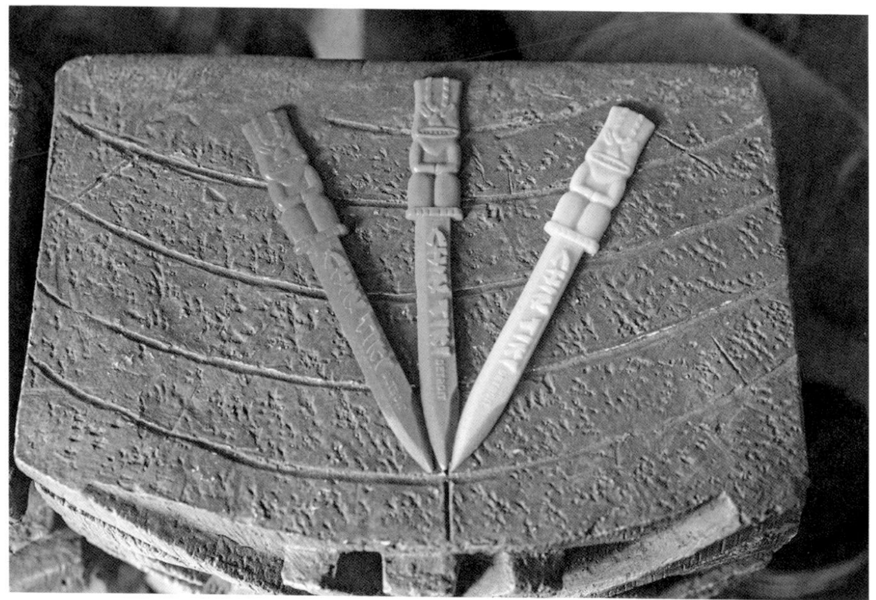

On November 27, 1969, the Chin family was in the news again. A *Detroit Free Press* article reads, "Marvin Chin's father, Joe Chin will open the Mon-Jin-Lau restaurant on Maple at Stephenson Highway December 15. Blaine Perrigo, designer of Marvin's Chin Tiki designed the new eatery. The senior Chin, owner of the Wah Lee Import Co., is also father-in-law to actor Benson Fong, long-time Number Two Son of the Charlie Chan movies." The newspapers sure did get a lot of mileage out of Fong's association with the Chin family. According to the *HOUR Detroit* February 2008 issue:

> *Joe* [Chin] *would marry three times. His first two wives died. Then, in an arranged marriage, Joe, by then 60 years old, went home to China and brought back his third bride, 18-year-old Mon. Marshall* [Chin] *was the oldest son of their four children.*
>
> *In 1969, the corner of Stephenson Highway and Maple in Troy was out in the middle of nowhere. Mon Chin was an enterprising young woman, and she saw a future in the building that sat at that location, a lounge and restaurant named Chateau Gay. Its circular roofline of beams that all came to one point at the center, like a parasol, reminded her of the pagodas in China. The walls in the dining room had been built short and at right angles to one another, making little alcoves. They looked vaguely like a Chinese fan. She liked that too, so she bought the place.... When it came*

> *to naming the new restaurant, Mon assembled her name with that of her husband, Jin and added the Chinese word for house or place: Lau.... For the interior, she commissioned a commercial muralist named Blaine Perrigo, who studied the art and books of China and painted a series of allegorical tableaux, as well as a panel done with luminous portraits that now hangs in the bar.... Over the years, Mon Jin Lau has developed a loyal following and stayed on top of its game.*

Marshall Chin took over Mon Jin Lau more than thirty years ago. It is still in operation; his sons Bryan and Brandon are now the third generation of Chins to be involved in running the restaurant.

With the success of Chin Tiki, perhaps Marvin was itching for a new project. In 1969, he moved Chin's Chop Suey a stone's throw down Plymouth Road and turned it into a Polynesian sit-down restaurant. Using the same type of décor and creative ingenuity, Marvin built a mini, less lavish version of the Chin Tiki. Inside, canopies of thatch hang above green button and tuck-upholstered booths. A line of banquettes splits the restaurant into two dining spaces; an airy bamboo screen uses jade-colored ceramic tiles to differentiate the space. Artificial plants and flowers are tucked in along the screen, giving the space a splash of tropical ambiance. Just inside the door along the front wall is a Blaine Perrigo mural that extends to the working waterfall. Tall tikis are nestled around the tufa rock. Bamboo matting covers the walls and ceiling; beautiful lampshades made of shells hang alongside rattan lampshades in various shapes and sizes. Located at 28205 Plymouth Road in Livonia, Chin's Chop Suey is still in operation.

Meanwhile, the Chin Tiki continued to pop up in local newspapers. On May 31, 1970, the *Detroit Free Press* reported:

> *Chin Tiki is a bit of Polynesia in downtown Detroit. Pass under the torches, between the carved doors and a tiny Oriental will lead you over a rippling stream and through the jungle. Cozy rooms divided by bamboo and tikis make up the restaurant. Waitresses are sarong wrapped and though some seem to be quite Nordic, the overall effect is of eastern mystery. Wicker baskets have been made into light fixtures and the rooms are wall to wall original decorations. The drink menu lists dozens of exotic monsters with smoke and gardenias and an occasional orchid for garnish. Ninipo and Smokey head a show of Pacific dance and song on Thursday and Friday nights. Balamaki, rumaki, gai sub*

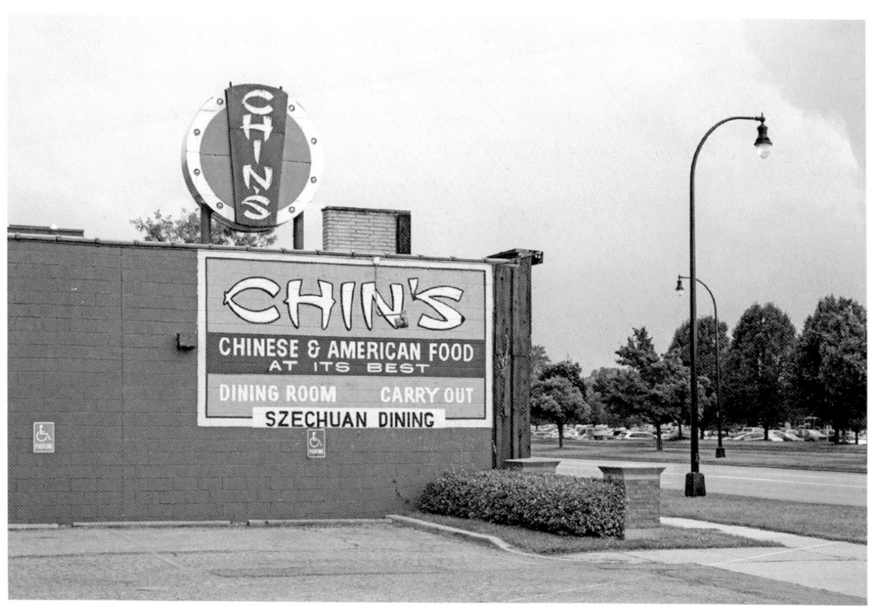

Chin's Chop Suey on Plymouth Road in Livonia. *Photo by Nick Hagen.*

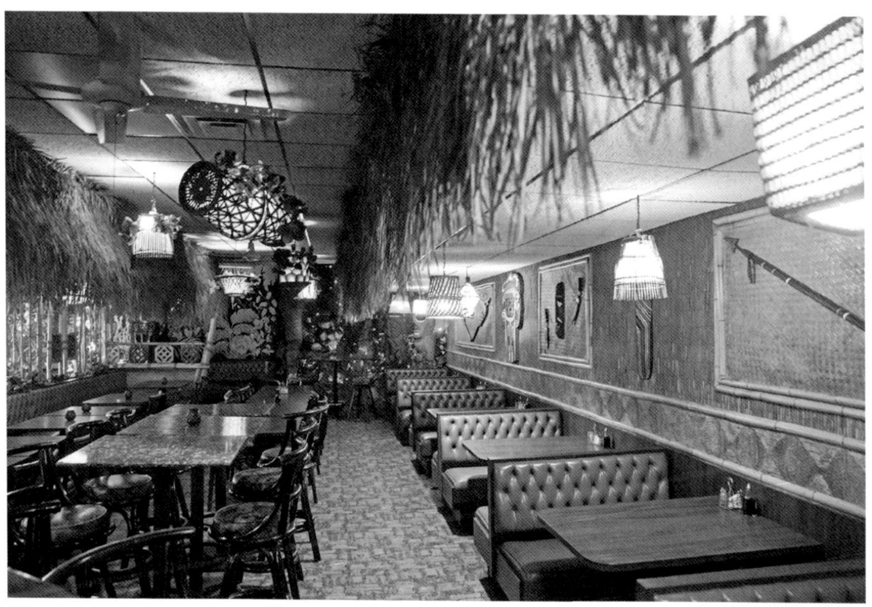

Interior of Chin's in Livonia. *Photo by Amy Sacka.*

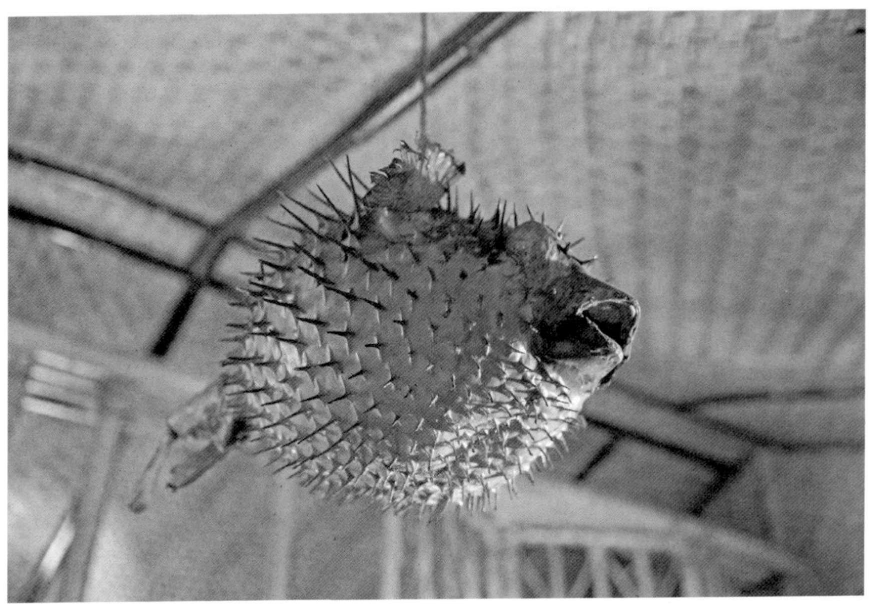

A blowfish hangs from the ceiling at Chin's. *Photo by Amy Sacka.*

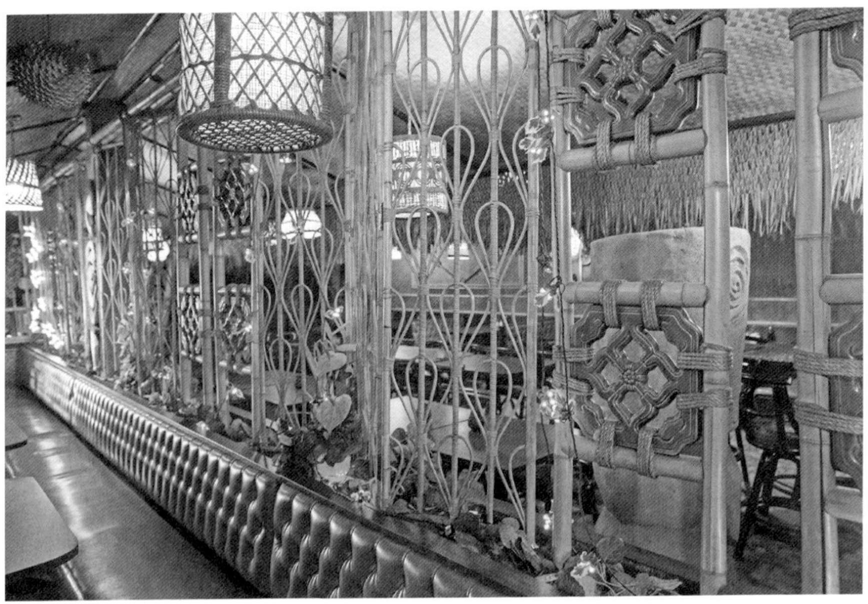

The room divider at Chin's uses many of the same elements Marvin used at Chin Tiki. *Photo by Amy Sacka.*

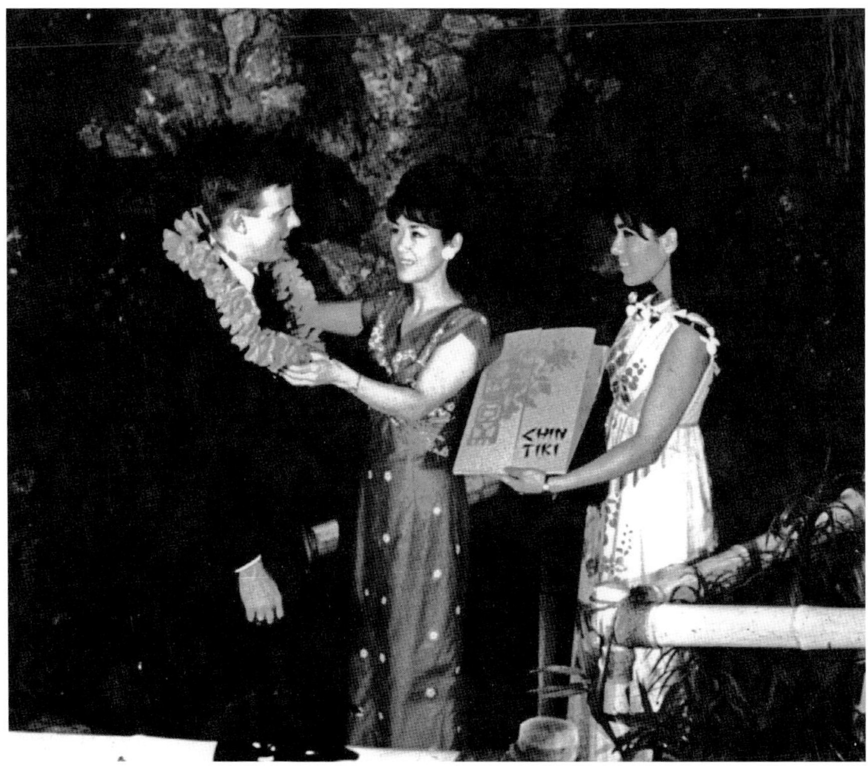

Seating hostesses greet a diner. *Courtesy of Kim Fujiwara.*

> *gum Samoan on the menu means that there are dishes of minced celery, bamboo shoots, celery pimentos to go with the Japanese and Filipino beer. 2121 Cass (962-1434)*

Marvin Chin was featured in the June 15, 1970 *Detroit Free Press* as "This Week's Man of Ideas." In it, Marvin talks about his goal of building an assembly-type machine for making egg rolls and turning the idea into a fast-food franchise chain called Tiki Huts. The article also states, "Chin no longer operates the Jackson Bar. Its liquor license (and apparently prime asset) has been transferred to Chin's-Livonia which recently began serving drinks for the first time. Using Chin Tiki as his model, Chin is now expanding the Livonia establishment into a larger building bearing Polynesian motifs."

All of Marvin's restaurants had built up a loyal clientele and were doing well; people loved everything about the Chin Tiki, from its tasty

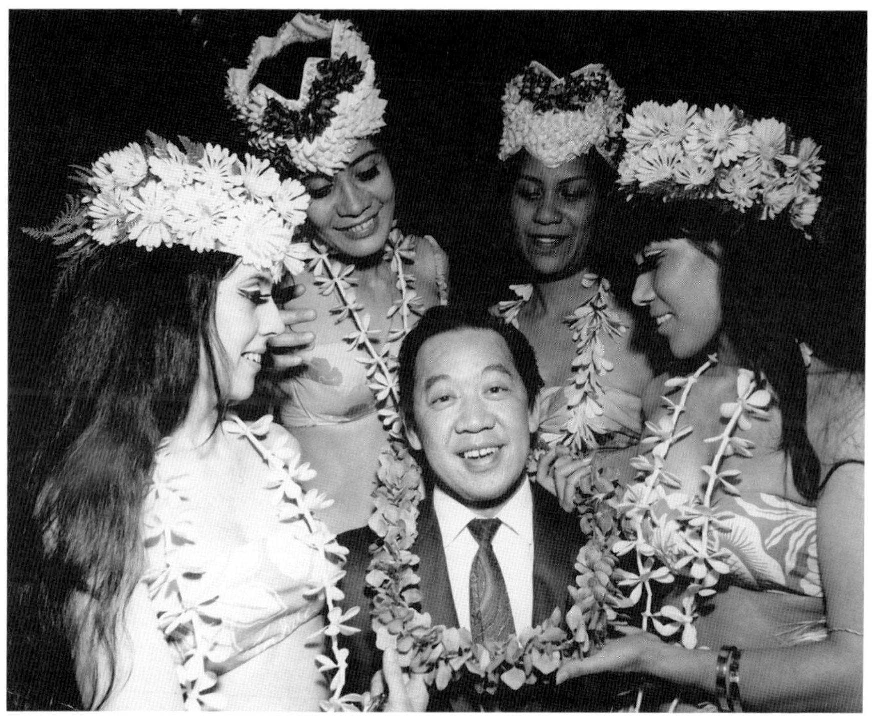

Above: Polynesian dancers surround Marvin Chin. He looks very happy. *Courtesy of Kawehilani.*

Opposite: Marvin's hand-drawn designs for a new restaurant, perhaps Port O' Three. *Chin family collection, photo by Amy Sacka.*

food and unique flower-topped cocktails to the South Seas décor and live entertainment. It appears once again Marvin had become restless and began a new project out in Bloomfield Hills in the former Devon Gables spot on Telegraph at Long Lake. This time, he had two partners—childhood friend and commercial architectural designer Wah Yee and another personal friend who was a physician. Marvin had a grand idea to create a "new concept in dining"—a restaurant that served a unique combination of seafood, Polynesian and Japanese cuisine under one roof. This was to be his biggest undertaking yet; again, Marvin would be the designer. His plan was to build three completely different atmospheric restaurants under one roof—a ship serving seafood, a Polynesian room that was to top Chin Tiki and a Japanese-themed room. Receipts from Oceanic Arts reveal thousands of dollars spent on décor using many of the same type of items used in Chin Tiki. Marvin used the same graphics and

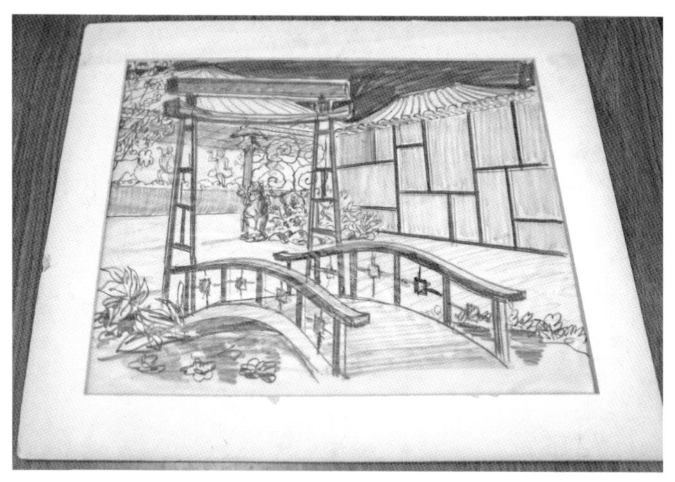

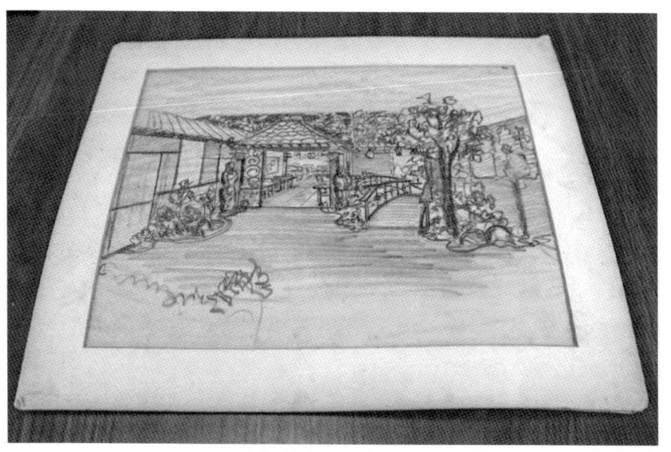

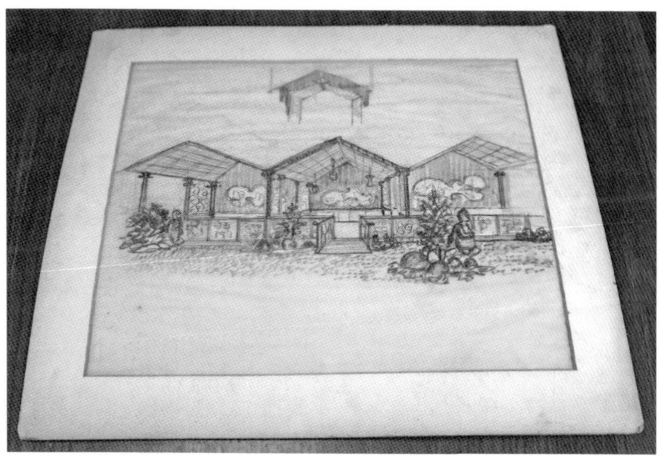

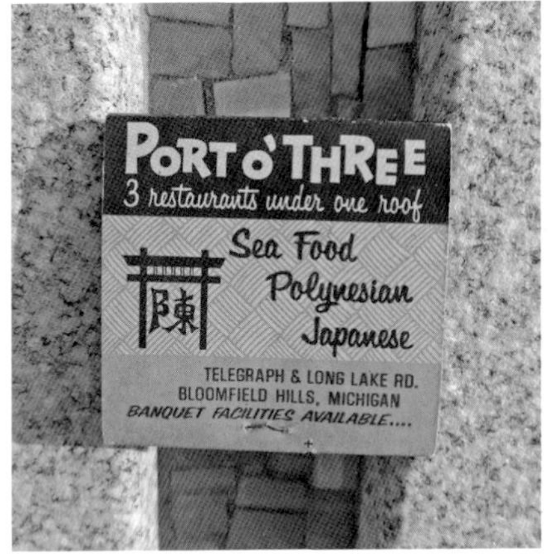

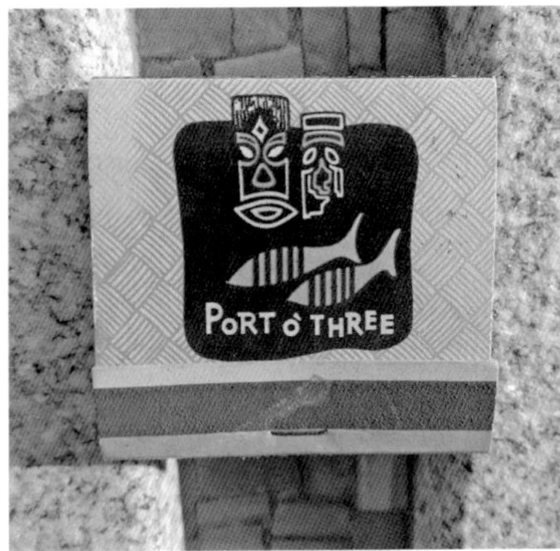

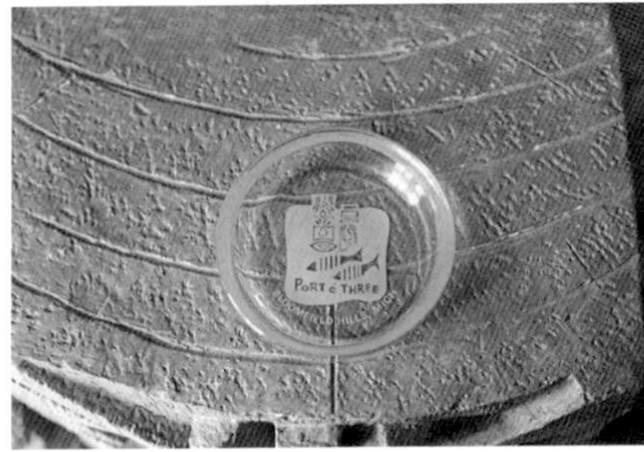

Above, left: Back of Port O' Three matchbook. *Author's collection.*

Above, right: Front of Port O' Three matchbook. *Author's collection.*

Left: Port O' Three glass ash tray. *Private collection, photo by Nick Hagen.*

cocktail menu as Chin Tiki, simply changing the name. Chuck Thurston printed a review in the June 9, 1972 *Detroit Free Press*:

> **Aboard Port O' Three for Polynesian Feast** *Two signs point to the difficulty the latest Marvin Chin restaurant is faced with. One, "Port O' Three" suggests bigness. The other, reading "Help Wanted" indicates that service may be predictably poor. Both indications are correct. Port O' Three, Long Lake at Telegraph is large—even though the Japanese third is nowhere near completion—and the shortage of busboys leaves empty glasses on the table right down through dessert.*
>
> *Francis, the maître d', does the best he can as he oversees two dining rooms, two kitchens and a covey of banquet facilities, but he lacks lieutenants to keep things ship-shape in the Ship Room and the Polynesian Room. Of the two, the Polynesian Room is the smaller, more intimate and easier to manage.*
>
> *The Ship Room is built to look like a ship with most of the passengers sitting on the maindeck and a few up on a raised portion at one end that*

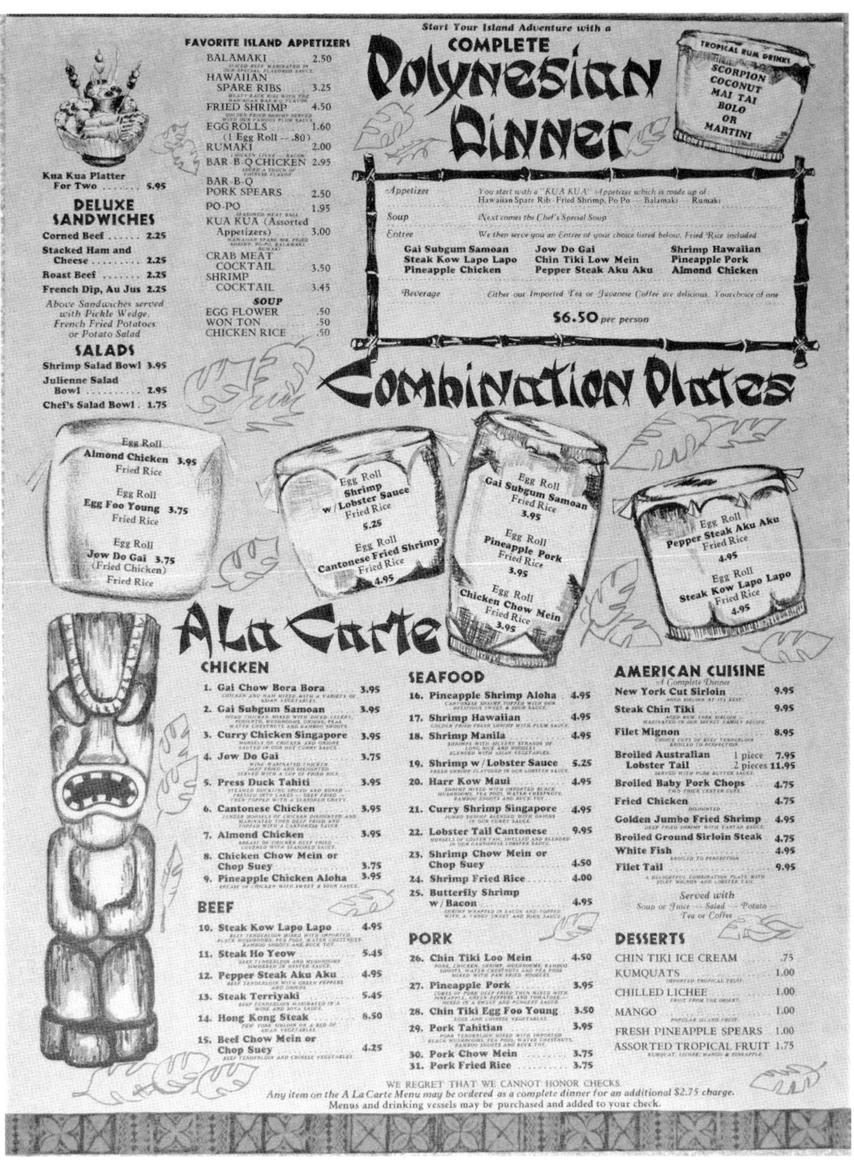

FAVORITE ISLAND APPETIZERS

BALAMAKI	2.50
HAWAIIAN SPARE RIBS	3.25
FRIED SHRIMP	4.50
EGG ROLLS (1 Egg Roll -- .80)	1.60
RUMAKI	2.00
BAR-B-Q CHICKEN	2.95
BAR-B-Q PORK SPEARS	2.50
PO-PO	1.95
KUA KUA (Assorted Appetizers)	3.00
CRAB MEAT COCKTAIL	3.50
SHRIMP COCKTAIL	3.45

SOUP

EGG FLOWER	.50
WON TON	.50
CHICKEN RICE	.50

Kua Kua Platter For Two 5.95

DELUXE SANDWICHES

Corned Beef	2.25
Stacked Ham and Cheese	2.25
Roast Beef	2.25
French Dip, Au Jus	2.25

Above Sandwiches served with Pickle Wedge, French Fried Potatoes or Potato Salad

SALADS

Shrimp Salad Bowl	3.95
Julienne Salad Bowl	2.95
Chef's Salad Bowl	1.75

Start Your Island Adventure with a

COMPLETE Polynesian Dinner

Appetizer — You start with a "KUA KUA" Appetizer which is made up of: Hawaiian Spare Rib, Fried Shrimp, Po Po — Balamaki — Rumaki

Soup — Next comes the Chef's Special Soup

Entree — We then serve you an Entree of your choice listed below, Fried Rice included

Gai Subgum Samoan	Jow Do Gai	Shrimp Hawaiian
Steak Kow Lapo Lapo	Chin Tiki Low Mein	Pineapple Pork
Pineapple Chicken	Pepper Steak Aku Aku	Almond Chicken

Beverage — Either our Imported Tea or Javanese Coffee are delicious. Your choice of one

$6.50 per person

TROPICAL RUM DRINKS
SCORPION
COCONUT
MAI TAI
BOLO
OR
MARTINI

Combination Plates

Egg Roll
Almond Chicken 3.95
Fried Rice

Egg Roll
Egg Foo Young 3.75
Fried Rice

Egg Roll
Jow Do Gai 3.75
(Fried Chicken)
Fried Rice

Egg Roll
Shrimp w/Lobster Sauce
Fried Rice
5.25

Egg Roll
Cantonese Fried Shrimp
Fried Rice
4.95

Egg Roll
Gai Subgum Samoan
Fried Rice
3.95

Egg Roll
Pineapple Pork
Fried Rice
3.95

Egg Roll
Chicken Chow Mein
Fried Rice
3.95

Egg Roll
Pepper Steak Aku Aku
Fried Rice
4.95

Egg Roll
Steak Kow Lapo Lapo
Fried Rice
4.95

A La Carte

CHICKEN

1. Gai Chow Bora Bora	3.95
2. Gai Subgum Samoan	3.95
3. Curry Chicken Singapore	3.95
4. Jow Do Gai	3.75
5. Press Duck Tahiti	3.95
6. Cantonese Chicken	3.95
7. Almond Chicken	3.95
8. Chicken Chow Mein or Chop Suey	3.75
9. Pineapple Chicken Aloha	3.95

BEEF

10. Steak Kow Lapo Lapo	4.95
11. Steak Ho Yeow	5.45
12. Pepper Steak Aku Aku	4.95
13. Steak Terriyaki	5.45
14. Hong Kong Steak	8.50
15. Beef Chow Mein or Chop Suey	4.25

SEAFOOD

16. Pineapple Shrimp Aloha	4.95
17. Shrimp Hawaiian	4.95
18. Shrimp Manila	4.95
19. Shrimp w/Lobster Sauce	5.25
20. Harr Kow Maui	4.95
21. Curry Shrimp Singapore	4.95
22. Lobster Tail Cantonese	9.95
23. Shrimp Chow Mein or Chop Suey	4.50
24. Shrimp Fried Rice	4.00
25. Butterfly Shrimp w/Bacon	4.95

PORK

26. Chin Tiki Loo Mein	4.50
27. Pineapple Pork	3.95
28. Chin Tiki Egg Foo Young	3.50
29. Pork Tahitian	3.95
30. Pork Chow Mein	3.75
31. Pork Fried Rice	3.75

AMERICAN CUISINE

A Complete Dinner

New York Cut Sirloin	9.95
Steak Chin Tiki	9.95
Filet Mignon	8.95
Broiled Australian Lobster Tail, 1 piece	7.95
Broiled Australian Lobster Tail, 2 pieces	11.95
Broiled Baby Pork Chops	4.75
Fried Chicken	4.75
Golden Jumbo Fried Shrimp	4.95
Broiled Ground Sirloin Steak	4.75
White Fish	4.95
Filet Tail	9.95

Served with Soup or Juice — Salad — Potato — Tea or Coffee

DESSERTS

CHIN TIKI ICE CREAM	.75
KUMQUATS	1.00
CHILLED LICHEE	1.00
MANGO	1.00
FRESH PINEAPPLE SPEARS	1.00
ASSORTED TROPICAL FRUIT	1.75

WE REGRET THAT WE CANNOT HONOR CHECKS.
Any item on the A La Carte Menu may be ordered as a complete dinner for an additional $2.75 charge.
Menus and drinking vessels may be purchased and added to your check.

Port O' Three menu selections. *Author's collection.*

> *resembles a poop-deck. Ropes and rails and furled sails complete the illusion. It all but rocks. Naturally the specialty is seafood.*
>
> *Exotic drinks that smoke and float flowers sell for $2.50 to $3 and all taste, to a scotch drinker, like melted jello. Wine comes in goblets for 90 cents.*
>
> *Diners make their own salads at a well-stocked salad bar on the poopdeck.*
>
> *In two trips to Port O' Three we found the food well prepared and served piping hot to the table. Even broiled salmon steak, a quick cooler, came on hot. Daily house specialty is unidentified on the menu and a waitress must be queried. It was red snapper with mushroom sauce last Friday and was excellent.*
>
> *Up front, reservations are handled efficiently and the valet parking is fast both in and out. Dinners range from $4 to $8.45. All orders are fried in butter for an extra quarter.*

Not exactly a glowing review. Marlin Chin later said the interior was enormous and extravagant, the most ambitious of all of his father's creations. Sadly, there are no published photos of Port O' Three; it disappeared from the restaurant section of the newspaper after 1972. Unlike the Chin Tiki, Port O' Three opened and closed without fanfare.

The remaining years of the 1970s were unkind to Detroit; businesses left, factories closed, crime increased, people bolted to the suburbs. Chin Tiki hung in there, surviving mostly on lunchtime dollars. "By the dawn of the '80's the 'Paris of the Midwest' was mired in an economic crisis. And thus, one day in 1980, Chin bolted the door to his Polynesian paradise and left it untouched for more than two decades….'The city closed. I went with it,'" he says in the 2003 *Metrotimes* article.

Journalist Sarah Klein wrote the article "Freaky Over Tiki" for the *Metrotimes* of September 24–30, 2003. She put a notice on tikicentral.com looking for Detroit-area tikiphiles, inviting them to join her. The article states:

> *For two decades, the Chin Tiki remained in limbo, a source of fascination for locals and visitors who drove past the striking exterior and wondered what treasures lay inside. And not too long ago, one of those gawkers turned out to be a Hollywood hotshot.*
>
> *While scouting locations for Eminem's semiautobiographical film* 8 Mile, *production designer Phil Messina stumbled across the Chin Tiki, and was entranced. Universal Studios then contacted Chin and contracted use of his facility for filming. During a brief scene in the movie, the Chin Tiki is featured as a favorite hangout of Eminem and his crew. During filming, Chin stopped by. His long dormant club was bathed in light once again, crammed*

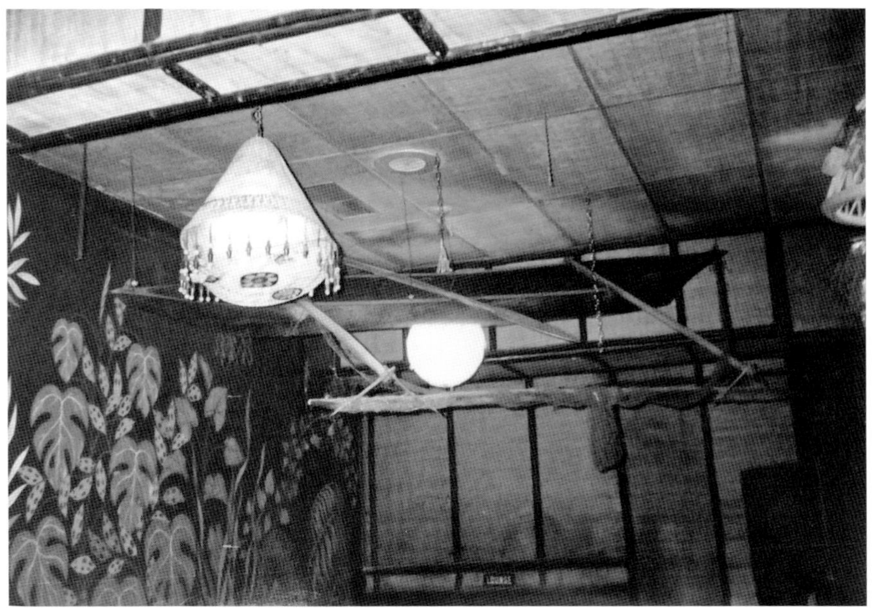

Chin Tiki interior post–*8 Mile. Courtesy of Tim Shuller.*

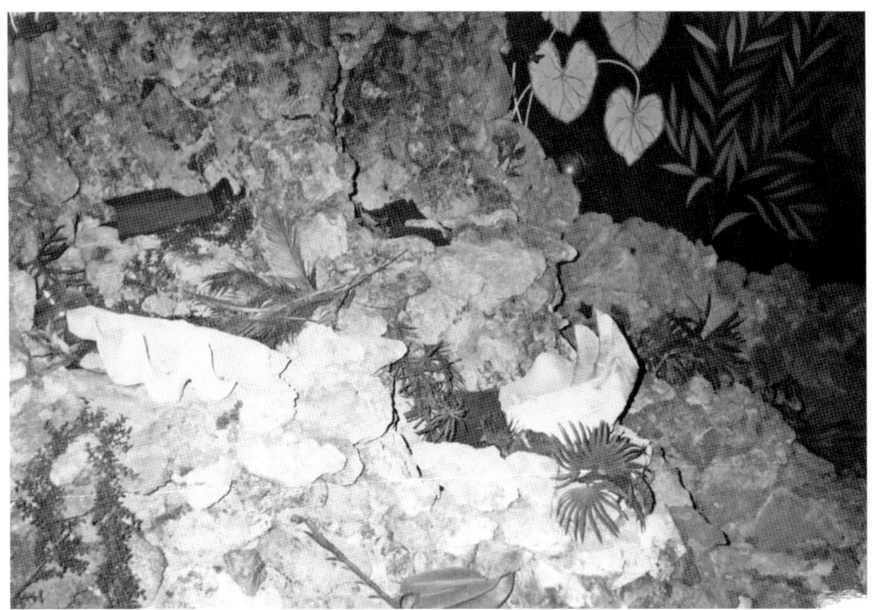

In 2003, the waterfall was long dried up. *Courtesy of Tim Shuller.*

> *to the bursting point with young kids drinking, laughing, pulsating with life. "It was inspiring," says Chin. "With all those kids dancing, there was all this energy. And I thought, why don't I open up again?"*

As Marlin Chin describes what it was like to have Hollywood swoop in and use the shuttered restaurant for a movie set, a smile spreads across his face. He points out that movie executives like using places that are closed up because they have full use of the facility any time of the day or night. The movie crew moved a lot of the décor from the main floor to the upstairs where they were shooting; they crowded as many things into the space as they could. And that ultra-cool bar with the Chinese coins embedded in Lucite on the bar top? That was the original bar out of the Mauna Loa. Nobody knows where the Hollywood set found it, but after filming, they gave it to Marvin. While rummaging through the building, Marlin recalls finding boxes of brand-new tiki mugs; stacks of new, unfolded menus; order tickets; and business cards. It really was a time capsule. Marlin and a former employee and friend of the family got to be extras in one of the scenes in the bar—what fun. He tried to persuade the movie crew to get the torches working again on the exterior of the building, but it didn't happen. The grin now encompasses his entire face as he remembers how amazing the building looked all lit up again. When asked what the movie experience was like for him, he says, "It was great!"

On that September day in 2003 when Sarah Klein arrived at Chin Tiki to do the interview and tour of the building, it was still arranged as it was for the filming—that's to say, it was not as it was during the fourteen years it was open. Fortunately, photos exist from that visit. The article continues:

> *Stepping into the Chin Tiki today is like walking into a time capsule. Inside the cold, damp and musty interior, half-full liquor bottles are piled among boxes of moldy drink umbrellas. The menu caddy still holds the yellowed drink and food menus, and a rusty metal rack holds the timecards, curled inward with age. A dirty Hawaiian shirt is draped on a Donna Reed era blender, while a lone, ratty sarong hangs in a dingy closet. A cluster of 5-foot Tikis are huddled in a corner, ghostly lit by a lone construction lamp.*
>
> *Chin is an affable old fellow with a rounded face and watery eyes, happily spinning yarns about the heyday of his tropical mecca. Flipping open a scrapbook, Chin points to a worn photo, dated 1969, of a coquettish young lass with teased hair and fat false eyelashes, draped in a blue sarong that creeps up midthigh.*

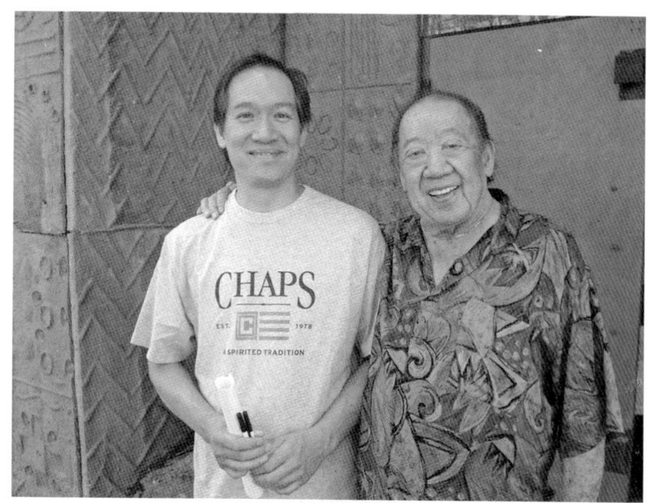

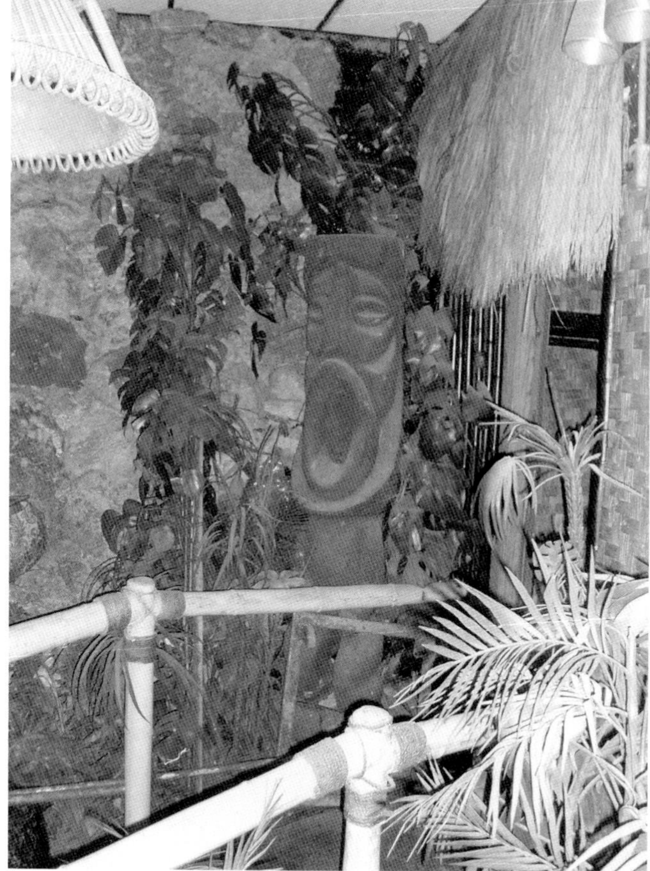

Top: Marlin and Marvin Chin. *Courtesy of Louis Devaney*.

Bottom: The bamboo bridge in 2003. *Courtesy of Louis Devaney*.

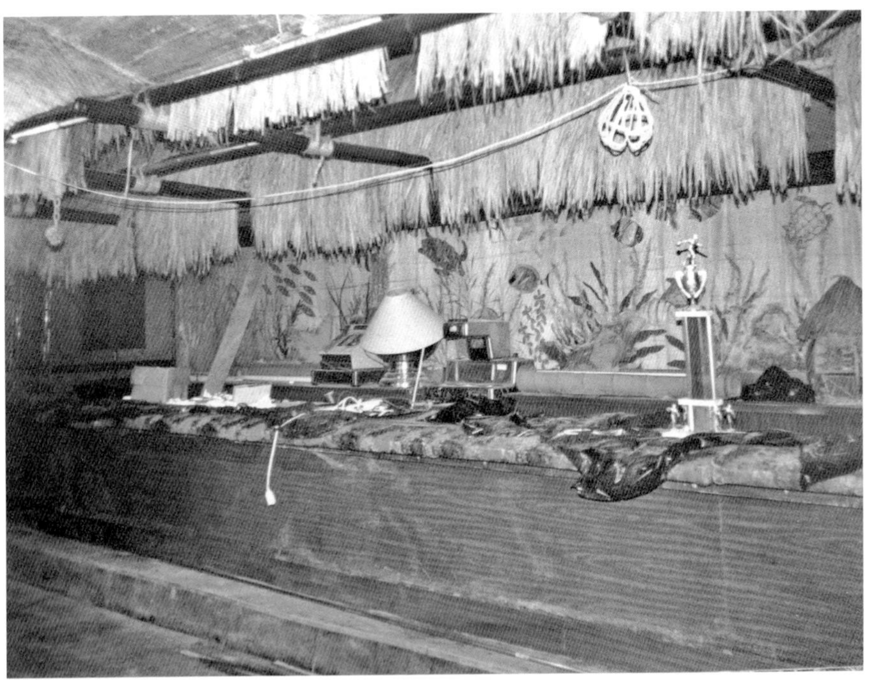

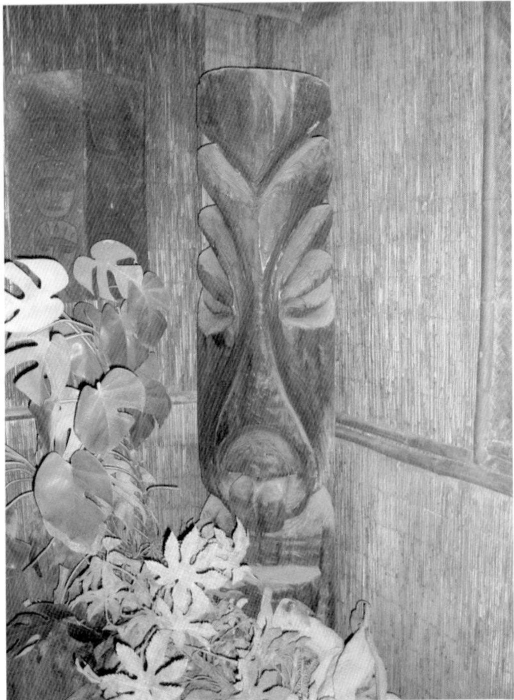

Above: The Chin Tiki bar in 2003. *Courtesy of Scott Schell.*

Left: Dust-covered tiki and artificial plants in 2003. *Courtesy of Louis Devaney.*

Opposite: A cluster of tikis as seen in 2003. *Courtesy of Tim Shuller.*

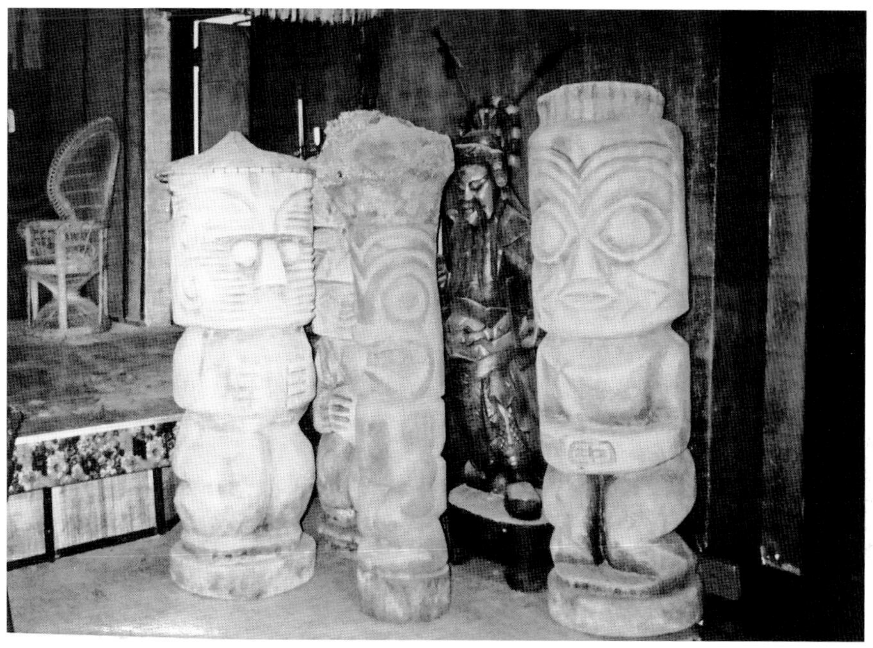

"They always like the girls running around in sarongs," he says with a smile.

He fondly recalls the real gardenias that floated in the Chin Tiki's custom drinks, often served in seashells or coconut husks.

After Universal finished their filming, Chin returned to the bar with hopes of reopening it. He received a nasty surprise. Chin claims the crew severed his electrical wiring and damaged murals, and that extras stole memorabilia, including Tiki mugs, matchbooks, and autographed photos from celebrities who frequented the establishment in the '60's.

Chin says he was paid $20,000 for use of his facility but says the cost to rewire and replace stolen items will be significant.

He began working on restoration midsummer, with doors finally open, the curious flocked to the site, full of queries. On any given day when the door is open, passers-by rubberneck and some immediately do a U-turn. Chin says he has inquiries every day from pedestrians who stop by and want to know the fate of the bar....

The Chin Tiki has been closed longer than it was open, and neither nature nor time have been kind. Although the upstairs portion is in good condition, thanks to the cleaning efforts of Universal. The downstairs has suffered considerable water damage and rotting. The plumbing needs a

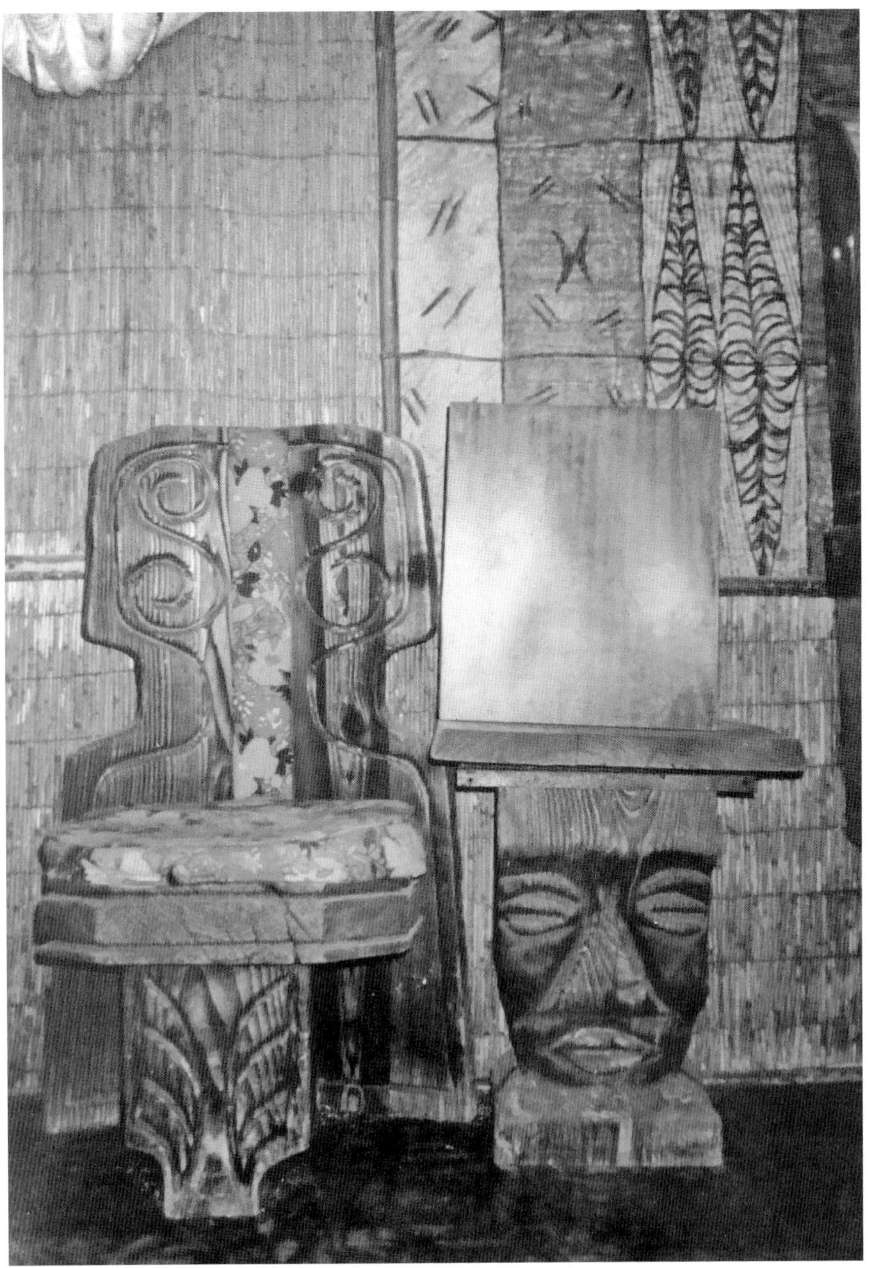

Above: A pair of decorative chairs in 2003. *Courtesy of Tim Shuller.*

Opposite, top: Demolition of Chin Tiki in 2009. *Courtesy of Dave Chow.*

Opposite, bottom: Chin Tiki is erased from the streetscape in 2009. *Courtesy of Dave Chow.*

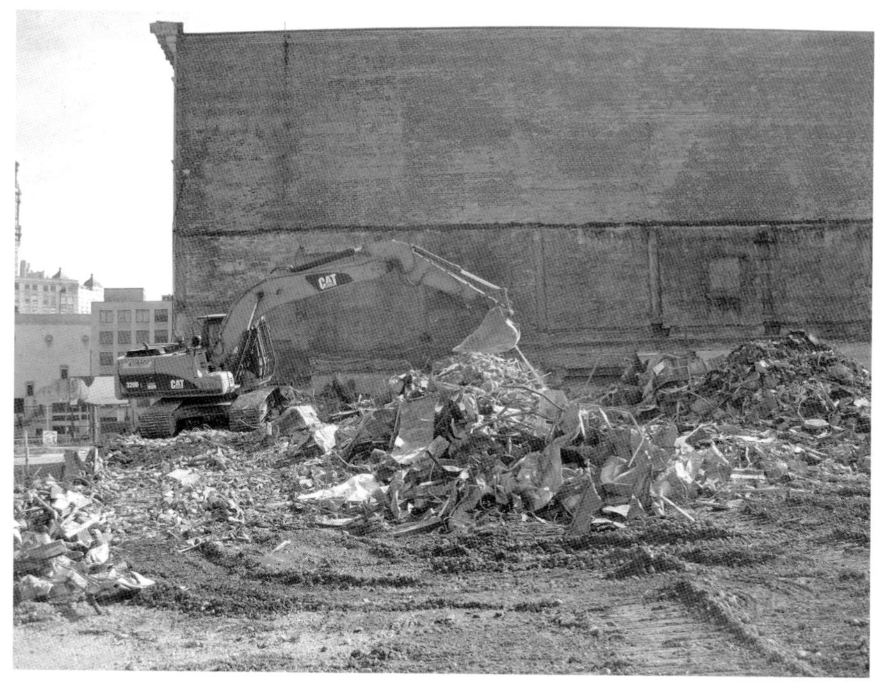
CAT

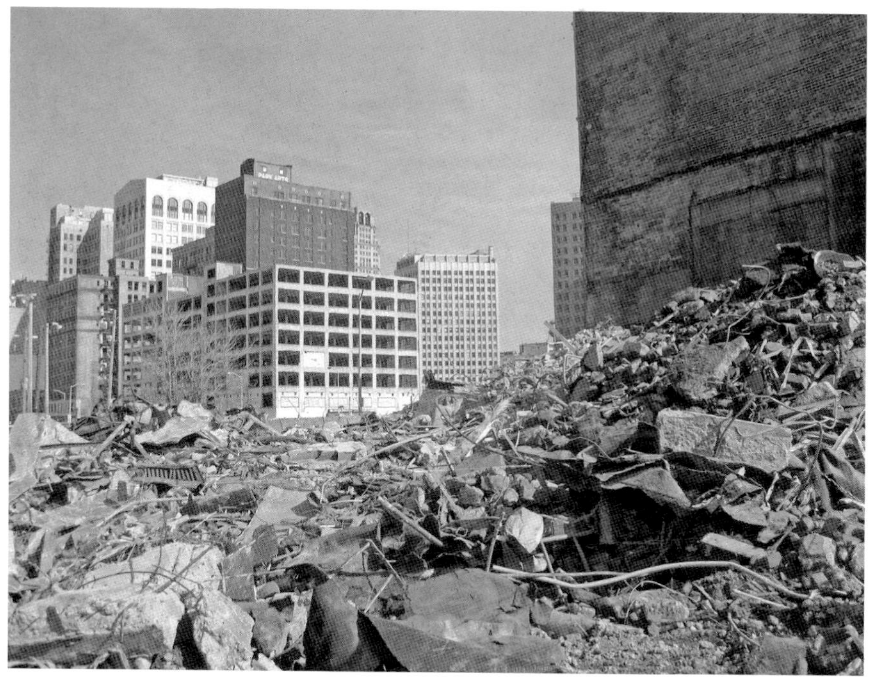

> *complete overhaul; Marvin no longer has a liquor license for the Chin Tiki and doesn't own the adjacent parking lot....*
>
> *"I would just like to see it open again, instead of just sitting here, paying taxes on it," says Marvin Chin, as he takes a seat in a carved Tiki chair and gazes at his dimly lit creation. "People really loved this place. They remember it. There's nothing else like it, there never was."*

Marvin Chin passed away in 2006. The Chin family decided to sell the building to Olympia Development LLC, which is owned by the Illitch family. Much of the Polynesian décor was sold off by the Chins; the remaining items were moved into storage or relocated to Chin's in Livonia. Olympia determined the building was unsuitable for development and proceeded to tear it down in 2009. Locals who had gotten word of the demolition showed up at the site and watched as the once-fantastical Polynesian paradise in the heart of the Motor City was reduced to a pile of bricks and mangled steel.

Marvin Chin did more than create a tiki palace. He built a gorgeous tropical fantasyland where everyone felt welcomed. When people began arriving from all over the country to work at the Mauna Loa, Chin Tiki became their hangout. Marvin, George Nakashima and Robert Fenton were friends. There was no competition between the two restaurants; many of the employees were friends too. People who worked for the Chin family still express their affection for Marvin and the people who ran Chin Tiki. Blaine Perrigo did more than paint and decorate; when in town, he would often act as host, greeting guests as they arrived. He is described as charming and being good with people; many of the young employees even called him Uncle Blaine. Some of the former employees have maintained a lifelong relationship with the Chin family. For the people who never got a chance to go there, we feel like we missed something special. For the people who got to experience the magic of Chin Tiki, it's something they will never forget.

Chapter 7

THE MAUNA LOA

The Mauna Loa has always been shrouded in mystique. Perhaps it's the long list of Detroit VIP investors, the $2,225,000 price tag, the pearl-diving girls or the fact that one of the most elaborate Polynesian restaurants in the world was on the auction block after only four years in business.

The story begins with a vision in 1964. The visionary was Robert L. Fenton, a prominent Detroit attorney, political activist, financier and agent to local sports figures. The March 13, 1966 *Detroit Free Press* had this to say about Fenton:

> *During one recent week, Fenton, 36, took Gail Cogdill, a handsome as well as an occasionally windy Detroit Lion, to New York to talk about television commercials. While there they bought Milt Plum some sweaters he'd been wanting. He also considered buying a radio station; checked to see how many times he could touch his toes; began accepting construction bids on his upcoming $1.5 million Polynesian restaurant in Detroit; and practiced law. In the latter endeavor, he flew once to Dallas and drove once to Lansing; and any number of times carried his brief case to the London Chop House. He negotiated for Wayne National Life Insurance Co., of which he is also a director, and for other insurance firms in Wisconsin and California; and counseled, cheered and chided as needed a dozen professional athletes who are his clients. A year younger than Mayor Cavanagh, Fenton is much like him in outlook and manner, soft spoken;*

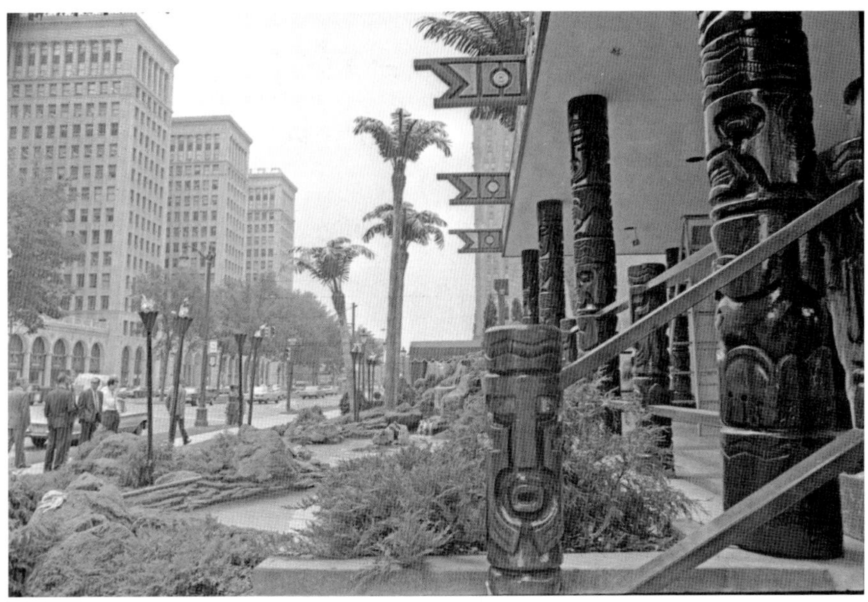

The Mauna Loa facing West Grand Boulevard. That's the General Motors Building across the street. *Courtesy of Walter P. Reuther Library, Archives of Labor and Urban Affairs, Wayne State University.*

> *outwardly controlled; buoyant in his approach to what seem impossible tasks; adept at banter, but intense. He is a lawyer-financier, the senior partner of Fenton, Nederlander, Tracy & Dodge; and the action in Suite 2555 of the Guardian Building is unrelenting.*

Now that we know a little bit about Robert Fenton, the man behind the Mauna Loa, let us explore how the idea for a Polynesian restaurant in Detroit came about. This is an excerpt from an interview with the *Detroit Free Press*:

> *The restaurant happened because Tiger pitcher Hank Aguirre talked about a new Mexican restaurant for Detroit. The thought led to Polynesian food. Fenton pondered about the number of Detroiters, including himself, who continually appear at Don the Beachcomber's in Los Angeles, and Trader Vic's in San Francisco. He found the restaurant owners interested in talking franchises. "That's no fun. You're nothing more than a flower pot" he said. Consulting surveys made on Detroit as a location, he decided to build independently in the New Center area, on West Grand Boulevard near Woodward. Once budded, the idea bloomed: "Get your fanny out of bed," he said to a hospitalized friend, "We've got to learn how to make egg rolls."*

There's fine dining

Top: Pontchartrain Wine Cellars bar, where cold duck was introduced to U.S. Below: Exterior of Mauna Loa.

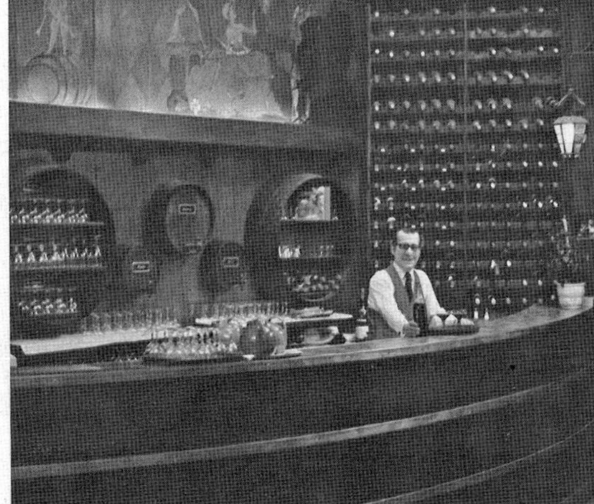

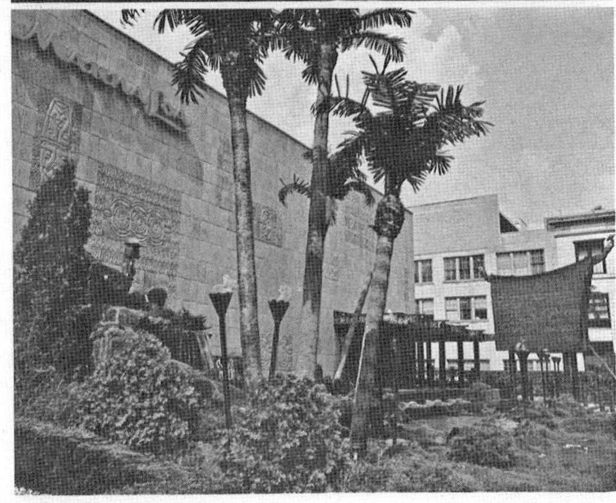

The Pontchartrain Wine Cellars is often described as the kind of small restaurant that everyone wishes was on a corner down every street . . . a little place with distinctive food, charm, friendliness, excellent but unobtrusive service, and that indefinable warmth that can be measured only by the low, steady hum of patrons obviously enjoying themselves.

"The Ponch," as many loyal downtown Detroit patrons call the little restaurant huddled in a building almost 90 years old, is more of a bistro than French restaurant. It serves a variety of dishes, among them a few French specialties, which have proved the choice of clients over many years. There is no attempt at haute cuisine. It's not that kind of place.

But few large, pretentious restaurants anywhere can claim a more loyal following. The clientele comes largely from workers in downtown Detroit's financial district . . . secretaries, advertising men, attorneys, businessmen . . . and also from visitors attending conventions and other events in Cobo Hall, Cobo Arena and other buildings in Detroit's Civic Center area.

The Pontchartrain Wine Cellars deserves national acclaim if only because it is the ancestral home of the "Cold Duck," that combination champagne-still Burgundy delight which now is becoming popular across the country. Jack Ross, head bartender at the Wine Cellars for some 17 years, estimates that he's served about 2.5 million Cold Ducks. For years only the Ponch, and then a few other Detroit restaurants, served Cold Duck. Now, vintners throughout the country are bottling it and restaurants and bars almost everywhere are adding it to their lists. The drink, properly served in a champagne glass, derives from an old German wine festival custom of pouring the last wines . . . red and white . . . together for one final quaff. Joan Collins, former proprietress of the Wine Cellars, introduced the drink in the United States.

Somehow, a Cold Duck at the Ponch just tastes better than anywhere else. Trays of them leave the small, curving bar, particularly when secretaries in the downtown area celebrate payday with lunch at the Wine Cellars.

Incidentally, Cold Duck at the Ponch is a combination of New York State champagne and California still Burgundy. The

18

The July 1970 *Dodge News Magazine* mentions the Mauna Loa in "Fine Dining in the Motor City." *Author's collection.*

And under the spell of this candid approach, 28 associates, mostly Fenton's friends, took out their checkbooks. Wielding the financial ladle of the Mauna Loa will be a number of stars sometimes in the soup themselves: Cogdill, Milt Plum, Lindsay and Aguirre; plus a scholarly leavening of bank vice presidents, insurance men and auto executives. Trusting, but cautious, one remarked before uncorking his pen: "You may be a great corporate attorney Fenton, but you don't know beans about running a restaurant." "What we needed," said Fenton, "was a manager able to successfully cope with Oriental chefs and all their cousins." So he stole Jerome L. Cohen from a West Coast chain of Polynesian Restaurants. Cohen ran the Chicago and New York Playboy clubs before going native. Soon after, George Nakashima, of Beverly Hills, designer of the most posh American Polynesian eateries, began trampling the Detroit snows envisioning palm trees against storm-blown skies. Nakashima had not, at first, been keen about Detroit. "I telephoned him one afternoon, told him to catch a plane, spent three hours traveling and two hours talking. If he weren't convinced, he'd be home the same night," Fenton said. Nakashima reluctantly arrived. He was toured from Cobo Hall out the freeway, through the packed Fisher Theater, past the General Motors and Burroughs buildings, to the site of the restaurant next to the emerging St. Regis Hotel. The two men talked until 4 am in Fenton's office. Nakashima took the job and became an investor. The Mauna Loa will be a smash, says Fenton. A place of poetry-food, shimmering waters and authentic monkeypod teak; with prices low enough so secretaries can lunch there the day before payday; and a place to "escape the rigors of living." Fenton wants his new restaurant to be a place of escape. "People should feel they're on a quiet island" with a bridge back to the mainland.

The team was now assembled. There were fifty stockholders in all; Walter Burkemo and Al Kaline joined the investor list in addition to the earlier named members of the Detroit Lions, Tigers and Red Wings. Commentators Roger Stanton and Wayne Walker each had a piece of the pie. The Big Three were well represented: Eugene Bordinat Jr. of Ford Motor Co.; Chilton Drysdale, Buick dealer; Peter Epsteen of Epsteen Pontiac Sales Co.; Byron J. Nichols Jr., son of Byron J. Nichols Sr., vice president at Chrysler; Dorothy Withers and Roland Withers of General Motors and Buick Division. The investment group dubbed The Syndicate also included radio personality J.P. McCarthy. The remaining $1.1 million came from the Bank of the Commonwealth.

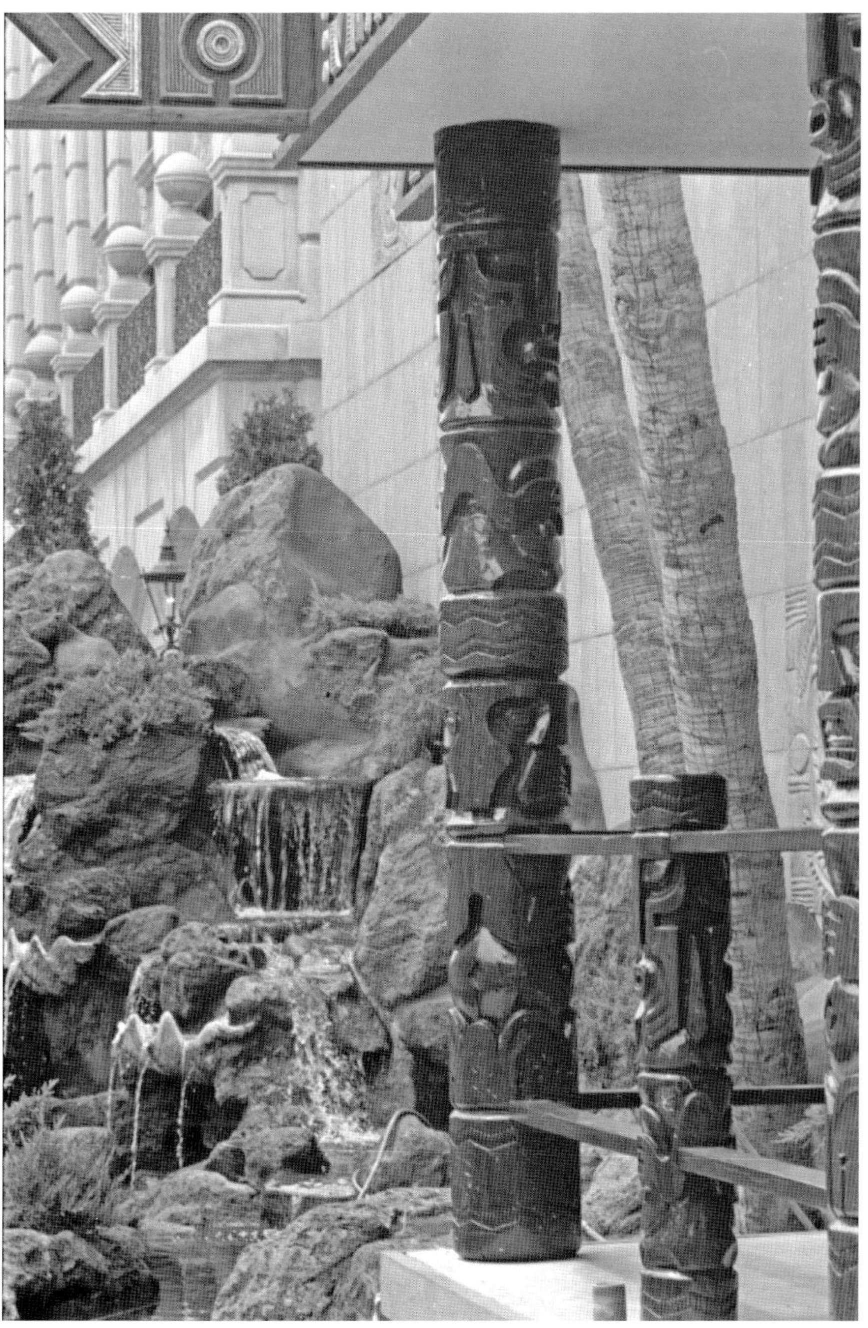

View of the waterfall in front of the Mauna Loa. *Courtesy of Walter P. Reuther Library, Archives of Labor and Urban Affairs, Wayne State University.*

Marvin Diamond compiled an impressive (if somewhat Orientalist) press release for the Mauna Loa. It begins:

> *One of the world's most elaborate restaurants, the $2¼ million Mauna Loa, will open its doors to the public at 11 a.m. Saturday, August 12* [1967]. *The Mauna Loa is nestled on a man-made lagoon at 3077 West Grand Boulevard at Cass. A waterfall rushes down a hill of volcanic lava into the lagoon. Patrons will pass under a thatched hut then through the restaurant's massive doors for a make-believe trip through the Pacific Archipelago and India. While dining at the Mauna Loa, Detroiters will not be surprised to find members of the Detroit Tigers baseball team, Lions football team, radio and TV personalities, civic leaders and faces made familiar through the business pages of Detroit's papers.*
>
> *The foyer is a ceremonial hut with a red box hanging from the roof. In the islands, when a Polynesian swain takes his sarong-clad maiden into this hut, it indicates they are going to be married and spend the rest of their lives together.*
>
> *When the diner asks "Is it real?," no matter what he is pointing to, the answer is "yes." The heroic island figures are authentic. So are the tiki poles with island carvings that support the ceiling. The blowfish that glow red, blue and green are real blowfish. The enormous war canoe (one of five) came from Samoa. The 1,250 Chinese coins imbedded in the bar are real. The bar tables are brass-bound hatch covers from trading schooners. The four-bladed fans that twirl languidly from the bar ceiling came from a Hong Kong saloon. The brass lamps, the ship's compass, the spears and shields are all real. The Chinese writing carved into some of the columns really say something and chances are your waiter will be able to translate it for you.*
>
> *Yes, that's real water cascading down the lava falls and running in the stream beside your table. Take our word for it. If mi-lady puts her slipper-clad foot in the stream, she'll find it's real deep and she'll be real wet.*
>
> *If you eat in the Papeete Room, the Tonga Room, the Lanai Room or the Maui Room, your Oriental waiter will be mandarin-jacketed. In the Bombay Room, a turbaned waiter will make you feel like a member of the British Foreign Service. It is only in the Bombay Room that we find something that is not real—the 3,000 gems that are imbedded in the filigreed teakwood panels are not real gems—they are Zircons.*
>
> *The Mauna Loa has two complete kitchens (American and Oriental), plus a third kitchen for the banquet room. Kurt Mecklenburg, who has cooked everywhere from the Bavarian Alps to Singapore and has directed the*

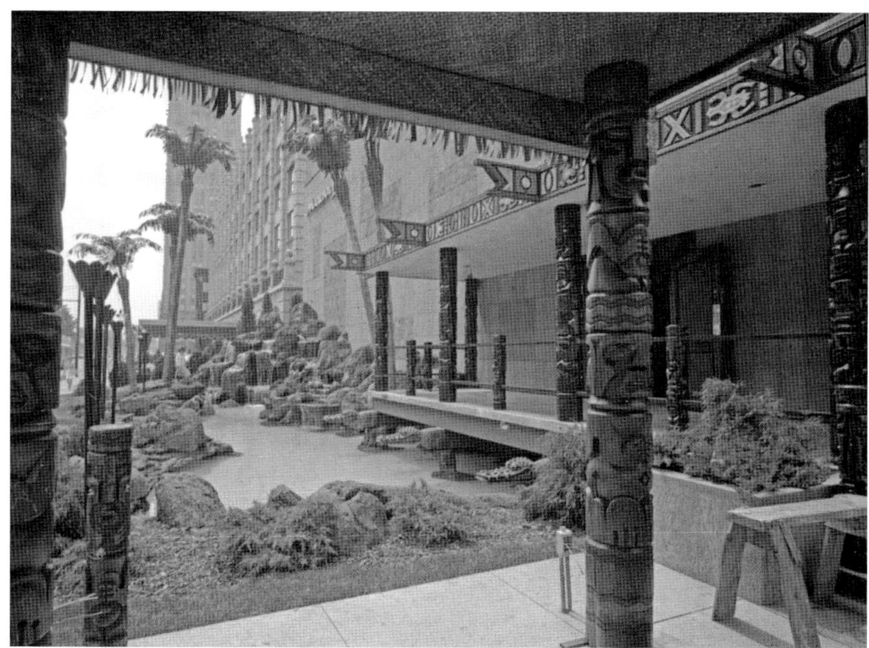

Above: View of the lagoon at the Mauna Loa. *Courtesy of Walter P. Reuther Library, Archives of Labor and Urban Affairs, Wayne State University.*

Right: Mauna Loa plate, salt and pepper shakers, Polynesian Pidgeon mug, knife, spoon and special occasion menu. *Author's collection.*

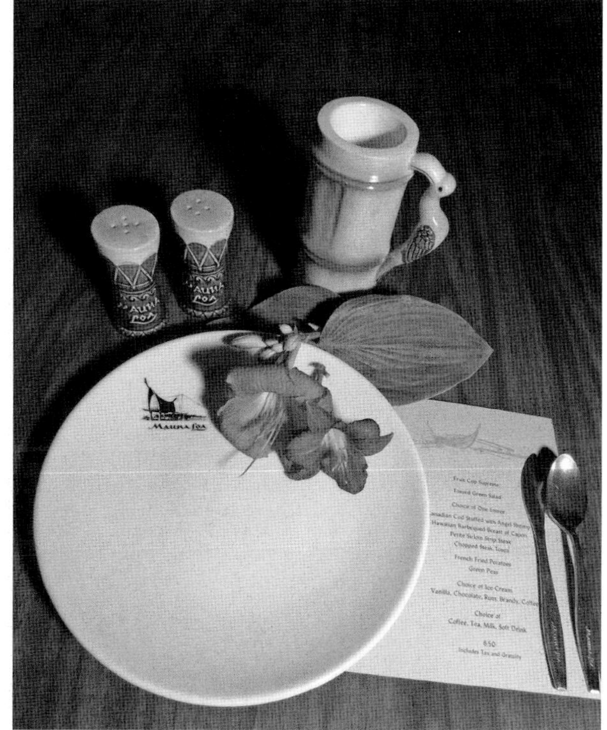

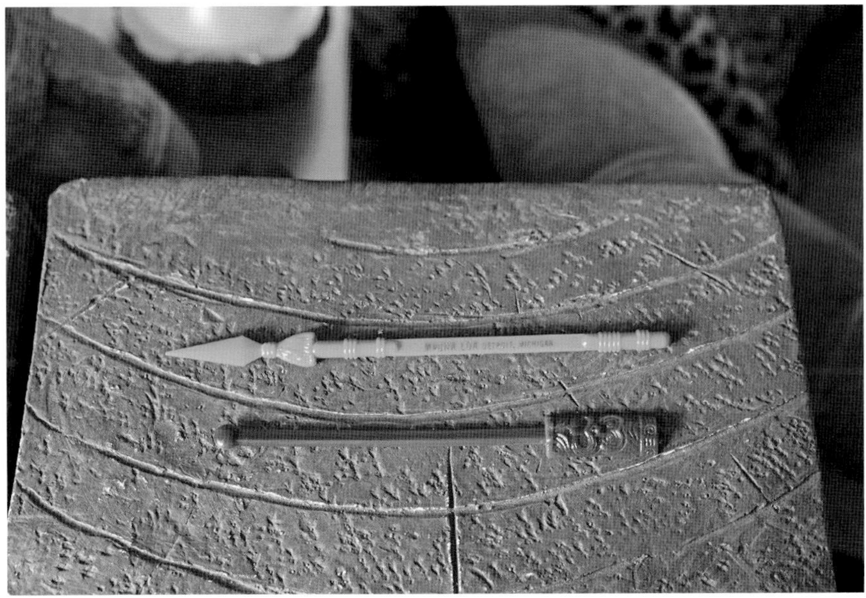

A common Mona Loa swizzle stick and a rare spear. *Private collection, photo by Nick Hagen.*

> *food services for the sleek ships that bring American products to the Orient and bring all of those motorcycles back here, is Executive Chef.*
>
> *The only areas of the restaurant off limits to patrons are the service bars where island drinks are mixed with precision from secret formulas. You may ask the waiter for the recipe for any of the exotic dishes and Kurt Mecklenberg will see that you get it. But if you ask the waiter for the ingredients of your island drink, you will only get an inscrutable Oriental smile.*
>
> *And just when you think you have seen everything, you come upon a volcanic pool where a sarong-clad diver is about to submerge and search for pearls.*
>
> *And you still haven't seen the banquet facilities which can accommodate groups from 12 to 450. The banquet décor is Mediterranean. The banquet room has an enormous Bar-B-Que pit which can accommodate a luau, New England clambake or Texas barbeque.*

Doesn't that sound magnificent? After reading that introduction, who would not put down the paper, run to the telephone and dial TR 5-7800 and make a reservation? Also included in the press release is a fact sheet; here are the highlights:

> *Décor: Authentic Pacific Archipelago, 5 waterfalls, 3 island ponds, Indian Room, huge island pool*
> *Food: All the exotic dishes of the Islands plus Indian food, plus full selection of the finest American food.*
> *Parking: Room for 400 cars*
> *Exotic Building Components: 500 tiki poles, 25 heroic island figures, 1,250 rare Chinese coins imbedded in plastic in the bar, 40 hatch covers from ocean freighters for use as bar and table tops, 40,000 lineal feet of bamboo, 250 tons of lava, 3,500 pounds of thatching, 5 war canoes, 75 spears and paddles, 7 palm trees.*
> *Countries Contributing Materials: Hawaii, Guam, Panama, Puerto Rico, Virgin Islands, Honduras, Nicaragua, Costa Rica, New Guinea, Australia, Indonesia, New Zealand, Philippine Islands, Solomon Islands, New Hebrides, Fiji Islands, Samoa, Singapore, Thailand, Burma, Ceylon, India, Cambodia, China, Taiwan, Japan, Hong Kong, Macao*

Under "Service," it mentions specially trained waiters except in Shanghai Lil Room, where there will be costumed waitresses. Wow, they had a Shanghai Lil Room? I'm thinking Busby Berkeley's *Footlight Parade*; I wonder if that was the inspiration behind it.

Fenton wanted only the best for the Mauna Loa, as is evident in the pedigree of his key hires. John S. Karydes was the catering manager. B.F. Enriquez, formerly of Washington's Mayflower Hotel, was the assistant manager. Kurt Mecklenburg was a chef from West Germany, and Jimmy Mark was a Chinese cook. Jerome L. Cohen, the general manager of the restaurant, was assistant general manager and general manager for Playboy Clubs International; he worked in both the Chicago and New York clubs. From there, he was snatched up by Stephen Crane Associates, the Luau Company, as their managing director of the Kon Tiki Ports Sheraton Chicago Hotel. He then became regional management supervisor of three restaurants located in Montreal, Cleveland and Chicago. That is an impressive résumé. Mixologist Joe Spada created the secret recipes for the exotic rum-based drinks and oversaw the recruitment of bartenders. Joe (aka Sinbad) reached out to men he had worked with all over the country; bartenders came from Los Angeles, Palm Springs, Dallas, Chicago and Las Vegas. All these men were put on the payroll months before the restaurant opened to lock them in. Being new to the area, many of them stayed at the Leland Hotel in downtown Detroit.

M. George Nakashima probably had no idea how much his life would change once he got to Detroit. On a professional level, he was about to embark on two of the most prestigious projects of his career: the Mauna Loa and the renovation of the Mai Kai in Fort Lauderdale, Florida. On a personal level, he was reunited with bartender and friend Joe Codilla from his days at the Luau; both would end up marrying women they met at the Chin Tiki and spend the rest of their lives in the Detroit area. First, let us take a detour to Beverly Hills, California, in the 1950s, the force, Stephen Crane. Following a brief marriage to Lana Turner and bit parts in three films, Crane entered the restaurant business. Taking note of the wild success enjoyed by Don the Beachcomber's and Trader Vic's, Crane bought out The Tropics in Beverly Hills; hired restaurant designer M. George Nakashima and art director and Bay City, Michigan native Florian Gabriel; and created a Polynesian palace known as The Luau. The Luau opened on Rodeo Drive in 1953. Movie stars, Hollywood notables, locals and tourists alike flocked to The Luau, making it an immediate success. It was so successful that in 1958, the Sheraton Hotel chain lured Crane into opening a string of Polynesian restaurants in its hotels to directly compete with the Hilton's Trader Vic's. Continuing his relationship with Nakashima and Gabriel, Crane opened Kon Tiki restaurants in Sheraton Hotels across the United States and Canada. Crane also worked with the pair on his Ports O' Call restaurants. All of the ceramics such as mugs, bowls and salt and pepper shakers were designed in-house; mug designs have been attributed to Gabriel.

M. George Nakashima had been busy creating lush, tropical tiki restaurants for years before he got the call from Fenton. At this time, he was no longer employed full time by Stephen Crane Associates. Throughout his career, Nakashima purchased much of the authentic decorative items for his projects from Oceanic Arts in Whittier, California. According to its website, Oceanic Arts is "the world's largest supplier of tropical and Polynesian décor." The shop opened in 1956. Co-owners Robert Van Oosting and LeRoy Schmaltz sold everything needed to properly outfit a Polynesian palace. They imported objects and materials across the South Pacific, from Hawaii to New Guinea. What they didn't buy, they carved themselves—Tahitian support posts, South Sea island paddles, shields and masks. An Oceanic Arts invoice from January 5, 1967, shows the Mauna Loa purchase of multiple blowfish, authentic New Guinea shields, shake totem, ancestral mask and skull hook, Solomon Island plaited spears and hand-carved ship figureheads, totaling $1,694.00. That was just a drop in the decoration bucket.

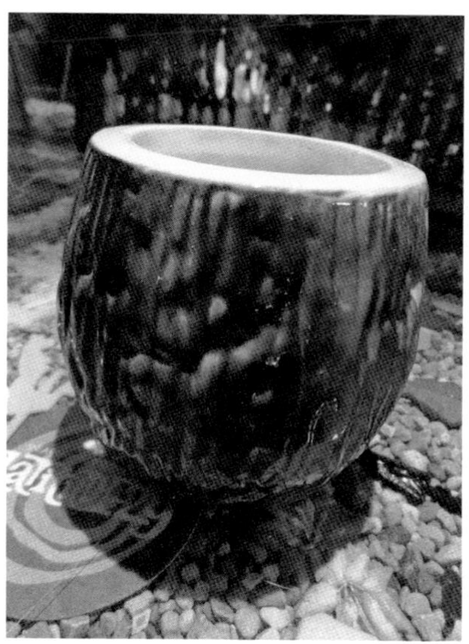

Right: Mauna Loa coconut mug. *Courtesy of Tim Shuller.*

Below: Oceanic Arts invoice. *Courtesy of Oceanic Arts.*

OCEANIC ARTS

IMPORTERS • MANUFACTURERS • DESIGNERS • CONSULTANTS

901 W. PHILADELPHIA WHITTIER, CALIFORNIA

phone 693-1643 area code 213

INVOICE NUMBER 2365

sold to MAUNA LOA RESTAURANT
2555 GUARDIAN BUILDING
DETROIT, MICHAGAN

ship to MAUNA LOA RESTAURANT
3077 W. GRAND BLVD.
DETROIT, MICHAGAN

DATE	YOUR ORDER NO.	SHIPPED VIA	F.O.B.	TERMS
JAN 6,1967	9781-G.N.	TRANSCON JAN 5,1967	WHITTIER	2%/10, NET 30 DAYS

QUANTITY	STOCK NO.	DESCRIPTION	PRICE	UNIT	EXTENSION
6		Blowfish, 28/30"	20.00	ea	$120.00
2		Blowfish, Large, Unusual spineless type	20.00	ea	40.00
8		Blowfish, 25/27"	18.00	ea	144.00
1	4269	Authentic New Guinea Shield, Sepic area			225.00
1	5584	Authentic New Guinea Shake Totem, Sepic area			160.00
1	5592	Authentic New Guinea Ancestral Mask, Sepic			62.50
1	4727	Authentic New Guinea Skull Hook, Sepic area			62.50
1	#1	Handcarved Ships Figurehead, Redwood,Painted			300.00
1	#2	Handcarved Ships Figurehead, Redwood,Painted			300.00
1	193-A	Authentic New Guinea Shield, Oldish, Sepic			190.00
6		Solomen Island Plaited Spears, selected	15.00	ea	90.00
					$1694. 00

- Orig Bill of Lading Enclosed.
- Following on Back Order: 2 Marquesan Oars
2 Sarawak Shields

THANK YOU

PAID
JAN 23 1967
NO. 656

YOU MAY DEDUCT $ 33.88
ONLY IF PAID BY JAN 16th.
FREIGHT & SALES TAX NET

INTEREST CHARGED ON ALL PAST DUE ACCO...S. SHOULD LEGAL ACTION BE NECESSARY TO ...FECT COLLECTION OF THIS ACCOUNT, DEBTOR AGREES TO PAY ALL COURT COSTS ATTORNEY'S FEES INCURRED BY SUCH ACTIC... ...ETURNED ITEMS SUBJECT TO 10% HANDLING CHARGE.

buyers in: TAHITI, SAMOA, FIJI, NEW GUINEA, AUSTRALIA, AFRICA, HONG KONG, JAPAN, THE PHILIPPINES

Blueprints of the Mauna Loa reveal the architect's name as George Pelham, head AIA architect, and M. George Nakashima, restaurant designer. A first glance at the architectural drawing is dizzying—the curvy shape of large pools, tropical foliage, waterfalls cascading down into streams crossed by plank bridges. U-shaped booths are found clustered in groups or lining walls. The fine details—such as the location of drains in the pools, conveyor coatrack with portable remote control, location of the pump and filter for the exterior pool, service stations, lava stone overhangs, bamboo screens, posts and railings—give us a clearer picture of the intricacies involved in the build-out. Between the blueprint, a small number of interior photographs and personal descriptions, we can put together the layout of the restaurant. The building rose behind a man-made lagoon surrounded by real lava rock. Tiki torches stabbed the landscape as weatherized palm trees rose from Michigan's earth. You may be asking yourself, what exactly is a weatherized palm tree? Basically, the only parts of the palm trees that are real are the trunks; they were pumped full of asphalt under pressure, and the palm fronds are pure plastic. The total cost for the eight exterior palm trees was $12,000.

The restaurant entrance was marked by a huge New Guinea–style thatched hut supported by carved wooden poles—an unexpected sight in Detroit, especially in the winter. Patrons passed through massive doors ready to embark on a fantastical trip through the Far Pacific. Once inside the windowless structure, there was nothing indicating you were in the Motor City any longer. On the right, an elevator waited to lift patrons to the Mediterranean-style banquet room on the second floor, and stairs were to the left. Pushing farther in, you entered the grand foyer designed as a Polynesian ceremonial hut with a red box hanging from the roof. From the far right, the distinct sound of water came from a tropical pool complete with stones and sand-textured cement—a glimpse of what was to come deeper into the restaurant. Here you could check your coat, wander into the gift shop and access the corridor to the restrooms. After checking in with the maître d', you'd pass the chopstick display; a right turn would lead you to the bar known as Shanghai Lil's, and bam, just like that you were in Polynesia. Four-bladed fans from a Hong Kong saloon twirled from the ceiling. Bar tables were brass-bound hatch covers from trading schooners. The one-of-a-kind canopy-covered bar stretched about twenty-five feet across the room diagonally, the top a dazzling display of 1,250 Chinese coins embedded into plastic. Mixologist Joe Codilla recalls water spilling placidly down the waterfall located behind the bar as he was whipping

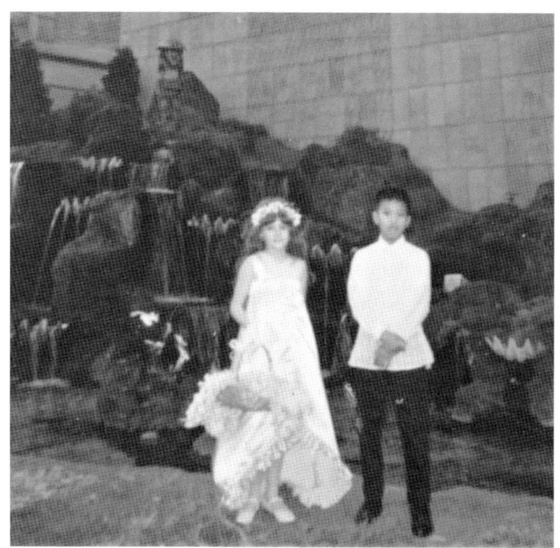

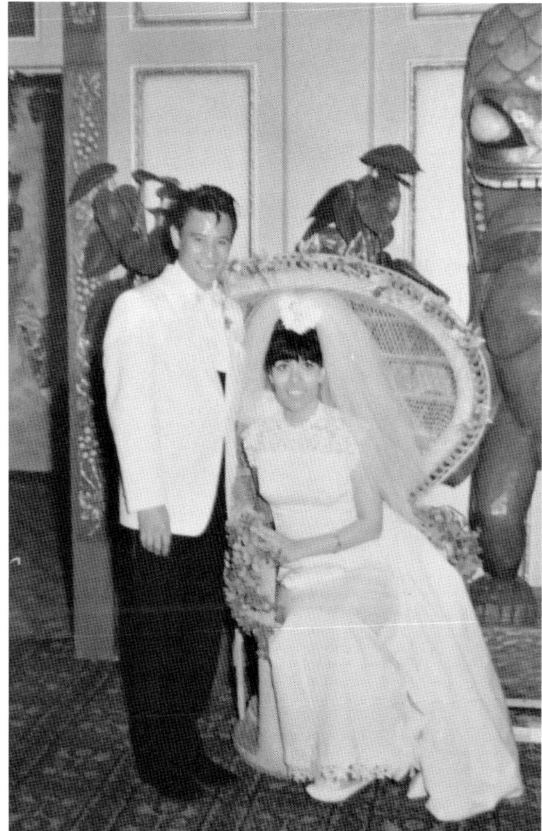

Top: A flower girl and ring bearer pose for photos in front of the Mauna Loa waterfall. *Courtesy of Kawehilani.*

Bottom: This bride and groom had their wedding at the Mauna Loa in the Mediterranean-style banquet room on the second floor. *Courtesy of Kawehilani.*

up Scorpions, Tahitians and Daiquiris. Drinks would be served in sixty different types of glasses and ceramic mugs.

If you instead walked straight, you would enter the main dining area, which

> *is divided into intimate areas through varying floor levels and ceiling treatments. The main floor resembled a native village in the islands with thatched roofs, walkways, bridges and streams. Elaborately carved posts, a war canoe, shields and other Polynesian art objects add atmosphere. The Polynesian restaurant on the main floor will seat 300 persons.*

You have one large, open space all under a single roof. The addition of screens, passages, carved poles, water and bamboo divides it up into smaller, quaint spaces. For example, the Tonga on the right is at ground level, and the Tahitian to the left is elevated one foot. From here, it gets even more interesting. A river meanders throughout the restaurant; koi swim at a languid pace. You enter an open area where a huge main pool flows by four waterfalls and a stream into consecutive pools; a giant shell rests in the final pool. The sound of gushing water had to be intoxicating. The falls were lit up, and ferns and lush greens imitated nature. It is here where a pair of oak plank bridges crossed the stream—one leading to the Lanai and Shangri-La Room and the other to the Garden Room. The Shangri-La had banquette seating; the Lanai was seemingly more extravagant, with booths lining the lowest part of the waterfall and continuing the length of the wall to the left as you came off the bridge. Here, there were tall, carved columns, greenery and multiple tikis. A July 4, 1967 *Detroit Free Press* article states:

> *A real problem was posed by the need for authentic worn wood pilings for one of the Mauna Loa's several pools. After a long search the determined decorators finally found dock pilings that had just the exotic character they wanted from an old dock being replaced in a quiet corner of the world known fondly to bon vivants as Belle Isle.*

The Garden Room was the main attraction; this is where the deep lava pool was located and where you could watch a Polynesian girl dive for pearls. While other tiki palaces around the country entertained their guests with floor shows featuring live music, native dancers and fiery torches, it was only at the Mauna Loa that customers could walk up to a sarong-clad maiden and place an order for a pearl, which she would then retrieve from

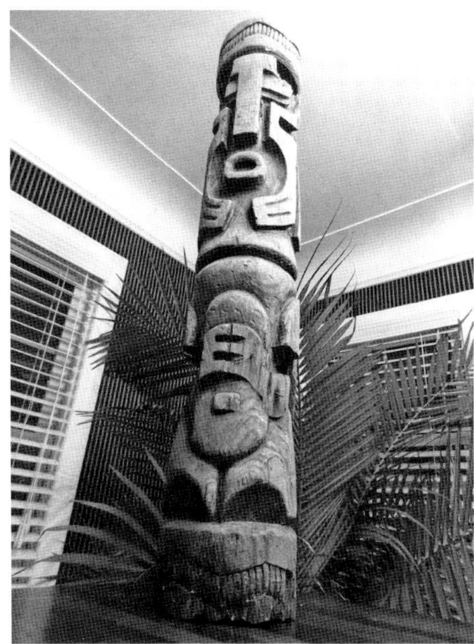

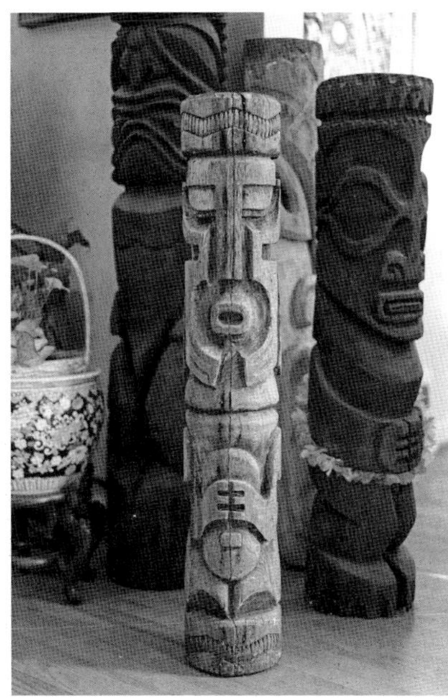

Left: Hand-carved post from the Mauna Loa. *Courtesy of Zach Roberts.*

Right: Mauna Loa post. *Private collection, photo by Nick Hagen.*

the pearl-bearing oysters. That's probably one of the reasons Nakashima called it one of the two most elaborate Polynesian-type restaurants in the country. The Garden Room used the U-shaped booths in clusters of four; the deep lava pool was the central focus. At over twenty feet wide and ten feet deep, it featured a platform and a ledge from which the girls would dive. The drawing shows a ladder that it seems was used to climb out of the water in the shallow area. The blueprint shows lava stone overhangs, a waterfall leading to a smaller pool, carved railings and numerous tropical plants. A June 11, 1969 *Detroit Free Press* article says, "Micky Lolich warmed up for his heartbreaking stint against Seattle by stopping off briefly at the Mauna Loa to watch Princess Liana dive for pearls. The princess is really Jan Ricca, the pearls are genuine though not very cultured. If the kind of luck Lolich encountered keeps running, he might want to trade jobs with the princess." Kim Fujiwara relayed a story in which his sister, who was nineteen at the time, told their mother, Helen Fujiwara, that she wanted to become a pearl diver at the Mauna Loa. Helen, who worked as the hostess at Chin Tiki at the time, told her no way. It was at the Chin Tiki that Nakashima met Helen while he was working on the Mauna Loa. They

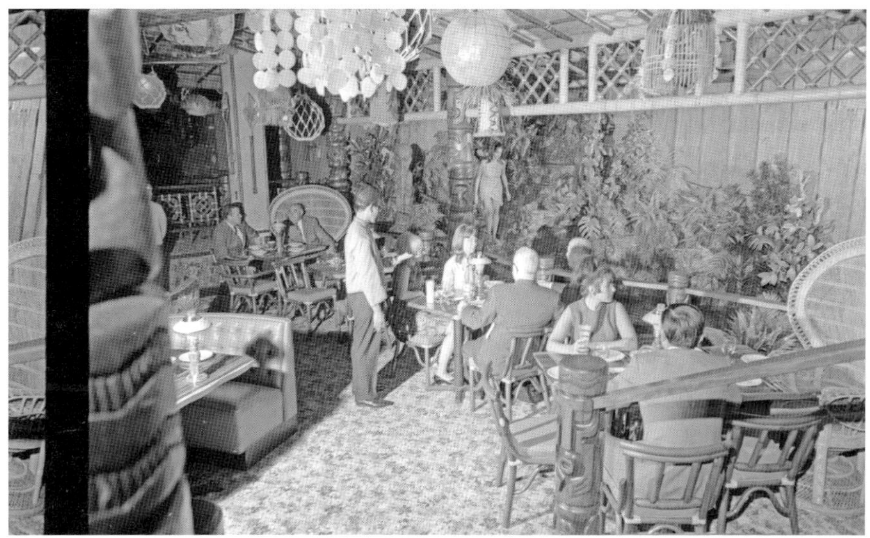

In the Garden Room, a pearl diver stands at the edge of the deep lava pool. *Courtesy of Walter P. Reuther Library, Archives of Labor and Urban Affairs, Wayne State University.*

started dating and eventually married; Nakashima spent the next forty years of his life with Helen in the Detroit area.

The standard rule of tiki décor is to never leave a blank wall or open space. Photographs and newspaper accounts confirm this was the case with the Mauna Loa. Carpenters, plumbers and electricians worked side by side installing water features, handsome tiki poles, columns, Chinese soapstone, lava rock, cinnamon sisal, colorful tiles, speckled bamboo, rice straw and rich wood weavings covered with hand-wrapped rattan peel. Designers arranged furniture, spears, paddles, carved wooden figures and other decorative items; any remaining empty spaces were filled with some kind of flowering plant or greenery. The bamboo was imported from Japan, the Philippines and Formosa—twice. Termites were discovered in the first shipment, and it had to be replaced. This was just one of the setbacks incurred getting the place up and running. There were lighted waterfalls flowing from nearly every corner and even behind the huge bar and romantic lights glowing from stuffed blowfish, shells and papier-mâché globes. The *Bay City Times* was especially proud of native son Florian E. Gabriel's part in the Mauna Loa. A Sunday, August 20, 1967 article had this to say:

> *A former Bay Citian can confirm the authenticity of the elaborate Polynesian décor of Detroit's newest, luxurious restaurant, the Mauna*

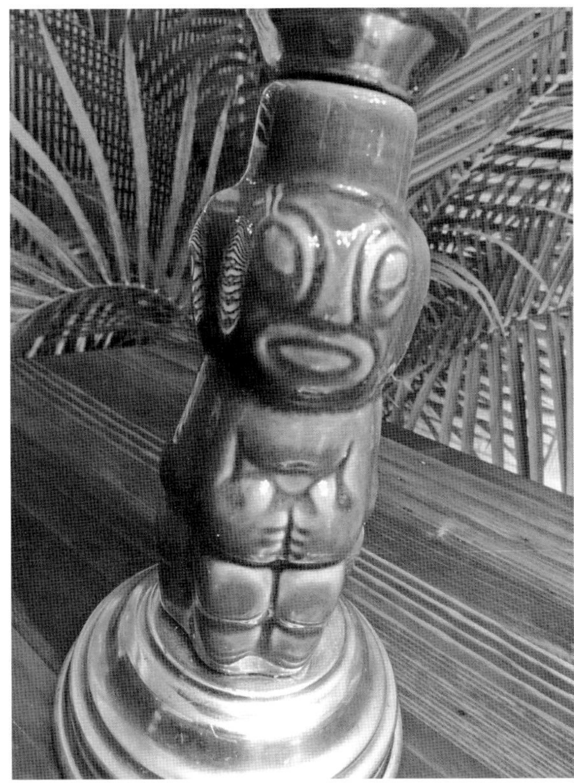

Left: Mauna Loa lamp base. *Courtesy of Zach Roberts.*

Below: The Garden Room details: tiki posts, table lamps and the seated pearl diver. *Courtesy of Walter P. Reuther Library, Archives of Labor and Urban Affairs, Wayne State University.*

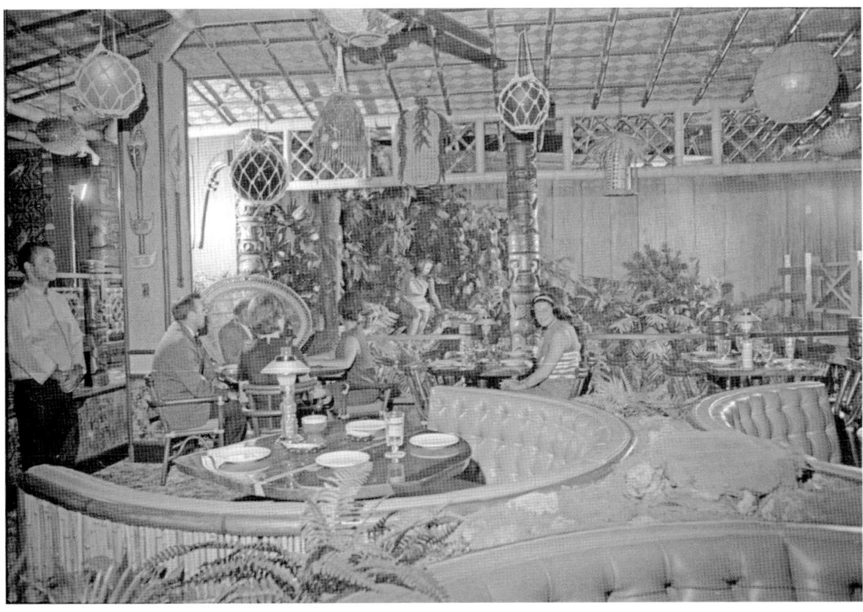

> *Loa. The interior design, said the 1945 graduate of Bay City Central High School, "is a fusion of many exotic locales," all authenticated since the plans were begun two and one half years ago. The heroic island figures and the tiki poles with carvings are authentic, as are the glowing blowfish and an enormous war canoe from Samoa. The Bombay Room, formal dining area, has 3,000 zircons imbedded in the filigreed teakwood panels that surround a sacred elephant shrine. Turbaned waiters serve diners there.*

Everything about the Mauna Loa was special and unique; the cover of the dinner menu was extraordinary. The same hut that marks the entrance to the restaurant also graces the cover, and colorful flora and fauna appear as if they came straight out of a tropical jungle; even the font feels like it came from the islands. The text on the inside cover is framed by bold renderings of fruit and sea life; the story takes us on a Polynesian trip through time. One paragraph reads, "Decorating our rooms are authentic war weapons from the Sepik River area of Dutch New Guinea, the Philippines and other Pacific islands, figurines from Cambodia, temple dogs from Nepal, outriggers from Samoa, lava and feather rock, blowfish and Japanese fish floats…" Speaking of menus, you might be wondering what dishes they served. Hot appetizers included Shanghai Crab Roll, Rumaki (water chestnuts and spiced chicken livers, rolled in crisp bacon), Hikoki Tidbit (the Polynesian meatball), Nuku Hiva Drums (specially prepared chicken upper wings, a masterpiece of culinary art) and Kau Kau (an appetizer selection consisting of Hawaiian Ribs, Rumaki, Bali Miki, Puffed Shrimp and Hikoki Tidbits). Main dishes from the Orient included Beef Bock Toy (beef with water chestnuts and Chinese green vegetables), Pork Peu Peu (Polynesian meatballs with green peppers and pineapple sweet and sour), Chicken Akipou (breaded breast of chicken with mixed island vegetables), Lobster Cantonese and Shrimp Tango Roa (diced with pea pods, water chestnuts and mushrooms, served on a bed of crisp noodles, topped with almonds). Lobster was the most expensive at $5.75; pork and chicken dishes were under $4.00. Special salads included the Mauna Loa Luau for $2.75 and the Crabmeat Soroya (crisp hearts of mixed lettuce, King crab meat, crunchy shrimp chips with a tangy garlic dressing) for $2.75. There's an entire page of Specialties from Foreign Lands: France, Mexico, Romania, Tahiti, Russia, Japan, Greece, Italy and Hawaii. The most expensive dishes come from the American Broiler: Filet Mignon for $6.75, Prime Strip Sirloin Steak for $6.75 and Baby Back Ribs for $4.25. Second-most expensive was the Lobster Shrimp Mornay at $6.25. Don't forget the Indian Curry Dishes available in Bombay (hot) or

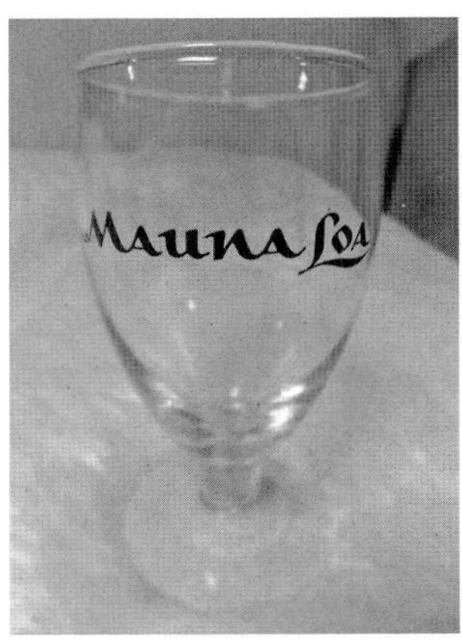

Mauna Loa glass. *Courtesy of Tim Shuller.*

Madras (mild). Entrées were served à la carte; rice, noodles, soups and salads could be added for an additional charge. Dessert consisted of ice cream and sherbet; flavors included coconut-pineapple, aged brandy, Brasilian coffee, chocolate-cinnamon and Key lime. The Orange Blossom Flambé sounds pretty fancy—a stuffed orange with brandy ice cream flamed with orange brandy at your table.

It's cocktail time! Mauna Loa tiki mugs are highly sought after by collectors. Like the Luau and Kon Tiki mugs, Florian Gabriel did an exceptional job creating unique, colorful, original, some say iconic designs. While many restaurants' signature tiki mugs were finished in a single-color glaze, Gabriel's designs went a step further by applying individual colors to the figures. The Bird Bowl and Ku mug for Stephen Crane Associates are perfect examples. For the Mauna Loa, Gabriel created a golden-brown bamboo mug with a pastel-colored parrot forming the handle for the Polynesian Pidgeon cocktail. The Drum mug was a simple drum with a tan glaze on top with a brown-glazed body accented with red; the handle is a drumstick. The Cauldron has a charcoal gray body with red, orange and yellow flames coming from crisscrossed brown logs; a brass-colored handle is fitted across the top. The Mauna Loa served the Coco Aku in a coconut mug. Bob's Rum Barrel was served in—what else—a rum barrel mug. I have to assume the "Bob" is named after Robert Fenton, just as the Steve's Rum Barrel was named for Steve Crane. All of these mugs are double-wall constructed. The most common Mauna Loa mug is the one used to serve the Baha Lana: an almost-black glazed tiki character sticking out his tongue. There's something very appealing about this little guy; it makes me wonder what he's up to. Each of these mug designs is identified by the "Design by Mauna Loa Detroit" and the gold "HF Japan" sticker on the bottom. Also bespoke for the Mauna Loa were the Drum salt and pepper shakers, sugar bowl, condiment set and Boat ash tray. Again, these have the "Design by Mauna Loa Detroit" on the bottom. Perhaps these items would have been sold in the gift shop.

The plain brown paper cocktail menu cover isn't much to look at other than the rendering of the restaurant entrance. The inside is quite lovely, with color photographs of cocktails in their designated glass or mug. A

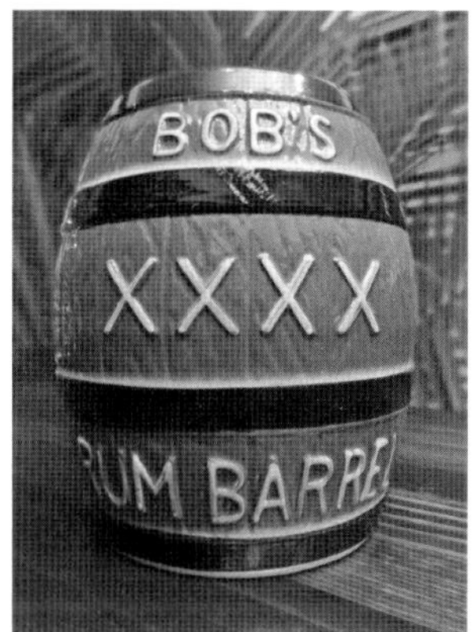

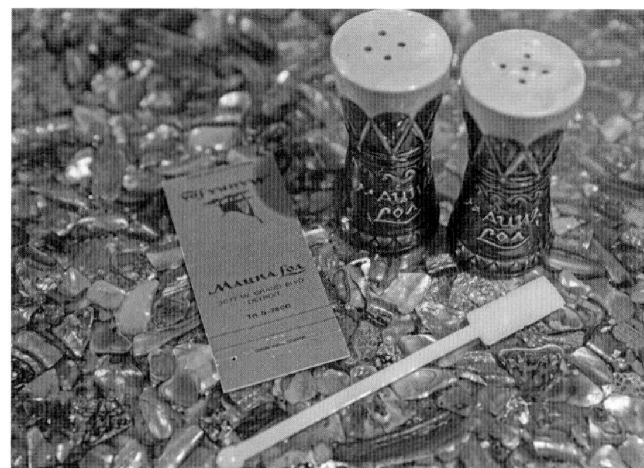

Left: Bob's Rum Barrel mug designed by Florian Gabriel. *Courtesy of Zach Roberts.*

Right: Souvenir matchbook, swizzle and salt and pepper drums. *Author's collection.*

list of drinks on the inside cover is cleverly arranged to vertically spell out "Welcome to Mauna Loa." One of the photographs is taken on lava rock; you can see water flowing over rock in the background. Orchids, lilies and Birds of Paradise are placed around the drinks; perhaps this photo was taken by one of the waterfalls inside the restaurant. There are photos of eighteen cocktails, with descriptions, including the Mauna Loa, Zombie, Tiger Shark and Tropical Itch. Another sixty-four cocktails are divided up with the heading "Choose the spirit to suit your mood." These are listed without description. Under "Mild" you can find the Blue Hawaii or Firefly; "Medium" offers the Pearl Diver; "Strong" lists the Cobra's Fang. The Coffee Grog comes under the "Hot" listing. Drink prices start at $1.50; a Polynesian Pidgeon cost $1.75. On the high end, This Is It! is the most expensive drink at $2.85, and the Mauna Loa, a "nectar for the gods erupting in a cloud of smoke," is $2.65.

Who went to the Mauna Loa? The goal of the investors was to create

> *a richly appointed establishment that will draw patronage from a wide segment of the dining public. "Exclusive" is regarded as almost a dirty word. So the striving is for what can truly be called popular prices. A luncheon buffet table offering 50 salad items luau style will carry a $2.50 tab. A "Polynesian delight" featuring two specialties, fried rice and tea will be $2.25. At dinner there will be such attractions as smoked pork loin Tohua Tabu for $4.75 and lamb casserole Ramadur'a at $4.10.*

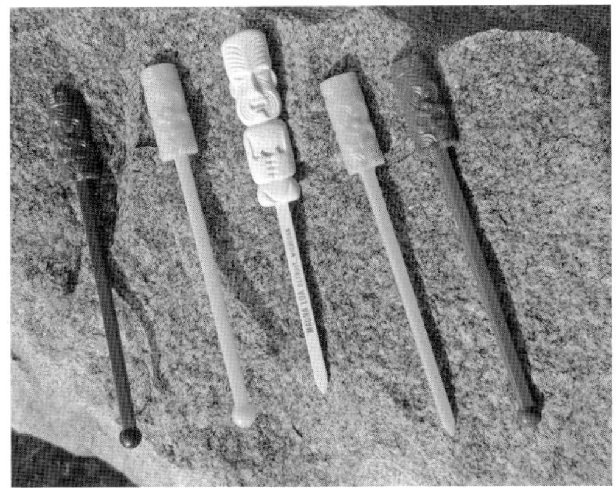

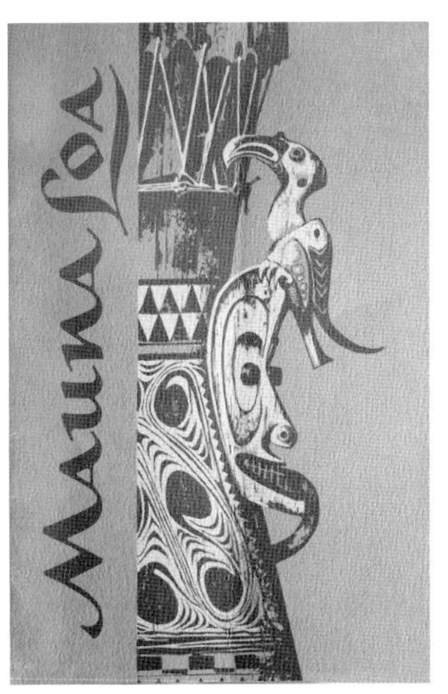

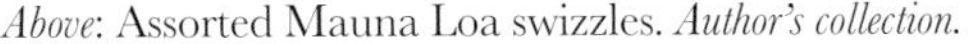
Above: Assorted Mauna Loa swizzles. *Author's collection.*

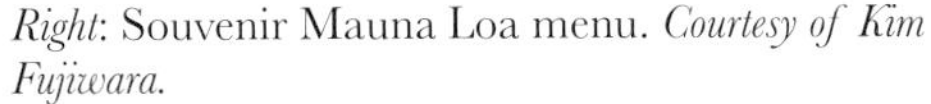
Right: Souvenir Mauna Loa menu. *Courtesy of Kim Fujiwara.*

They succeeded in attracting a luncheon crowd of businessmen, secretaries and other workers from the New Center area. Dinnertime diners were a mix of local, suburban and out-of-town guests, not to mention the investors themselves. The Mauna Loa could be found in the entertainment section of local newspapers, tourist magazines and dining guides as a suggestion for a night on the town; it was also a popular dining spot for Fisher Theatre–goers. Going to the Mauna Loa was a big deal and often marked special occasions such as birthdays and anniversaries. It's where you took guests when you wanted to impress and delight them. The Mauna Loa served as a venue for the presidential campaign of 1968 when, on August 2, Vice President Hubert H. Humphrey gave a speech at a gathering titled "Founding Members of Citizens for Humphrey." His stop in Detroit was aimed at garnering support and donations to help him secure the Democratic nomination. Social columns were filled with events that took place at the Mauna Loa: an eightieth birthday party for retired judge Arthur Lederle, Wayne State University alumni events, political fundraisers and class reunions. Students from local high schools were welcomed with a special menu for dinner after the prom. If you speak to anyone who went to the Mauna Loa, they use adjectives like amazing, wondrous, spectacular, exotic, astonishing. Some cannot even find the words to describe the experience, but the faraway look in their eyes tells you it was something special that made a deep and lasting impression.

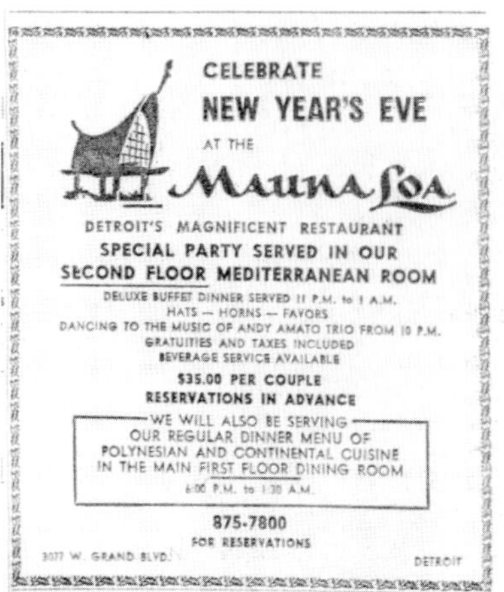

Newspaper advertisement. *Author's collection.*

From all appearances, the restaurant was highly successful; articles would appear in out-of-state newspapers boasting the $2.25 million price tag, the opulent décor and the impressive receipts. The restaurant held New Year's Eve celebrations in the Mediterranean Room, hosted graduation parties and fed swanky local celebrities. In January 1969, business was seemingly doing so well that there was an announcement in the newspaper: "The Mauna Loa crowd are getting ready to branch out in the eggroll-to-go business. They'll soon be opening a Chinese fast food shop on Woodward called 'The Little Red Pagoda.' With an eye on the national franchise possibilities." The Little Red Pagoda did indeed open at 2280 North Woodward on Sunday, June 21, 1970, according to the *Daily Tribune*. Investors Mel Farr, Dick Purtan and Nick Eddy were on hand for the opening. In January 1970, United Airlines held a shindig at the Mauna Loa to announce its first nonstop 4,500-mile jet service from Detroit to Honolulu beginning on June 1, 1970, in addition to five other daily flights to Hawaii. The 1970 book *Detroit: A Young Guide to the City* dubbed the Mauna Loa "the Disneyland of Detroit restaurants."

What went wrong? That's a question people continue to ask more than fifty years after the Mauna Loa closed. The timing of the restaurant opening may have been the first major hurdle. All was well when they started construction in 1965; nobody could have imagined the civil unrest of the Detroit riots in July 1967. Fires burned, buildings were looted and the National Guard was called in. A month later, the restaurant opened not far from the epicenter of the rebellion. People were hesitant to go downtown; many who lived there fled, vowing never to return to the city. The Mauna Loa could without a doubt pull people in for the one-of-a-kind experience, but for most folks, it was a special occasion–only type of place. Fenton often talked about the importance of keeping prices low enough for the average person, but it wasn't possible to compete with your average family restaurant or diner. Then there were the forty-nine investors. For years, rumors floated about investors showing up with groups of friends and associates, treating them to a night out "on the house." It dramatically cut into the profits. By

1970, most say the tiki craze had run its course, and places like the Mauna Loa had become a novelty. Most likely, the final nail in the coffin was the United Auto Workers (UAW) strike against GM. To this day, it is the longest strike in UAW history, lasting sixty-seven days, from September to November 1970. GM headquarters was located almost directly across the street from the restaurant—say a two-minute walk—making it an attractive and easily accessible lunch spot. The *Holland Evening Sentinel* of October 16, 1970, reported:

> *In Detroit, the white-collar executives are staying away from Sak's Fifth Avenue and a pitcher of martinis at Shanghai Lil's now goes for a dollar, if it goes at all. Effects of the United Auto Workers strike against GM, now in its second month, are continuing to depress local economies and collectively, the national economy. In Detroit, merchants in the snazzy New Center area around GM Headquarters report executives and their wives are buying less, even though the white-collar crowd is still on the job. "I used to have large parties of GM people and their clients, but not now," Richard Enriquez, general manager of the lush Mauna Loa restaurant said. "Their expense accounts are being cut down and there is no one for them to bring in here to wheel and deal. Everybody around here is being hurt by the strike." The Mauna Loa's Shanghai Lil's bar is offering martinis at one dollar a pitcher to try and revive luncheon business, which Enriquez said is down 15 to 20 per cent.*

The June 20, 1971 *Detroit Free Press* broke the news:

> *The Posh Mauna Loa restaurant in the New Center area, in which several prominent athletes are listed as investors, has gone into receivership. The restaurant was built in 1965–66 at a reported cost of more than $2 million. Restaurant operators asked federal court for 21 days in which to gather complete statements about the firm's affairs. Detroit attorney Allan Schmier, who filed the petition, said he was optimistic the company could meet its debts. "This is a holding action while we restructure finances," he said. "The restaurant's revenue decline is just part of the general business condition." The Mauna Loa petition said it owes taxes of $108,171 with creditors due another $1,225,682. The petition asked for protection from the federal court because the Internal Revenue Service, the city treasury office and the State Department of Revenue "have threatened to padlock the premises by reason of tax liability due and owing."*

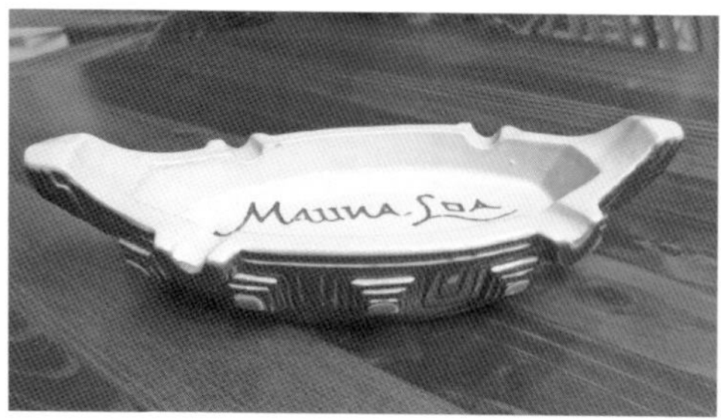

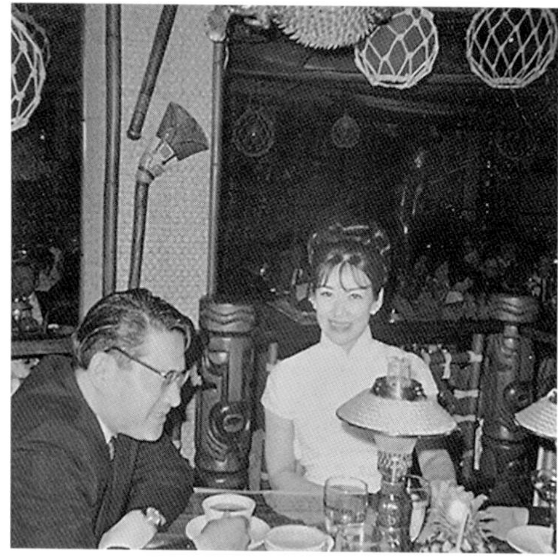

Top: Mauna Loa ash tray. *Courtesy of Zach Roberts.*

Bottom: George Nakashima and Helen Fujiwara enjoy a night out at the Mauna Loa. *Courtesy of Kim Fujiwara.*

On October 13, 1971, the *Detroit Free Press* published a small article with the headline "Mauna Loa on the Block":

> *Definite end of the road for the plush Mauna Loa Restaurant? Firm of lawyers representing Bank of the Commonwealth has sent letter advising that the bank "proposed to sell at public auction on October 22, 1971, at 10:00 o'clock a.m. all the equipment, furnishings, decorations and fixtures contained in the restaurant building known as the Mauna Loa Restaurant, covered by security agreement dated December 1, 1966, between 49 individuals and the Bank."*

On December 19, 1971, a public auction notice showed up in the *Detroit Free Press* announcing assets of the Mauna Loa would be auctioned off on Wednesday, December 29, at 10:30 a.m. by L.M. Koploy Company. After less than four years in business, it was aloha, Mauna Loa.

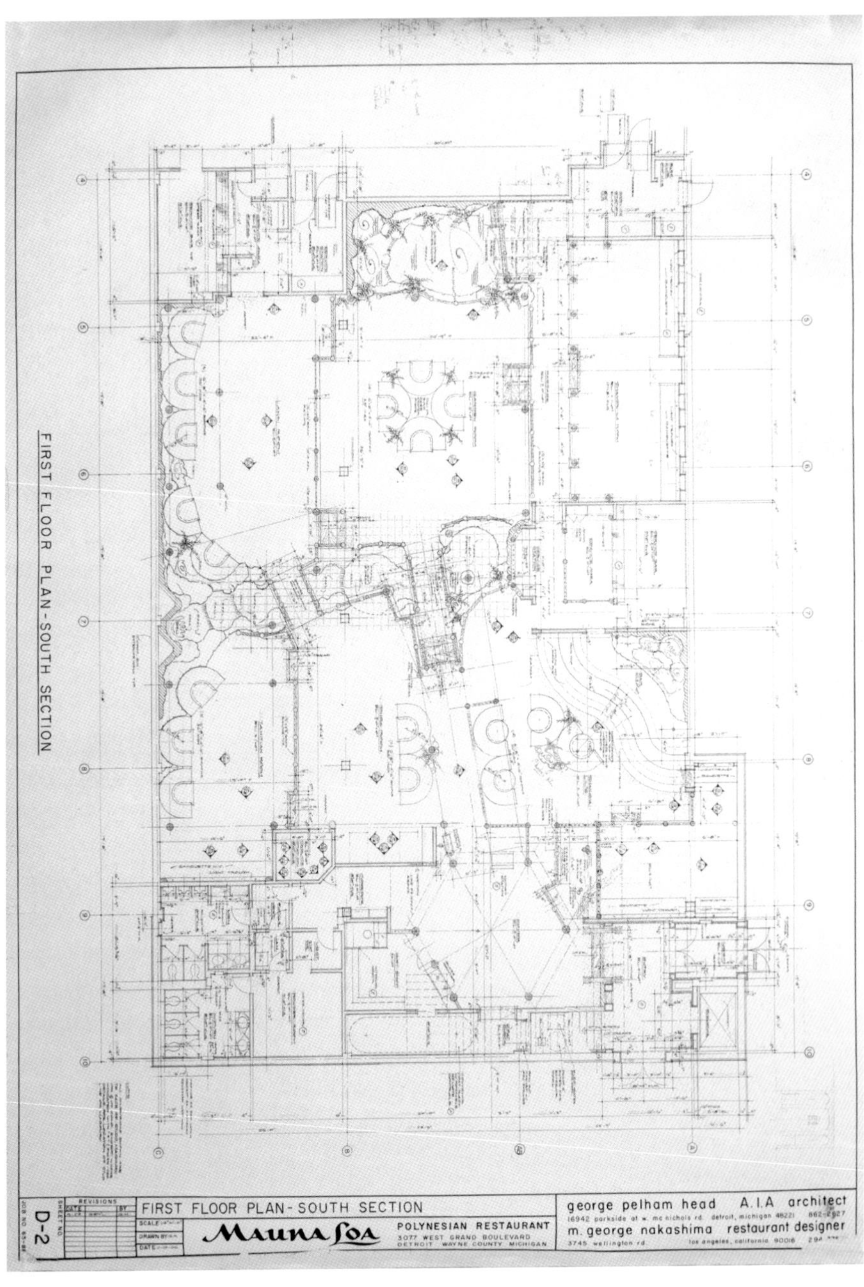

Mauna Loa blueprint. *Private collection, photo by Nick Hagen.*

The building was used again for a short time when the Clam Shop moved from its tiny space at 2675 East Grand Boulevard into the shell of the old Mauna Loa in 1975. It did not last long. According to a June 2, 1976 article in the *Detroit Free Press*, the Clam Shop had a fire on April 15, 1976, and the IRS seized the business for back taxes. The building was eventually demolished.

As for M. George Nakashima, when his work was finished with the Mauna Loa, he went right to work on the Mai Kai addition/renovation in Fort Lauderdale, Florida. Once that was done, he began getting more work in the Detroit area, allowing him to settle down here. Toward the end of his life, he began getting the much-deserved recognition from tikiphiles for his contribution to the genre. He would appear at organized tiki events and enjoyed talking with enthusiasts. Nakashima passed away in 2004 at the age of eighty. When asked what people remember most about him, the response is always the same: he was the nicest guy in the world.

Chapter 8

TRADER VIC'S

Trader Vic's was the last to arrive on the Detroit tiki scene. The Statler-Hilton Hotel building the restaurant called home was going through a turbulent time when Vic's arrived. The hotel started out life as The Statler. According to HistoricDetroit.org, it was designed by George B. Post in the Italian and Renaissance Revival styles. It was Detroit's most expensive and luxurious hotel at the time and the largest in the Midwest when it opened on February 6, 1915. President Franklin D. Roosevelt and Zsa Zsa Gabor stayed there, as did Harry Houdini in October 1926, when he collapsed on stage at the Garrick Theatre. He was taken to Grace Hospital, where he died.

In 1954, the Hotels Statler Co. stockholders wanted out. In August 1954, Conrad N. Hilton announced that his company was buying controlling interest in Statler Hotels Inc.; by October that same year, Hilton owned all Statler hotels and two office buildings. The Detroit location's name was changed to the Statler-Hilton in January 1958. By the early 1960s, hotel occupancy was declining in Detroit, and as early as 1961, Hilton started exploring the sale of three of the oldest, least profitable Statler hotels: Detroit, Buffalo and Cleveland. Around this time, Hilton decided to modernize the Detroit location, adding wood paneling and drop ceilings and converting public rooms. In an attempt to land more banquets and conventions, the Statler added the largest convention area in Detroit. The website continues, "The renovation did much to strip the hotel of its original opulence but did little to change the hotel's declining business."

In August 1968, Hilton Hotels announced it would spend another $2.5 million to add a swimming pool and luxury suites and to remodel guest rooms. In January 1969, Hilton announced that a Trader Vic's Polynesian restaurant would replace Café Rouge.

On July 1, 1969, the *Detroit Free Press* revealed:

> *A group of 26 Detroiters led by three attorneys have purchased the Detroit Hilton Hotel from Hilton Hotels Corp. The announcement was made by Barron Hilton, president of Hilton Hotels Corp. and Fred Gordon, Davis A. Kaplan and Alan B. Grass of the Detroit law firm of Bizer, Sommers and Gordon. The 905-room hotel will continue to be managed by Hilton Hotels Corp. under a long-term management contract, it was announced. "We believe this relation of our corporation with local investors will be of benefit to the hotel and community at large," Hilton said. The Detroit Hilton is in the midst of a $3.5 million renovation. The hotel's rooms and Washington Blvd. façade are being redone. A Trader Vic's restaurant is planned for the Bagley Ave side of the hotel, and the top three floors are being converted into a luxury area.*

The group renamed it the Detroit Hilton, which was "the first time in 54 years that the name Statler was not associated with the landmark." To Detroiters, it would forever be The Statler. A July 20, 1969 article drums up more interest in the project:

> *If you wonder where Detroit Hilton's Café Rouge, longtime luncheon hangout has gone—it's been traded to Trader Vic's. The lobby level restaurant has been closed and boarded and is being replaced by an exotic new place to be known as Trader Vic's Luau Room for private luncheon and dinner parties. Frank W. Telch, general manager, says the spiffy place will open in early November prior to December completion of a $3.5 million face-lifting, which includes all guest and private rooms. Trader Vic's will take up the entire Bagley side (with a new Polynesian façade with tiki gods, no less). Barron Hilton, president of the worldwide chain, has been quoted as envisioning the Detroit pad as "one of the best appointed in the Hilton system."*

On October 30, 1969, the headline in Chuck Thurston's column in the *Detroit Free Press* reads, "Trader Vic's Talks About His New Detroit Restaurant":

> *Bergeron is in town to talk to the Rotary and to look over the boards, plaster and straw matting that will be shaped into the 275-seat Polynesian restaurant in the Detroit Hilton. The 13th Trader Vic's will be for people who want an adventure in eating out. There will be no entertainment in Trader Vic's but table conversation and canned music. Table accessories will be the expensive originals that have been copied by other Polynesian restaurants around the country. Two kitchens, one Chinese and one American will prepare food for both tastes.*

Finally, Trader Vic's opened. The December 10, 1969 *Detroit Free Press* proclaimed, "A Little Piece of Polynesia Comes to Detroit Today":

> *Detroit will have a Trader Vic's come Wednesday when Victor Jules Bergeron opens another in his chain of noted Polynesian restaurants in the Detroit Hilton. Bergeron, who was in Detroit to supervise the opening, is a salty, peg-legged trader who is right at home in the atmosphere of grass skirts, straw mats and outrigger canoes. But he's never roamed the South Seas. And he most certainly did not lose his leg to an unfriendly shark, as legend has it. "That story about the shark has been going around for years, and it's a lot of nonsense," says Trader Vic. "I fell from a roof when I was a boy and injured my leg. Eventually it had to be amputated." Trader Vic's*

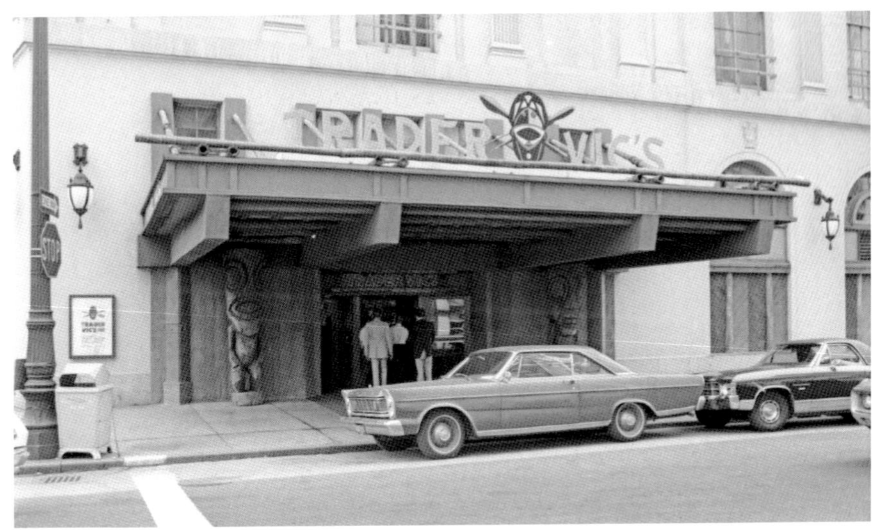

Trader Vic's entrance on Washington Boulevard in the Detroit Hilton Hotel. *Courtesy of Walter P. Reuther Library, Archives of Labor and Urban Affairs, Wayne State University.*

will occupy the old Café Rouge in the Hilton, extending the entire Bagley side of the building.

Today his 16 restaurants—scattered across the globe are famous for their Oriental and Polynesian foods and he trades an incredible assortment of decorations and souvenirs gathered by his team of genuine traders in Tahiti and Samoa, for dollars.

Knowing exotic rum drinks are a trademark of the Trader Vic's, we asked about the origin of the Mai Tai, the most famous in the world. "Yes, I originated it and don't let anyone tell you different," he boomed. "The Royal Hawaiian Hotel in Honolulu wanted me to come up with some different drinks so I mixed some good rum with fresh lime juice, orgeat liqueur and orange curacao, put it in a fancy glass with ice and named it Mai Tai for two of my Tahitian friends."

At 67, the Trader has now turned over most of the business end of his enterprises to members of his family, and he and his wife Helen enjoy various forms of leisure. "I'm chairman of the board now and my eldest son, Vic Jr. [Joe] *is president of the restaurants and the food products company. The younger boy, Lynn is vice-president and manager of the San Francisco Trader Vic's. It's good to see them take hold and there are 10 grandchildren to take over someday." Apart from the restaurants, Trader Vic Food Products produces and markets across the country a line of 75 drink mixes and Oriental condiments.*

Throughout 1969, 1970 and 1971, Trader Vic's was regularly listed in the entertainment section of the newspaper; one ad called it the "Land of Enchantment." In 1973, Trader Vic Bergeron released a book titled *Frankly Speaking: Trader Vic's Own Story*. In it, he writes, "Then Hilton asked us to go to Detroit. Downtown Detroit. Nobody in Detroit goes downtown because they feel that if they do, they'll never get out again. It's one lousy location, but I think it will grow pretty steadily." In an article titled "Vic Tells On Detroit," the *Detroit Free Press* of June 18, 1973, reports, "This cavalier treatment naturally ruffled some fur in the Detroit Hilton front office, where manager Arthur Gimson reports that Trader Vic's annual gross is just over two-thirds of a million dollars." "Trader Vic's is open on Sundays," Gimson says, "after hometown Lion's games the place is packed....Trader Vic's is serving 10 percent more in the first part of 1973 (its fourth year) than in 1972."

Meanwhile, according to HistoricDetroit.org, the hotel continued to struggle, and Hilton pulled out of the deal in 1974. The move prompted the name to be changed again; it was now called the Detroit Heritage Hotel. On

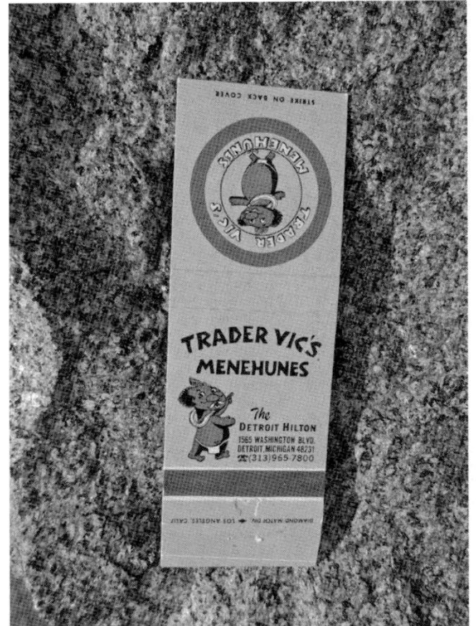

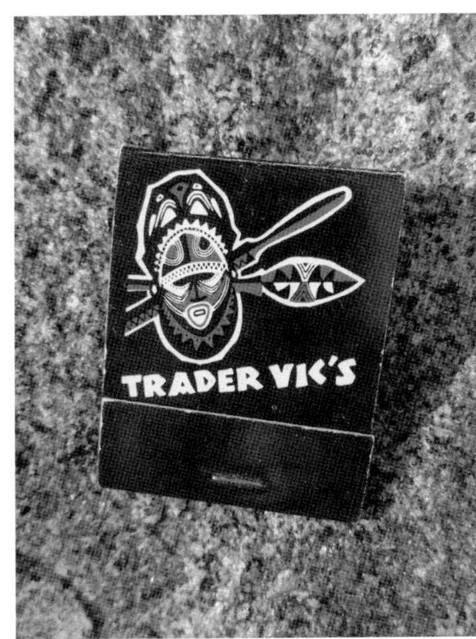

Left: Trader Vic's Menehunes Detroit souvenir matchbook. *Author's collection.*

Right: Trader Vic's at the Detroit Hilton matchbook. *Author's collection.*

April 9, 1975, the *Detroit Free Press* announced the closing with the headline "Aloha, Vic": "Trader Vic's will close April 20. All the decorations inside the restaurant will be shipped to San Francisco." By June 1975, the hotel's occupancy rate was averaging only 20 percent. Unable to pay its taxes and bills, the hotel was on the brink of closing for several months. On October 15, 1975, after the hotel's utilities were cut off, the Heritage Hotel owed nearly $150,000 in back taxes, which led to foreclosure in 1979. In 2005, "the grandest hotel on Grand Circus Park" started to come down ahead of the Super Bowl and All-Star Game. The hotel was taken down floor by floor. The last of the hotel was brought down in late October 2005.

Part III

THE AFTERLIFE

Time marched forward, and the South Seas craze slowly faded away. Gone from everyday life were exotic cocktails, loads of bamboo and thatch and the idea of a life of leisure under palm trees. Elaborate, atmospheric restaurants were replaced with themed establishments. Bellbottoms, fringe and flower prints replaced Hawaiian shirts and grass skirts. In our homes, housewives no longer had to make everything from scratch; help came in boxes, cans and ready-to-heat frozen dinners. Bartenders followed suit. Instead of using fresh-squeezed juices and house-made syrups, they purchased large tin cans of citrus juices and dry or bottled mixes; cocktails became overly sweet and unrecognizable from the originals.

With the closure of many tiki restaurants and bars, those who embraced the tiki lifestyle were forced to form an underground society. They built home tiki bars and named them and created original custom cocktails to share with friends at regular gatherings. These like-minded enthusiasts kept the culture alive and well. Websites, Facebook pages and Pinterest gave collectors a place to show off their homes and collections and connect with one another. After collecting dust on flea market and antique store shelves or being sold by the box in garage sales, tiki mugs, menus and other ephemera began showing up on eBay auctions, bringing a pretty penny to sellers' pockets. Tiki events were being held at iconic restaurants still in business. Here in Detroit, the Cat's Meow has hosted the annual Christmas Tiki Party at Chin's in Livonia since 2006. The Detroit Area Art Deco Society hosted a tiki event including live music by Roland Remington at the now-shuttered Zenith restaurant inside the Fisher Building in 2015.

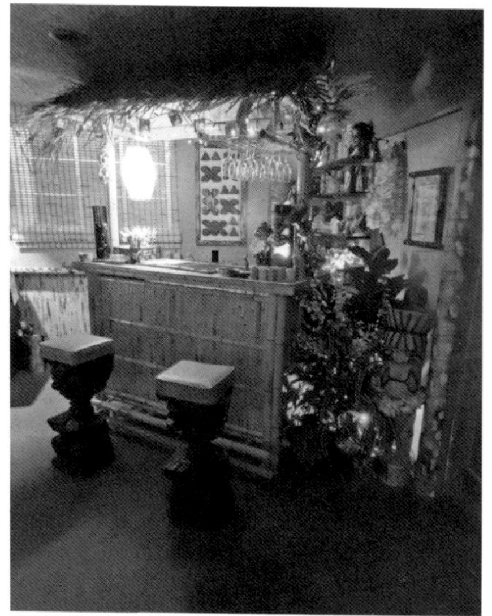

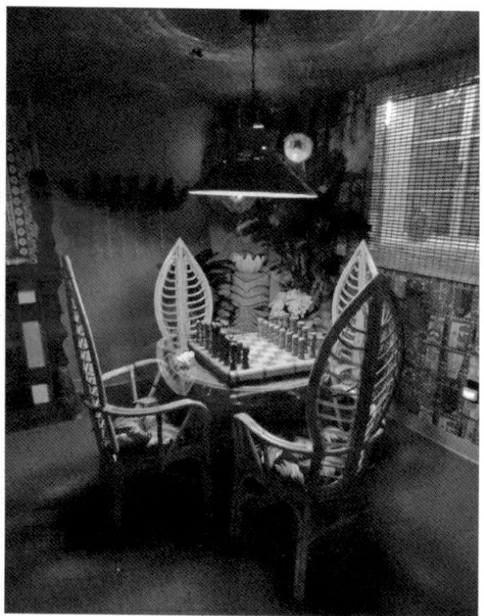

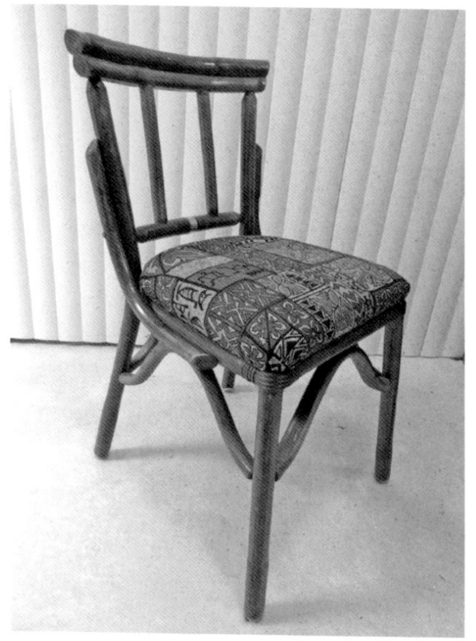

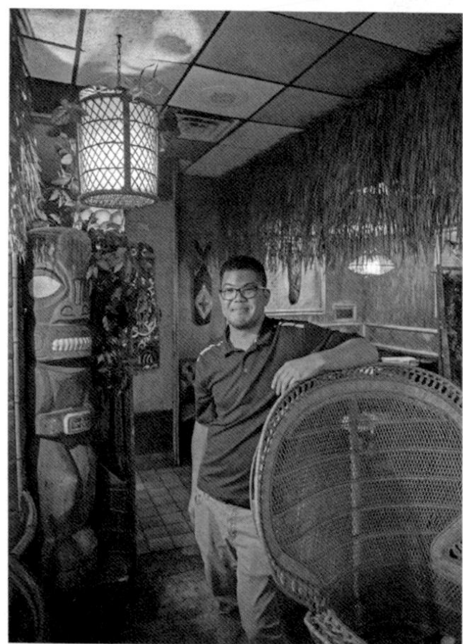

Top, left: Home tiki bar. *Private collection.*

Top, right: Tiki-themed room. *Private collection.*

Bottom, left: Original Chin Tiki chair. *Courtesy of Tim Shuller.*

Bottom, right: Marvin Chin's grandson Steven Lim. *Photo by Amy Sacka.*

Opposite: The now-closed Zenith in the Fisher Building. *Author's collection.*

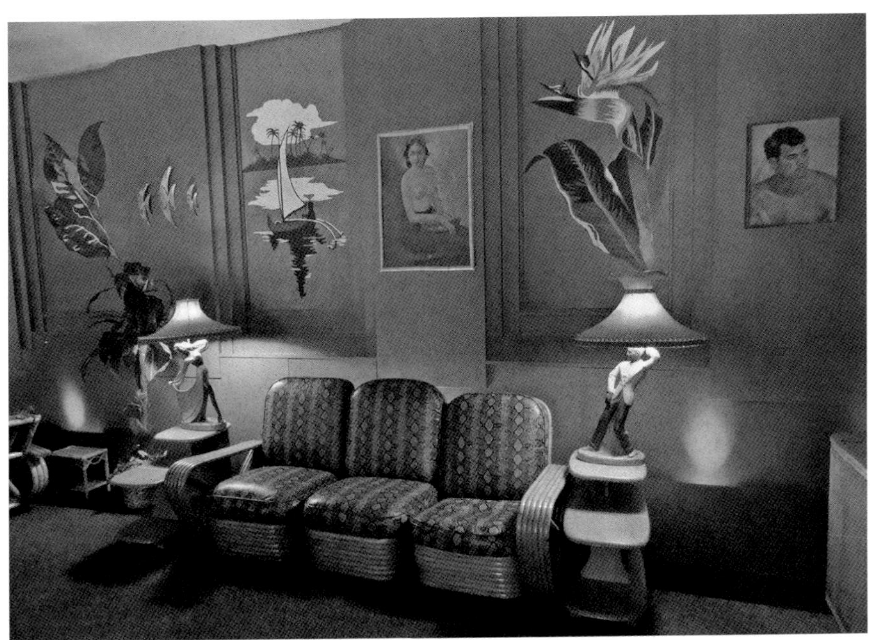

The resurgence of the craft cocktail movement allowed young bartenders to reach into the past and re-create staple tiki drinks such as the Mai Tai, Painkiller and Scorpion, once again using fresh-squeezed juices, house-made syrups and high-quality rums. These young guns of the cocktail world put their own spin on the classics, introducing a whole new generation to tiki and Polynesian culture. Tiki made a comeback; new bars have opened; ceramic artists are back to work creating original mugs for venues and the masses.

In 2017, two new tiki bars opened in Detroit. Mutiny at 4654 Vernor Highway calls itself a "dive" tiki bar. Local ephemera hangs on the walls, and skilled bartenders create exceptional cocktails, entertaining patrons as they look on. Lost River at 15421 Mack Avenue also pays homage to Detroit's former tiki palaces in atmosphere, memorabilia and a classic tiki cocktail menu. Max's South Seas Hideaway is a Mark Sellers, Martin Cate and Gecko Joint located at 58 Ionia Avenue SW in Grand Rapids, Michigan. The interior is a nod to the original transformative style of the tiki bar. Clientele is a mix of those with a longing for the old days and those who are curious and want to experience drinking a Mai Tai while sitting in a Polynesian-themed space.

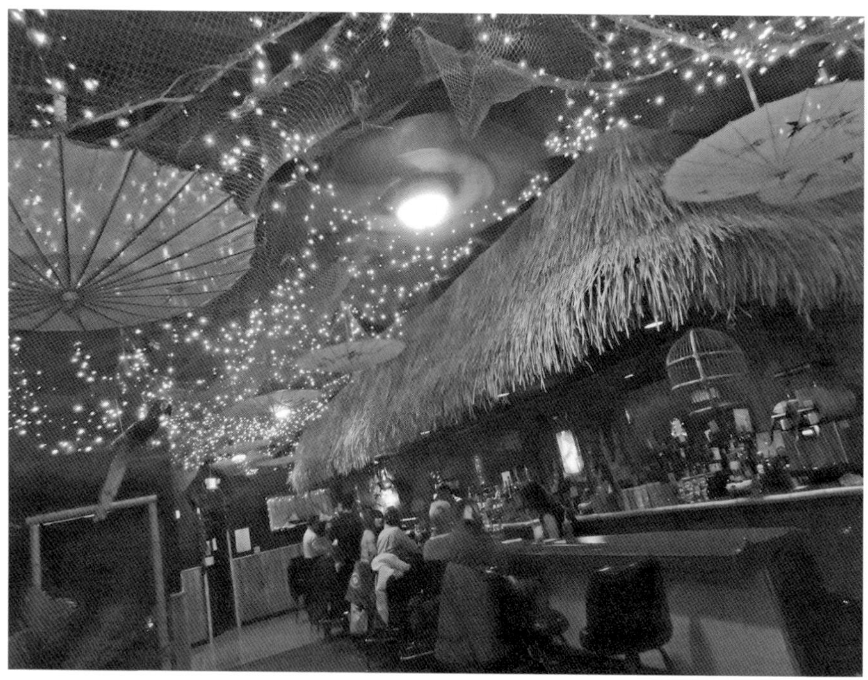

The Mutiny Tiki Bar is one of several bars and restaurants in Detroit operated by the Detroit Optimist Society. *Author's collection.*

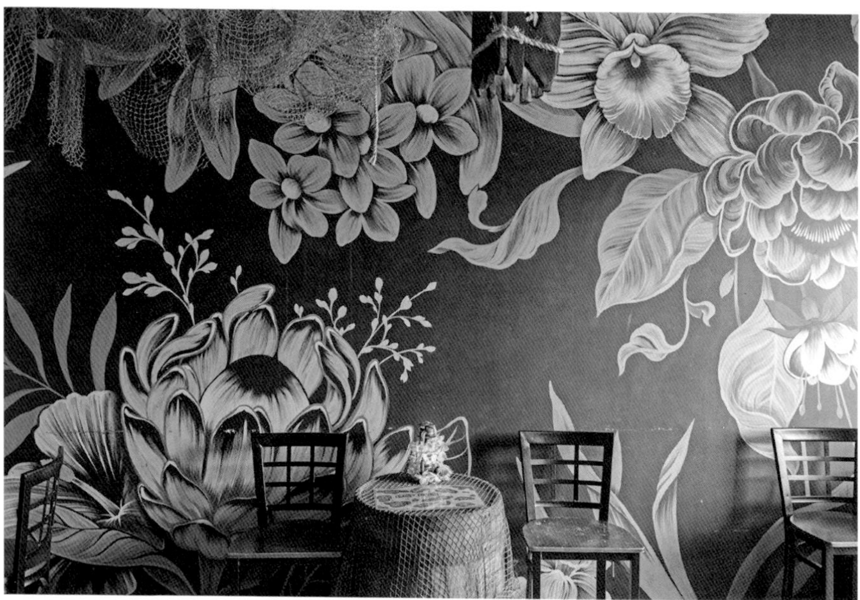

Mural by Ouizi at Lost River Tiki Bar in Detroit. *Photo by Nick Hagen.*

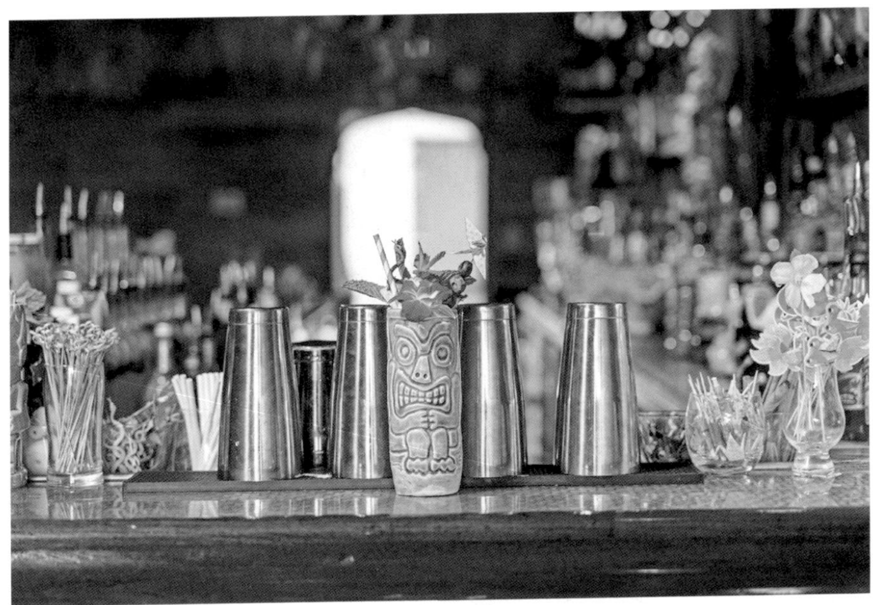

Above: Lost River Tiki Bar on Mack Avenue in Detroit. *Photo by Nick Hagen.*

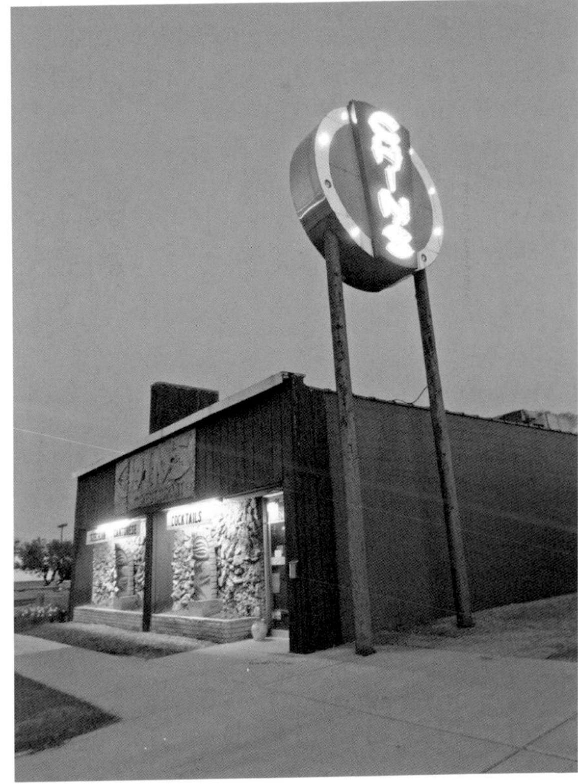

Right: Chin's Chop Suey in Livonia. *Author's collection.*

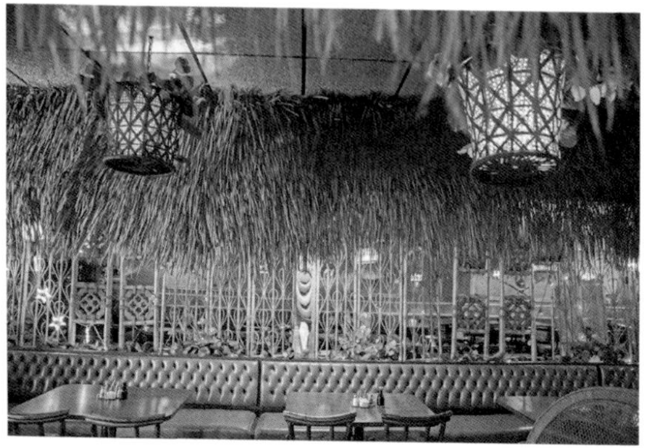

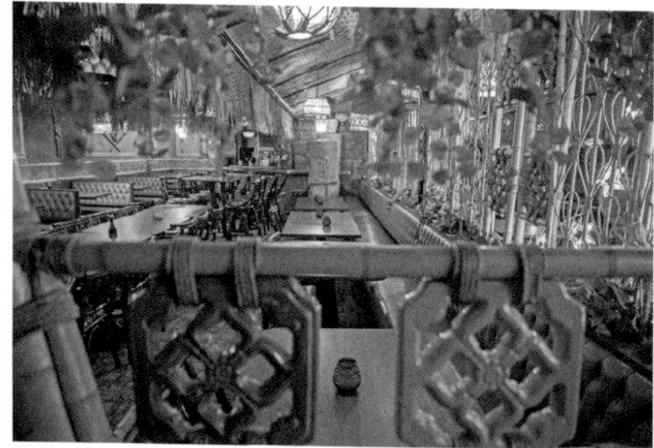

Chin's Livonia dining room.
Photos by Amy Sacka.

For those wanting a truly authentic experience, Chin's Chop Suey is still open and continues to be operated by Marvin Chin's son Marlin and his grandson Steven Lim; his wife, Kitty, still makes an appearance now and then. The waterfall no longer runs; Marlin said they could never get the water to stop splashing onto the carpeting. Lit up in red, it now resembles a volcano. The original bar from the Mauna Loa is stationed at the back of the left side dining room, and rescued tikis from Chin Tiki are huddled together behind the bar. Other items from Chin Tiki have found a new home at Chin's as well. Walking through the door and into the restaurant is like passing through a time warp—isn't that wonderful?

The pandemic has taught us how vulnerable food and drink establishments are. For now, these places remain open; I, for one, hope they are here to stay.

INDEX

B

Barton, Fred 33, 44, 48, 50, 51
Bay City Times 102
Bergeron, Victor Jules 16, 115, 116
Buick 90

C

Chin, Marlin 56, 63, 78, 80, 124
Chin, Marvin 52, 53, 54, 56, 58, 61, 62, 63, 69, 70, 73, 76, 80, 86, 124
Chin's Chop Suey 54, 70, 124
Chin Tiki 52, 54, 56, 58, 61, 63, 64, 68, 69, 70, 73, 78, 80, 83, 86, 96, 101, 124
Chrysler 90
Club Bali 26, 27
Crane, Stephen 95, 96, 105

D

Daily Tribune 108
Detroit Free Press 18, 23, 26, 53, 54, 56, 58, 64, 68, 69, 70, 73, 76, 87, 88, 100, 101, 109, 110, 112, 114, 115, 116, 117
Detroit Hilton 114, 115, 116
Detroit Lions 63, 90
Detroit Red Wings 90
Detroit Tigers 20, 25, 63, 92

E

8 Mile (film) 52, 78
Eminem 78

F

Fenton, Robert 86, 87, 88, 90, 95, 96, 105, 108
Fong, Benson 53, 54, 63, 69
Ford Motor Co. 90

G

Gabor, Zsa Zsa 113
Gabriel, Florian 96, 102, 105
General Motors 90

H

Hawaiian Gardens 33, 35, 36, 40, 42, 43, 44, 48, 49, 51
Herald Advertiser 44
Holland Evening Sentinel 109
Holly, Michigan 31, 33, 34, 35, 36, 41, 43, 44, 46, 48, 50
Houdini, Harry 113
Hour Detroit 52

L

Lost River 121

M

Mauna Loa 10, 41, 49, 80, 86, 87, 88, 90, 92, 95, 96, 98, 100, 102, 104, 105, 106, 107, 108, 109, 110, 112, 124
Metrotimes 78

N

Nakashima, M. George 31, 62, 86, 90, 96, 98, 101, 112

O

Oceanic Arts 63, 74, 96

P

Pontiac 90
Port Huron Times Herald 24
Port O' Three 76, 78

R

Roosevelt, Franklin D. 113

S

Scorpion Chin Tiki 68
South Pacific (Tales of) 28

T

Trader Vic's 16, 88, 96, 113, 114, 115, 116, 117
Tropics, The 18, 21, 22, 23, 25, 96

W

Wah Lee 52, 69

ABOUT THE AUTHOR

Renee Tadey was born in Detroit and continues to reside in the metro area. She is passionate about all things vintage, from automobiles and architecture to film, clothing, home furnishings and lifestyle. She is especially fond of Mid-Century Modern design. She and her husband have traveled extensively throughout Michigan and the Midwest exploring and enjoying the Rust Belt cities; she has been blogging about their adventures for nearly a decade. This is her first book.